Celeb.
Pet Talking

with

'The Animal Psychic'

Jackie Weaver

Jackie Weaver

Celebrity Pet Talking

Jackie Weaver has always had an affinity with animals; she had often been aware of their thoughts and feelings but didn't really know why. A devastating illness changed her life forever and through her work she has changed the lives of countless animals. She listened to them, relayed what they said to their owners, and helped transform their lives. Much of her work is because people simply want to hear what their animal has to say, and Jackie gives them a voice.

With the help of these celebrities' animals they will show you how they really are just like little people in different bodies and know so much more than you would ever have dreamt of.

Jackie Weaver

Books by the same author:

Animal Insight

Animal Talking Tales

ISBN 9781780352244

First published 2011

Cover Image by Personaldesigns © Copyright 2011

Interior artwork by Jackie Fennell – www.jacksart.co.uk

About this Book

Jacky Newcomb: Sunday Times Best Selling author of '*An Angel Saved My Life*'.

"Jackie Weaver contacted me to see if she could interview my cats by way of a psychic animal reading. I have to admit, I do get asked to do a lot of things that I turn down, and felt this was likely going to go on the 'no' list, as I didn't know if I even believed in such a thing.

After exchanging a few emails I decided I would seriously think about it, after all she was prepared to travel to my home to do the reading. In the meantime Jackie sent me a copy of her first book and I have to be honest; I was completely blown away by the stories. Some were sad but many literally made me laugh out loud. Did the pets really say these things? I really felt they had, so invited her over.

Jackie arrived at my Midlands home and didn't even need my pets in the room although one of them joined us anyway. I was stunned - It really was just like she was having a conversation with my cats and telling me their reply! The insights she brought me were so interesting and amazingly accurate. Not only did she seem to connect with them they even passed their mannerisms over to her. My two cats are very individual and her conversations demonstrated this perfectly which you will read in this very fascinating book.

I felt very comfortable passing Jackie's details on to some celebrity friends for this book, what had they got to lose? Nothing at all, as you'll read for yourself. I know you'll enjoy this magical work as much as I did."

Jacky Newcomb.

Jenny Smedley - Radio and TV presenter, best-selling author, and columnist.

"There are, thank goodness, more and more of us who are able to connect with our spiritual partners, the animals that share this planet. Jackie has taken a huge step forward for those animals with this book, which will bring animal communication to the forefront - where it should be. Our connection with animals has to be accepted and they have to be respected if this world and the people who have temporary custody of it, are to thrive and progress in any kind of meaningful way. I salute people like Jackie who are pursuing this end with dogged determination and enviable courage. Jackie has proven her abilities over and over again and I really feel this book is the one that will give her the credit she deserves. Inspiring and often breath-taking, this book will lead you on an incredible journey you'll be so glad you took."

~~~

Barrie John - Multi Award Winning International TV Medium, Presenter, Broadcaster, Speaker and Columnist.

"Jackie has touched the heart of our animals, and makes us all aware that communication is important also for the living too. Animals are very intuitive and this psychic work is of great benefit to us all to help ensure that love, happiness and understanding are continued within our homes. Also, who would have believed that my dog would tell her about his love of a roast dinner on a Sunday?!"

Acknowledgement

For Bob, Sally and Stanley and all animals,
Thank you,
'You are my world'.
To all the celebrities in this book,
and for all the people who helped make
this dream a reality, I thank
you from the bottom of my heart.

Jackie Weaver

Contents

Jackie Weaver

Introduction

If someone said to me five years ago that I would be referred to as, 'The Animal Psychic', I would not have had a clue what they meant, or why that would be. I had an inkling about the fact that people could get information from animals but never in a million years thought we could actually have a conversation with them. I say, conversation; it is a telepathic conversation, but not really a lot different from a person using a mobile phone and hearing what another being has to say. The obvious difference is that the animal's voice is not heard out-loud, but conveyed to people's minds, very much like a thought. You can't see them, touch them, but thoughts are real to us; we have them every day.

This wonderful, and extremely, fulfilling work is not without its sceptics and quite rightly so. I am the type of person that if told something that, to be honest, sounds incredulous, I too would be looking for proof.

It was a chance comment by someone who said, "If celebrities believed in it, then everyone would!" Oh, if only that were true, but I understood her sentiments and it planted a seed in my mind. So, from that 'little acorn' eighteen months ago, this book is the result. I live in the real world and know that the public tend to follow, listen to and read about what celebrities do in their lives - it makes news and provokes interest. So, how on earth would a person like me achieve this? Yes, I have written two books and am recognised in the field that I work in, but that is miles away from contacting celebrities. Firstly, their privacy is closely guarded. Secondly, would they have any pets? Thirdly, would they believe what I do is possible? Finally, would they be prepared to let me talk to them, and their pets, and then write about it? Quite daunting really! It was a huge task but having had other challenging things in life to deal with, I started upon my quest to make this book a reality. Through the help of the 'celebrity platform' I just know that it *will* spread the word that being able to communicate with animals *is* completely, and utterly, true!

To say my life has been challenging is a bit of an understatement. I am still the right side of fifty, just, and I have not had an easy life in any shape, manner or form.

I lost my father to cancer when I was seventeen, which had a profound effect on my life, and I suffered from lack of self-esteem. Having been brought up on a farm, I then went in to veterinary nursing. I found solace with animals and little did I realise then that I could actually communicate with them – so many things make sense now.

I got married to Bob in 1995 and my life rolled along on its bumpy track, as most people's lives do. Little did I know, ten years later I would feel like I had been run over by a steamroller!

Although I was active and always outside, either riding horses or teaching people to ride, I was forever getting, or feeling, ill. I had constant stomach pains and then I got shingles, which really knocked me for six. I had become increasingly aware of a large swelling just below the sternum of my rib cage. This turned out to be my liver that had been seriously invaded by cancer, but the doctors were struggling to come up with a clear diagnosis. However, it was not just my liver that was involved, as I was to find out later.

In my life now, I often say to people that I believe when animals are going to come into your life, they will! In the midst of my deteriorating health, I went to the local vets to get some flea treatment for our dog, Bruce. I walked in and there was a lady standing waiting at the counter with a very pretty, but nervous, young collie sitting at her feet. I remarked how lovely she looked and those fateful words came out,

"She needs a home you know!" The lady went on to inform me that she had rescued this collie from a horrible and rather unsafe environment. She was visiting the place in an official capacity and apparently, it took her two hours to persuade the man to part with this poor little dog. To repeat this wonderful lady's words, "I wasn't leaving without her."

I went back home and told (note - 'told'!) Bob that I wanted this collie. I said that I had arranged for us both to go for a walk with her to see if she liked us. As you can imagine, immediately he responded with,

"But you are so ill - we can't take on a rescue dog in the middle of all this!" I admitted that it was probably the last complication we needed to add to our pile of woes but I was determined. I just knew that I had to help her, and I was going to!

Having got this little dog, that incidentally had not had one home but two, and was around seven months old, we changed her name to Sally. (It sounded very similar to her previous name and she responded to it just the same.) Anyway, it was very apparent that she was extremely anxious and scared, but we could see how much she wanted to love and be loved. We kept telling her we would not give up on her and that she was safe with us. (I did not know then about how much animals really can, and do, understand.)

Sally now became something else to focus on whilst I was still waiting to find out what type of cancer I had, and what lay ahead for me. This might sound selfish to some people but I believe that so many things are 'meant to be' so instead of going against the flow, just go with it. As I explained in my first book *Animal Insight*, it transpired that neither the lady nor I should have been at the vets at that time - I know it was fate and 'fate' I feel is something that cannot be ignored or controlled.

Sally was also a focus for Bob. Apart from finding the time to look after our two horses and Bruce, our other dog, and finding time to come to visit me, he also had to keep up his horse dentistry work to pay the bills. He couldn't wallow in self pity about the situation his forty-year-old wife was in (not that he is the type) but, he had to make the time, and have the presence of mind, to encourage this dog to learn to trust and let go of her fear. (At a later date, through an animal psychic, it turned out her past was a lot worse than we had ever thought).

I took a turn for the worse and landed back up in hospital yet again. The problem was that my liver was so enlarged that it was trying to burst out of its own viscous capsule – agony, to say the least! Unbelievably, more often than not, it would be on a Sunday that I would have a pain crisis. In fact, Bob used to exclaim, "What you will do to stop me drinking on a Sunday!"

This particular Sunday, the paramedics quickly arrived (our address had become a regular callout on their ambulance database) and promptly administered the usual high dose of morphine so that within five minutes I was totally oblivious to the pain and my brain was not acting quite as it should. The light was fading fast outside and the paramedics had to get me to the ambulance parked at the side of our house. Well, Bruce kept running up and down the wheelchair ramp showing much concern for me. Sally, however, was trying to encourage the ambulance men to throw a ball for her and this is why…

Sally had been so scared of strangers but I had very quickly found out that she loved playing with a tennis ball and so I had put this positive action into use by linking the action of someone giving her a ball with a certain phrase and, it worked! She could be barking furiously at someone but if I gave them a ball to throw for her, she instantly associated them as a friend and played happily, and silently.

Back to the ambulance - just as I was starting to lie down on the stretcher, hornets appeared from somewhere. I think they were drawn not only by our porch lights but also the ones in the ambulance. As they were buzzing around my head, I managed to say to the ambulance driver,

"Quick, swat them!" in my best drug-infused voice.

"No - *you* swat them!" he replied.

"I can't - I am the ill one here," I giggled in my druggy fog.

"Oh yeah, but I'm scared of them," he admitted sheepishly.

Bob quickly came to the rescue with a rolled up newspaper and batted them out of the ambulance for the both of us. (Before anyone thinks that nowadays I could just ask a hornet to 'please go away', I can't. I, like anyone, can say the words, but my work is to the subconscious and if it wants to carry on buzzing about – it will.)

Anyway, to continue - it was during that particular hospital stay that my health deteriorated very badly. I didn't even have time to get Bob to accompany me to see the head consultant who had come from Cheltenham Hospital (Herefordshire's Oncology Treatment Centre) to see me. He gently said,

"You do realise that you are very ill, don't you?"

I nodded as I sat there looking like 'Michelin Woman' (you know that advert for tyres) because my lymph system had stopped circulating and my body seemed to be inflating with its own fluid.

"We know you have cancer although we are still not quite sure which one but, sorry, we know you are stage four. Do you know what that means?"

"No," I mumbled as the tears rolled down my cheeks.

He explained, "The grade goes from good to bad; it goes from one, where is very first stage, to four, where it has spread throughout your body. We are going to send you to Cheltenham Hospital today as you need to start on chemotherapy right away."

He went on to tell me they had found cancer in my liver, spleen, and bones. There was also a large tumour growing in my stomach area. They had to do more investigations to establish which exact cancer it was.

Eventually I was diagnosed with non Hodgkins lymphoma, and not just one type, but two! Never been one to do things by half! (Having two types at once is extremely rare which is why they could not get conclusive results.)

The next part is rather a blur. Someone had to get hold of Bob as he was out working, and pass on the grim news. I had been on morphine patches for months so it was easier on me mentally than it was for him, and his family.

Amazingly, after a few weeks I started to feel slightly better - much to the surprise of the oncology team! Eventually I returned home, although I was to endure six more months of the strongest chemotherapy I could take.

It wasn't all bad. Yes, the treatment wasn't nice but I had a lot of laughs on the way. You know that saying, 'laughter is the best medicine'? I think there is a lot of truth to that. I learnt how to look for the positive in a negative, and still do. My first example of doing this was when I was losing my hair and my friend suggested that we do a 'head shave' and raise money for a cancer charity. It went ahead (no pun intended) - she had her blonde locks shaved off, Bob's head was also shaved and, as for me, I think I was actually quite relieved to see the rest of my hair go. We raised £3500 for charity and I will never forget the headlines in a local paper, complete with the 'before and after' photos, saying, 'Hair today, gone tomorrow!'

Although I berate my body for deciding to plonk the evidence of too much chocolate on my hips, its healing powers far outweighed the expectations of the cancer specialists and defied all medical reasoning.

During the hospital visit when I was told I was finally in remission, I casually asked my consultant if they had expected the cancer to go out of my liver and everywhere as well as it had. He replied, with all honesty,

"No, Jackie, we didn't think you would make it past four weeks - we never expected you to leave hospital! You should do the lottery; you have no idea how lucky you are!" Although quite shocked at the first line, I laughed at the second. They had got to know me so well by then and even when I was feeling ill I would try and make the effort to bring some cheer to their day. After all, they do such a mentally and emotionally challenging job – they deserve medals for the work they do.

By that time, my mind and thought pattern had changed forever. If you think you are dying, which I most certainly did, nature seems to 'click' a switch in your mind; you seem to gain an acceptance of what is happening and where you are supposed to be going. I look on it this way,

'This illness didn't take my life - it actually gave me my life.'

My brain was now open to all possibilities and the small things in life, many of which you cannot change, and are not of your making anyway, paled into insignificance.

As I said earlier, I had an inkling about animal communication as we used to recommend a lady, Julie Dicker, to our horse clients. I knew that she could get information such as their saddle was too tight, back problems and so much more, but I just didn't make the connection that she was actually being 'told' by the horses themselves. Whilst in remission I discovered that Julie had been battling cancer at the same time but, unfortunately, did not win her battle; however, she is well remembered for the fabulous work she did.

After this, a client contacted me to say that she had found another animal psychic, Beth, who was booked to visit her. She said she would let me know how it went and came back to me very quickly to say that Beth had been great and very accurate. I suggested to Bob that we book her for a visit as it would be lovely to know what our animals were thinking. This would be such a lovely treat. (Many people have communications done with their animals simply to hear what they have to say – it does not have to be for the sole purpose of finding out about problems they may be experiencing).

Beth was great and chatted to our horses first. She gave us information that she could not possibly have known – I was in awe! When we went across to our house, she uttered the words that have changed my life…

"You can do this, you know."

"Er, pardon?" I asked, bemused, "What do you mean?"

"I just know that you can do this too and, I can show you how!"

(Now that I do this work I come across this too; you often have a 'knowing' about someone and a lot of the time it is the person's animal that will tell us.)

With Beth's guidance, and (as I have said so many times before) it was like sitting down at a piano and suddenly being able to play the Moonlight Sonata. My life had been transformed and so many questions had been answered.

At one of my check-ups a few months later I sent a note to the consultant saying,

'I have won the lottery! It is not money though, but what it is I would not swap for a million pounds!' I am proud to say that I then proved animal communication was possible by means of a chat to the consultant's secretary's dog - and they actually sent a letter to my doctor about it! It said that they were extremely pleased with my progress and for them as a medical profession; they were simply amazed by what I had proven to them to be possible. I wonder how many other people have it on their medical records that they are psychic?!

I have to admit, most of my life I was rather like a square peg in a round hole and knew things but did not know how I knew them. On the farm and in my vet nursing work I used to find myself getting emotional but for no apparent reason. Over the years when I was holding horses for Bob to do their teeth I used to, for no explicable reason, get a wave of anger, frustration or sadness. Bob used to think I was sometimes being irrational and, to be honest, so did I! I would have been happily holding a horse, nothing had gone wrong, yet I was feeling awful.

In this work, animals do pass over their emotions to us, sad and funny ones. You may be wondering how this works. It works by telepathy, which is sending and receiving information via wavelengths through the air. Sounds impossible, doesn't it? Well, if you bear with me for a minute I will share a few thoughts with you. We all take the telephone for granted, so can you imagine what was said to the first person who suggested a mobile?

As the great Alexander Graham Bell said,

"I know not what this power is; I just know that it exists." That quote was pinned on my fridge for years. And so right he was. (I had to laugh; a journalist who visited my house spotted this quote. So, in an article it said, Jackie has the words... written on door of her fridge – just when I was hoping for more credibility, not less!)

The word and meaning of psychic is nothing to feel uncomfortable about; it means simply I, like many others, have a gift/skill to be able to use another part of my mind to tune into sources for information. Psychic actually means, 'a person sensitive to things beyond the everyday range of perception' so using telepathy I can have a conversation with an animal. Animals use it all the time – do you think horses only talk to each other when they neigh and that your dog has to bark to another to speak?

Being psychic/telepathic is far more common than you might think. How many times has the phone rang and you 'just knew' who it was? Psychic work has been, and is, used far more often than you may realise; psychics help the police, it was even used in the war and is used daily in life as guidance/mediumship for many people. There is so much evidence to support that when people and animals do pass over, they live on in spirit, or as I like to put it, 'go to Heaven'. We have Angels and guides to help us here on earth too. My easiest example of this is on those occasions when you are driving round a sharp bend and you just suddenly know to move tight to your side of the road. It is as if a voice told you (like a thought had been passed to you) and sure enough, someone was coming the other way, and more on your side of the road. (I can feel your heads nodding from here! Only joking).

I don't choose to do the 'people' side of things as my life is to work with animals and give them a voice to try to make a difference in their lives. When I 'tune in' (which is, basically, putting my mind to what I am doing) they pass me images, I hear information, and they manage to convey what they are thinking over to me. They give me their physical and emotions to feel; you would not believe how much I laugh with my work, animals can have a great sense of humour too!

Once you read about the wonderful times I have had with these celebrities, whose work is recognised through their various different walks of life, you will see for yourself how being an animal psychic works. I hope you will understand how through my efforts, with so much help from so many people and, not just the celebrities themselves, that this is seriously good news that needs to spread.

If animals can communicate with us, and they most certainly can, this would help solve so many problems and avoid many misunderstandings. This should make a huge difference to the lives of animals. This is a reality; there is no make-believe about it. After all, if it was, there is no way the personalities in this book would lend themselves to my cause and endorse what I do.

I know that I have beaten the odds with my health, although that has not all been plain sailing - since my cancer I have had two major operations and in fact, Bob laughs and tells people he thinks I am trying to leave him bit by bit!

So, if you think something is impossible, think again. We might not all achieve our dreams, but if you don't try, you most certainly won't.

If you don't think I have been laughed at for saying animals can 'talk', think again. I have put my head above the parapet so many times, and have on occasion, been shot down. I just bounce back up and keep going; the message I am trying to get out there is far more important than my feelings so I am pushing forward and doing the best I can do. I hope to inspire you, amuse you and warm your heart. I live by the concept of, 'nothing is impossible' and you know what - you would be amazed at what is!

As I said at the beginning, this book started as a little acorn before growing into its entirety. My hope is that it helps plant many more seeds for thought. Like the grand oak tree, it will give the strength and stability for animals knowing that we *do* know they can communicate and that we *are* willing to listen.

I have been blessed with help from so many people and thank each and every one of them for helping me make a difference for the animal kingdom and bringing me such happiness and fun on the way.

Jenny Seagrove

When Bob and I moved to a lovely hamlet in South Shropshire, England, nestled in a valley below the forestry we were delighted to say the least. What made the move even more wonderful is our neighbour, a lady called Veronica Thackeray, who is one of the most interesting I have ever had the pleasure to meet. Veronica is now in her early nineties (the naughty nineties as she likes to call it) and has a life story that would be sure to make a best-selling novel.

Not only is she a published author talking about rural life and so much more - she was in the S.O.E (Special Operations Executive) as a code breaker based in Egypt during the Second World War! This work was invaluable as depicted in the film *Carve her Name with Pride* starring the wonderful Virginia McKenna. Whilst talking about this project with Veronica she kindly offered to pass one of my books to Virginia, whom she has known for many years. Most of you reading this will link Virginia's name with the Born Free Foundation after her role in the film. Sadly, Virginia did not have any pets at the present time for me to talk to but, in a beautifully hand-written letter, said that she had spoken to her good friend Jenny. In

Virginia's own words, "Jenny is a wonderful person and a great dog champion", and now having met and talked to her many times, I couldn't agree more.

Jenny and I made contact and I quickly established that she knew all about animal communication and had even done a little herself! This was going to be delightful so I offered to chat to both of her dogs for her. Although we had planned to meet up in a few months we decided to do the chats sooner than that as there were a few pressing issues to discuss.

With pictures and details received, and the time arranged, I telephoned her. Just like the other lovely people in this book, she instantly put me at my ease and I had chosen to start with Louie, her six-year-old brown and white Springer Spaniel. He described himself as,

"A bit of a chap with lots of charm!" and stated that he was good at *stay*!

"That sounds just like him", Jenny enthused, "and, yes, he is very obedient."

Louie certainly wasn't shy. He informed us that he was really bright and always one step ahead and that he was not one of these 'silly' ones and had actually grown up very quickly! This was bold information as Springer Spaniels have the reputation for being slightly slower in the maturity stakes. Jenny said she thought he was right and he was ever such a clever boy. Louie then gave me a picture of him walking with a look of certain purpose and Jenny said,

"Yes, so true, but as he has declared how clever he is, could you ask him not to pull as I have tried to ask him and he is not listening." I explained that pulling was hurting Jenny's hands. This was quite difficult to discuss as he kept telling us how exciting his walks were and that he just wanted to get there. I pointed out that the more he pulled, the more Jenny had to keep slowing him down, so, in fact, if he went at a more sedate pace then he actually might get there faster! I used my 'bonding key' process to hopefully prick his subconscious. From Louie, his words for Jenny were 'Easy' to slow him down, coupled with 'Good Boy' if he responds and if he still isn't listening to try 'You're not helping.' I wished her luck on that one.

I asked Louie what he thought was fun? I burst out laughing as he seemed to be showing me Jenny throwing a ball that did not go in the right direction. I politely said to Jenny,

"Do you find that sometimes when you throw his ball that it doesn't go in the direction you would expect?" She laughed and said she knew exactly what he was showing me – when she takes him to the park, which is full of magnificent trees, sometimes the ball ricochets off one and goes elsewhere, quickly followed by an enthusiastic Louie.

Louie then volunteered that he was okay to be left alone and Jenny was not to worry. Jenny said that was true to a certain extent but could I ask him about being left in the theatre dressing room whilst she is on stage. Jenny explained she was talking about the Duke of Yorks in London where she was performing at that time. I asked him to show me how he felt and he made me feel rather on edge and as if he kept looking and feeling expectant. I could hear footsteps up and down a corridor. I passed all this over to Jenny and she said that she felt that he was edgy too. We established that her dressing room was in fact in a corridor but as it was further along it, this meant that there was a constant flow of people passing the door and this was what Louie was struggling with. He was worrying that people could come in when Jenny was not there who maybe shouldn't be in her dressing room at all. Oh bless him, he didn't realise that only people with permission were allowed in that area. So I asked him what would make him realise that they were friendly, no threat and indeed were doing no wrong? Immediately he presented me with a picture of those long and flat dog chews. Jenny said that sometimes she did give him them. So, by using them as a positive item we devised a system - Jenny was to break some up and put them in a jar so that people who entered could give him a treat and this would show that they were friendly and good because the only way they would know about giving him the treats was because Jenny would have told them! Also, I knew that he shared this time with his friend Millie, Jenny's other dog, and as she was completely relaxed about wherever she stayed, I suggested that he have a word with her too.

After that slightly serious discussion Louie made us laugh by noting that Jenny comes in looking one way and goes out looking the other!' We chortled and thought that was a good way of describing costume changes. When I asked him if there was anything important he wanted to share with Jenny, he said,

"Please tell her that I know I am her boy and that she would not let me go." These were beautiful words indeed but had a deeper meaning; Jenny had not been his first owner; she had actually got him when he was eighteen months old as the family he was with could no longer cope with having a dog. It was so lovely to hear how contented and secure he felt with her. He also said how much he adored Jenny's partner who unfortunately was allergic to dogs. Louie was so sweet about this and said although he would love a cuddle he quite understood and said it is fine to be admired from a slight distance. What a sweet boy.

I knew that I was going to meet Louie personally with Jenny in a few months time as the play *A Country Girl* in which she was playing the leading lady, was coming to Shrewsbury. Funnily enough, the leading man was Martin Shaw, who in *Judge John*

Deed, has a keen love interest in Jenny (aka Jo Mills) however, in this play, Jenny was to be his wife.

I thanked Louie for the chat and asked if he had anything he wanted to share with us before we gave Millie her turn. He most certainly did and it was a very poignant bit of advice about life and this is how it went.

"Sometimes in life you feel like you are on a moving escalator that suddenly comes to an abrupt stop but usually you *can* find a staircase!" A very clever way of pointing out not to give up as there is usually another way to continue your journey.

So over to Millie who had patiently been waiting her turn, which was quite surprising as I was about to find out that she was a prolific hunter and had the habit of getting in and out of places she shouldn't! The picture that Jenny had sent to me made me think Millie was actually bigger than she was. She was black in colour with that lovely 'I have been around a long time' grey muzzle.

"I am easy going and fit in anywhere," is how she described herself, and told me she was keen to please and also did that 'please stroke me' look and that Jenny got her 'by accident'. Jenny said that sounded just like her too. I was interested to know more about the 'by accident' line as, although I knew that she had come from an animal shelter she definitely was not giving me the impression that she had been a cruelty or neglect-type case. Jenny said that she hadn't been which was then confirmed by Millie saying,

"I simply got lost as I used to scavenge."

"Used to," laughed Jenny, "she still does, she is terrible." Jenny explained that at first, they had to keep a close eye on her as she would do a 'Houdini' as Jenny put it, out of the park. Apparently she would slip through the railings and go off like a bullet to check out the nearest bins and wherever else with the remote chance of a free feast. As most dog owners know, apart from the obvious getting lost, which is exactly what happened to her, is that should a dog eat the wrong thing, say, like a tasty chicken carcass – the chicken bones are lethal as they can pierce the intestines and, sadly, many dogs have lost their lives this way. There are many more that can be added to the danger list, corn on the cob, chocolate (mind you not many people throw out chocolate, well, certainly not from my house anyway!) and of course, poison put out for vermin - all inviting for a greedy dog just the same. Millie however, did stop her 'park escapology' – firstly she learnt to be more obedient and secondly, she's got too plump to get through the railings anyway!

On the subject of animal shelters - I have done work to help various rescue centres but the one I know more about than most is the *Dogs Trust* and I know that they do incredible work helping and saving so many dogs and cats. (Yes, they do help with cats too). I know sadly, and from personal experience, that some other animal centres only allocate a limited time they will keep an animal for. With the *Dogs Trust*, however, if they think an animal can be re-homed, then they will keep it for as long it takes to find them a new home. This all takes a lot of time, money and dedication and I know that Jenny is a Patron of theirs and huge supporter of their cause, as are many other animal loving celebrities. The work they do is invaluable and they keep all their supporters up-to-date with their monthly magazine, *Wag*. In one of their editions they highlighted my *Animal Insight* book which I hope triggered people's interest in animal communication and how we can try to help with rescue dogs. Something that I have heard time and time again from re-homed dogs is the question, "Am I staying here?" or the other, "Am I going back?" This might sound strange but some animals will try to keep their barriers up emotionally as they daren't believe that this wonderful home is theirs to keep. I equate this to a person having come out of a bad relationship and when they meet a truly lovely partner, sometimes they have that, 'too good to be true' feeling and are wary to let go should they lose that person again. Everyone can do this for a new dog to their home - just tell them in plain English what you yourself would want to hear, and make them feel secure so they can relax and enjoy life knowing that this is now their life and reality. This can work wonders, I promise you.

Jenny now knew for fact that Millie hadn't had a horrible previous home and asked if she missed that family.

"Oh no," she quickly declared, "my house is so warm and my bed so comfy!" She went on, "I am quite lazy really and I love my warmth, peace and quiet."(They were her priorities at this time of the conversation and I was sure she would go onto talk about her love for Jenny, well I was hoping so). I asked her, what was the best bit about her life?

"Eating!" No real surprise with that reply and Jenny saw the funny side. With that she also gave me the picture of her chasing something and looking up a tree, I suggested that she enjoyed a good squirrel chase?

"Oh yes," enthused Jenny, "I tell her they are tree rats and she runs like mad after them." Millie then told us, sometimes there are more than one which causes confusion when they split up and go in different directions. All was not lost according to Millie, who wanted to inform us that she could find them as they tend to poo so she can find them by their scent! Such good fun and exercise with no actual harm done to the squirrels at all. I have to say, whilst embarking on this celebrity quest; I never expected to learn the true art of determining a squirrel's whereabouts – so thanks Millie for that little gem!

One little animal that is not quite so lucky is the mouse - Millie is a dab hand at finding them and dispatching them. During one phone call at a later date with Jenny the way she said something still makes me laugh,

"Can you ask her how her eye is? She has had a run in with a broken plant pot whilst mouse hunting." Not funny about her eye, but the 'run in' bit instantly conjured up a funny picture of this broken plant pot making its fighting advance towards 'mouse-hunter' Millie! Fortunately Millie made me feel that her eye was fine with just a slight scratch on the eye ball but with no permanent damage done - this was basically the same as the vets conclusion, so Jenny felt relieved to hear this confirmed by two separate sources. (I now know that her eye did in fact heal with no further complications).

Suddenly I got that fantastic feeling when somebody with nails scratches your back in that certain way that makes you wriggle and squirm and plead with them to keep going. I could then see a hand doing this on Millie's back who was quick to inform us it was her favourite sign of affection, which I let Jenny know. Jenny confirmed that she did that and would do it even more so as she knew it meant that much to her.

On a more serious subject, which was one of the reasons for this phone call, Jenny wanted me to ask about Millie's right eye as she had been in a scrap with another dog, and its owner's foot as she tried to separate them. Unfortunately, in the panic of trying to separate the dogs the owner had been over-forceful and somehow managed to cause Millie's eye to pop out of its socket. Jenny was not walking Millie that day but, fortunately, Millie's walker rushed her straight to the vets so they were able to treat the problem quickly. According to Millie she could still see out of it but felt there was some damage to the peripheral vision on the outside. She seemed very un-phased by it and simply informed us,

"I just have to turn my head more!"

You would think by reading this that maybe Millie disliked other dogs, but this was not the case. She was friendly to other ones but not this certain dog. This other dog was a hairy mongrel who, according to Millie, was a 'cocky little devil' and she really didn't like him and with good reason according to her. Apparently this dog had been rather 'full on' with Louie on a previous occasion, and Millie had certainly not forgotten this although it was over a year ago! So, on spotting him across the park, she seized the opportunity, made a beeline for him to give him some 'full-on' attitude herself. I thought I would ask Millie,

"What did you gain from it?"

"I lost!" was her succinct reply. I had a discussion with her about doing it again and explained that things could be a lot worse, so please forget him and let bygones be bygones. I gave Jenny a bonding key (also to be passed to anyone else walking Millie), which I hoped would work and keep her out of harm's way. Mind you, I think the other dog's owner will keep a keen eye out for Millie appearing over any horizon in the future too.

"Does she realise how much I love her?" Jenny enquired. As soon as those words left her lips, Millie showed me a delightful picture of her 'Millie dance' with the words,

"I can make her smile!" Jenny immediately recognised 'the dance' and said it certainly did have the desired effect. Millie was on a roll now and declared, "I am absolutely adored!!" She explained that if she was somewhere with Jenny, that Jenny would always 'introduce' Millie to them, this made her feel very important and, in her own words, 'an integral part of Jenny's life.'

As I have said, this was done prior to me meeting Jenny so I knew that there were a few things that Jenny wanted to ask about. Having covered Millie's eye problem and about the other dog, I asked if there was anything else. Jenny paused and then said,

"Er, yes. She, for some reason, has taken to weeing under the piano, would you mind asking why?" I asked Millie outright, why she was doing it. Her response was swiftly given,

"It wasn't me that started it and is it wrong?" Immediately I thought to myself that I was pretty sure that Louie had not been guilty of such behaviour as surely Jenny would have noticed and asked about him first. So I simply repeated the reply to Jenny and asked if it made any sense to her. Jenny thought for a moment and then said,

"Actually, yes it does." She went on to explain to me that an old dog of hers had passed away peacefully under the piano and if her memory served her right, he had made a wet patch at that time. I explained that although it had been thoroughly cleaned I assume that there was still an odour that Millie with her strong nose could pick up. I set about explaining to Millie that what she was doing was wrong and was in fact a rather undesirable thing to do and could she please stop doing it. Although dealing with animal's 'toileting mistakes/problems' I know from experience can be very hard to solve, I asked Millie what Jenny could say to her to remind her that it was wrong, and Millie suggested that should she venture under the piano, Jenny should simply say,

"No more!" I also suggested that Jenny put an orange on the spot to deter her (a trick learned in my vet nurse days – this is even more effective with cats) and Millie suggested pepper would help - white pepper, not black! I wished her luck and she said she would let me know how it went.

I thought at this point we would ask her how she thought Jenny would describe her.

"A wonderful dog and very easy to look after!" I don't think she realises what a headache an 'escape artist' can produce but having listened to her, I thought this description was very apt. Jenny agreed but also said,

"Could you please explain my fear of losing her?"

"I will do my best," I replied but, on hearing that, Millie butted in with,

"I know, I know!" as though she had been told a thousand times before and then proudly told us that she 'went like a Gatling gun!' She sensibly offered that if she did get lost Jenny should stay in the same place as Millie said she was very good at backtracking and had successfully done that in the past. (She also suggested that Jenny blow a high-pitched whistle as she had superb hearing!) Jenny said that Millie was right and that she has worked her way back before but to try and help (with a bit of tough love) I did my usual thing - explaining that when animals were either with their owner or in a safe place that their owners had left them they would be safe away from things like traffic, people that steal dogs and from simply getting lost by venturing too far. (She knew the last one all too well). I ask them to try to imagine the feeling of never ever seeing their owners or other animal friends again - would it really be worth the risk? She responded for Jenny with,

"I know - I'd hate not to come back with you." She did however concede that if she had to go on a lead for her own safety, she would understand why Jenny was restricting her at that time. I don't know if this will really push into her conscious mind at the times when needed, but I had tried my best to point out the dangers to her and hoped it might help.

"What does she think of Louie?" Jenny ventured. "He is a good boy really, but sometimes he doesn't listen to me so I tell him again!"

"Too true" Jenny laughed and said she knew exactly what that meant. I asked Millie what she wanted to say to Jenny.

"You are a lovely owner - I'm not an accessory, I'm a person!" We both thought that was so lovely and just goes to show how they like being treated like little individual people. I spend my life telling people they are; just in different bodies.

We covered her few physical problems but, to be honest, for her age, she was in very good shape with many more years of mouse spotting and catching, I am sure. We finished the call and Jenny said she would confirm the date she was coming to Shrewsbury and we would arrange to meet up then. Our plan was to meet up to do the celebrity questions over a bite of lunch and combine the trip to the theatre for me and my next-door neighbour, Veronica, who, as I said, was the catalyst for me doing this with Jenny in the first place.

As I also mentioned at the beginning, Bob and I only moved to Shropshire in the past few years and I am still not terribly well acquainted with Shrewsbury and its surrounding villages, I am more of 'a country girl' myself too! On our caravan trips up the A5 to North Wales I was often drawn to a sign for a village called Montford Bridge, for whatever reason I had no idea. One day we decided to pull off and check out this village to satisfy my curiosity. It is very picturesque but I was actually hoping to find a tiny old-fashioned church or interesting landmark but it really was like a 'drive through' place. I was slightly disappointed but then forgot all about it.

Months passed then Jenny contacted me. We organised to meet on a Tuesday as she would not have a matinee performance that day. She was staying in a village North of Shrewsbury that, as usual, I had not heard of, but said I could look it up and we would sort something out. Jenny said she would call me and let me know when she (and Louie and Millie, of course) were at the house where they were staying. It turned out to be in a very rural place with great fields for the dogs to run, (apologies to any mice that might have been there!) but no pubs or suchlike. Jenny said,

"I did, however, pass a restaurant on the way to the theatre last night in a little place called Montford Bridge, do you know it?" My brain went into a whirr and I said I did and that that would be an ideal place to meet. It was now clear why I had been guided to go there in the first place - a quick pre-run was a very clever way of spirit guiding me.

On a lovely sunny day, Jenny and I pulled into the car park at exactly the same time and chose to sit at the outside tables with the dogs. As I said, I was surprised to find Millie was a lot smaller than I had expected but just as cute, and as for Louie, he was the big softy he had come across to me. Jenny said she would go and get us the menus and a drink and with that, turned to Louie and said, the way you would to another person,

"Louie, sit down and stay there." With that, this gorgeous Spaniel sat down and he didn't move, apart from his eyes following where she was going. I smiled and said,

"True to his word, he certainly is good at stay." Jenny nodded and finished tethering Millie to our table leg which would solve any thoughts of hers to either take off or decide this could be an opportunity for a bit of scavenging!

Jenny, I have to say, was delightful and came across as she had on the phone, warm and friendly and thought the world of her animals. It was so touching to see when we were talking about them that she would gesture to one as she was recounting a tale, so personal, lovely. She presented me with some great news - Millie had stopped weeing under the piano! I replied, with definite zest,

"Yes!" You know the type, with the accentuated 's'! I was delighted to hear such a good outcome and long may it last!

Also, the funny thing was Jenny's reference to Millie's stipulation of colour of pepper. It turned out that Jenny's carpet was white, so thank goodness white pepper was the order of the day as black would have made such a mess! I congratulated her on being so good about stopping doing it and asked her if she had anything else to add to the topic. In typical Millie style, she replied,

"Thanks, but the nice thing was I was able to blame someone else!"

After lunch we took the dogs for a walk in a beautiful field and, in the end, sat down on some luscious but dry grass. I have to admit, it did run through my head how surreal was this? Here was me, sitting in a field with a lady that people readily recognise from television. Imagine if someone said to me,

"What did you get up to today?" and I replied,

"Oh, I went to Shrewsbury, sat in a field with Jenny Seagrove chatting to her and her dogs!" It sounds funny put like that. It truly was such a lovely time and an unforgettable memory for me.

We let Millie take the lead on the celebrity questions when she had finished chatting and informing me about things that amused her like; how security conscious Jenny is, double-checking the door is locked twice etc.

For the question "What other job did she think Jenny could have done had she not been an actress?"

"Direct traffic!!" was her reply. I was laughing so much trying to deliver this line and quickly said I would find out why she had offered this. With Jenny laughing too, I explained that is was in fact intended as a compliment. Millie explained that Jenny is very clear and concise in the way she explains or directs people, encapsulated by this phrase from Millie,

"If you scream and shout, people don't listen but if you quickly point out the truth, they will see it!" How clever was that statement?! Well done, Millie. I asked Jenny if she had done any directing and she said that that side of the business really interests her too. For the contribution bit, she wanted to share a point on behalf of other dogs to say why often they were protective towards their owner.

"We feel the need to protect because we feel protected ourselves." I thanked her for that and said that it made a lot of sense and I understood her logic. I also told her that we, as humans, would understand this loyal thinking but, to be honest, we are so pleased to be able to look after and protect our pets that they should not need to feel that it has to be reciprocated. We want them to enjoy and relax in that feeling of security we aim to give.

I believe in 'life's timing' – things happen when the time is right and that is when it was meant to be. For various reasons it took me ages to be able to get round to writing this story up and I had even spoken to Jenny a couple of times in between doing so. The day after I wrote the above paragraph someone stopped me to give me confirmation of exactly what I was explaining. A gentleman stopped me to pass on the message to say the lady I spoke to the other day was so grateful and this is why.

About a week before whilst I was walking my dog, Sally, I stopped to talk to this gentleman. There was also a lady, who I didn't know, standing at the back of her parked car which was quite near to us. Whilst I was passing the time of day with this man, the sound of barking dogs erupted from her car. This lady kept trying to tell her two dogs to be quiet but to no avail. I stepped further back and apologised as I thought it was because they could see Sally.

"Oh no, it is not that, they never used to bark at anything but since my husband died a few months ago, they have been awful." I sympathised with her for her loss and I ascertained that this definitely had just started since the loss of her husband and she nodded. I decided to try to share my knowledge of a previous situation very similar to this that I had dealt with through my work. I know by experience there are many sceptics out there but I believe that even if people should laugh at me I should still try to give them the option to hear what I know to be true.

"I might be able to help you on this one," I ventured. "As strange as it may sound, and it does to many people, animals can understand what we say. My work is to talk to people's animals and help them if they need it." She didn't furrow her brow, she actually didn't change her expression at all, so I just kept going and said, "I have experienced this before and found this tends to be the dog's reasoning - because your husband has now gone, they think they are doing the right thing by asserting authority to protect you, hence the barking. As much as you are asking them to stop they feel that you need protecting and think they are helping by taking on that job." Still no words from her so I simply said, "Try telling them in plain English, (and don't worry, they will understand you) that you do not need protecting and that you would like to protect them as you did before. You appreciate their loyalty and thoughts but please stop barking as there really is no need." With that, I said goodbye to her and the gentleman and set off on my walk home wondering what kind of conversation would be going on now I was out of earshot.

I forgot all about it until the morning when the gentlemen stopped me and asked for my phone number. When I asked him what he wanted it for, he said,

"Oh, it is not for me, but you know Mrs …, you spoke to her dogs a few days ago and what you said would work, did! She is so pleased and would like to call you!"

So, apart from a delightful result for all concerned - by me being in the right place at the right time – it was not just an opportunity to help but clearly showed that animals can understand and change when told things. This is how the word about animal communication gets spread and this example truly bears out what the lovely Millie was trying to tell us.

So back now to our sunny field in Shrewsbury: Millie made me feel like she was blowing a kiss. Oh, how cute. The lovely thing about this was that Jenny shared with me that she often would blow a kiss to Millie - how wonderful I was able to return this loving gesture.

It was now back over to Louie who had been informing us that Jenny sometimes refers to him as 'young man'. Jenny agreed with this and, for fun, I asked him his thoughts on why she called him that and his reasoning was 'because she had had more birthdays than him!!' I know he thought this was really funny, and it was! He was comical but so polite with it. This he felt he needed to share with her,

"Please tell her I think she drives rather fast, if she doesn't mind me saying so." Jenny laughed again and said that he was probably right but she is very careful when they are in the car. I explained that she had taken note and will be extra careful from now on! Things like this make me laugh; it is like being told off by your children, whether they are right or wrong on the subject. On the subject of not doing things as one should; Jenny informed me that Louie did, at first, improve in the 'not straining on the leash' stakes, and listened to her use of the word 'easy' etc. Unfortunately, the effect didn't last and he was tugging her arm once again. I had another word with him about it. I pointed out that if Jenny was to heed his point and drive slower then could he possibly heed hers too?

Louie seemed to think that this conversation was such a great opportunity to express his sense of humour. The next question for her alternative job,

"A brain surgeon!" was his cheeky reply, quickly followed up with, "someone that cares for people, she is such a good listener you know, and has time for people, even if she is busy herself." This I hoped was right, although she might have wanted to be a brain surgeon – only kidding! We talked and Jenny said she does try to be as empathetic as possible; it is a busy world and sometimes people just have to make time to make a difference. The same goes for the work and causes regarding animals. Yes, it can be time consuming but if you can do something to help people or animals then, if possible, you should. I couldn't have put it better myself and I can see why Virginia McKenna suggested Jenny to me. I know through other animal communicators and healers that Virginia is still out there tirelessly working for everyday animals and not just the lions she is renowned for helping.

Louie's input here for this book I think encapsulates Jenny's tireless work on behalf of animals which takes on so many forms. These are the wise words Louie wanted share…

"Love and persistence does wonders." What a marvellous thing to say and it is so true - we do not have the given right for animals to just simply trust us; we have to earn their trust as we do with our human relationships.

After such a lovely afternoon we organised to meet after the show and I headed off to get changed and pick Veronica up. Although Veronica was ninety-two, she was still very nimble and was so excited about going to the theatre. She said it had been at least twenty years since she had been to one, and the last time was to a grand one in London. She had never been to the *Severn Theatre* in Shrewsbury, as neither had I and it took us about an hour to get there. We found our seats, fairly near to the front and settled down ready for the curtain to go up. To my utter surprise, Jenny, (as did the whole cast) spoke with an American accent, very different from her TV persona. The scene changes were done seamlessly by the actors themselves and I asked Veronica if she was enjoying it. I felt terrible – since her last theatre visit her hearing had diminished immensely and she could hardly catch a word. I offered to leave and take her home but she said she was happy to stay and 'just watch' and after all, she was so looking forward to meeting Jenny in person.

With the play over, and what a marvellous play it was, we set off to find Jenny. I decided to ask one of the theatre assistants for her guidance as; although I class Veronica as very sprightly, the *Severn* has quite a few floors. The assistant ushered us to a lift and into an area with tables. We waited and waited but there was no sign of Jenny but the assistant assured me that she would come out that way so we waited some more. After about fifteen minutes Veronica said it didn't matter and that she would quite like to get home. I was disappointed for her but bearing in mind she had listened to a 'silent' play I escorted her back down the lifts, outside and left her with some lovely people whilst I fetched the car.

We travelled back home and Veronica spent the whole journey regaling stories of her incredibly interesting life. She is such a character and even married the retired village doctor when they were both over eighty!! I got back into my own house and realised my mobile phone was still switched off (oh, could you imagine it going off during a play, a fate worse than death!) and having turned it back on, 'beep beep', and up came a missed call and a message from Jenny.

"Where are you? I can't find you." Oh, I could have kicked myself, I didn't think to switch my phone back on as I was too busy concentrating on looking after Veronica. Apparently we had been at one end of the building and Jenny the other! How very annoying. Still I had to laugh – there was me, a psychic, and Veronica who did intelligence work for Britain and between the pair of us, we couldn't find Jenny Seagrove at a local theatre!

Jacky Newcomb

"I'd contact Jacky Newcomb if I was you, she doesn't live that far from me and she is very approachable! I have met her on a few occasions and she is as she comes across in her Angel books - warm hearted and very sweet."

This was a chance conversation with a lady, Sue, who had emailed me having heard my name somewhere and simply wanted to tell me that she too was on the same 'animal wavelength' and liked what I was doing. So – with the wonders of *Facebook* I sent a note to Jacky explaining what and why I was wanting to do this Celebrity project.

We started emailing and I sent her my *Animal Insight* book so she could read about my work for herself. Within months, it was all was arranged (and with other personalities that she had so kindly put me forward to) and so near to the beginning of June 2010 myself and a friend Kim, to be my writer, set off on our 250 mile round trip.

As I have explained already, I decided to just let this run and see what the outcome was, and the reason I asked Kim, who I had met at a spiritual/holistic group, was because she kindly emailed me to let me know that Jacky had recommended my book in the *Chat it's Fate* magazine. So, who better to ask than Kim, who as it turned out wrote Angel poetry and had every book that Jacky had written, so a perfect choice.

Early on the Tuesday morning we set off with the sat nav on the dashboard and my Google printed maps complete with directions, just to be on the safe side! We were also going on North from Jacky's to meet her friend, Barrie John, and have a chat with his three animals too.

After a few, 'I don't believe you' incidents with the sat nav, we eventually conceded to do as it wanted and we actually arrived on time!

I believe there is no such thing as coincidence and 'signs' are put out for us should we be open enough to notice. Not that far before reaching our destination, there was a wheelie bin with 38 Main Street painted on it in big white letters – I gasped, that was my old address when I was a teenager! I laughed, and funnily enough, neither of us was nervous, we just knew all would be fine and were looking forward to it.

Jacky, with her beautiful, blonde, bobbed hair, prettily dressed with a long flowing skirt, greeted us like long lost friends and welcomed us into her office. I say 'office'; it is a beautiful light room where she works with meaningful pictures decorating the walls, and Angels and other beautiful objects adding class and atmosphere.

In trotted Magik, who is so petite, I had to have a quick re-check of her age. I had written down '5 yrs' yet she looked the size of 'five months', but she was actually just an amazingly small and dainty cat. She was jet black with big amber eyes and just the cutest little girl you would ever meet.

Although Jacky knew other animal communicators she had not personally had an animal reading before but, from my book, she knew how I worked. Magik immediately obliged by showing me a picture of her regularly just appearing as if from nowhere, accompanied by the expressive words 'Taa-dah' for the complete desired effect. Jacky smiled and confirmed this.

Well Magik, as small as she was, sure could talk and did her best to show that animal communication is real and informed me that she knew why I was there as Jacky had told her I was coming! With another nod and smile from Jacky, Magik then announced that Jacky had a 'very strong heartbeat' (close knowledge gained being held like a baby close to Jacky's heart) which I thought was quite a random thing to say.

"I actually do have a slight heart problem," Jacky informed us "but the doctors can't pin-point exactly what is wrong, so that is very reassuring to know – thanks, Magik!" As Jacky knew, the animals pass emotional feelings to me too, and when I told her that, according to Magik, 'there is an invisible chain between them' as she always knew where Jacky was in the house and I said that I felt there was a very strong bond.

"Oh yes," Jacky agreed, and put her hand to her heart and said, "Oh, I felt that too!" Magik had given us burst of emotion to share. I get to feel it most days from animals about their owners - I really do have such a wonderful job!

Magik put her 'serious hat' on for a minute and quietly informed me that,

"Tigger has been dropped, you know!" Tigger being the other cat, who presently was making his presence scarce, by staying upstairs. I thought the statement was a bit odd, so carefully asked Jacky if he was a rescue cat. She confirmed he was but really still a kitten as was just sixteen weeks old so I said we should come back to that later. In fact, I think that maybe

Tigger will want to enlighten us as Jacky had no idea what it was about, but intimated that, behaviour wise, it made sense.

"Can you ask her what she thinks of him?" Jacky questioned. Magik quickly responded with,

"He loves me, but he can be a bit grumpy!"

"Spot on," Jacky enthused, "that is exactly right; he licks Magik's head and then bites it!

Magik then took us back to her very young days, and I mean, very young - still on her mum's milk-bar! She went to great lengths to explain why she was so small, and said,

"I was different from the rest!" I looked to Jacky and she said,

"So true; She was small and, to be honest, not very pretty, the others were all boys and looked like 'magazine' cats" (I loved the magazine description – it depicted the journalist side of Jacky's work). Magik then showed me her being pushed out and really having to try to force her way through. I passed this over and Jacky said that she really didn't look terribly good with her tufts of dull, brown fur, so that is why she just had to have her.

"Aw, and just look at her now!" I couldn't help but say. With that, I distinctly heard the song 'There once was an ugly duckling...' and told Jacky and Kim, (who was writing ten to the dozen,) that my Dad used to sing that to me. (My Dad, who died when I was seventeen, made sure we knew he was on the journey with me too, I will come back to that later).

Magik took great delight in telling us that John, Jacky's husband, loved her too and so much so that she was sure he wouldn't mind having a picture of her in their bedroom! We laughed and although John was about to leave we had a quick minute to pose the question to him. His answer,

"No, I wouldn't mind at all, although not directly facing the bed would be preferable!" With John having left we were 'upgraded' to the sitting room to sit and relax on their sumptuous leather sofas.

I asked Magik to describe herself, and her reply took me quite by surprise.

"Very cute, very dainty – I could have been a ballerina!!" I told Jacky who said it made perfect sense as Magik would stand up on her tip-toes reaching for her hand and spins round! But in true animal style, would she give us a demonstration, of course not, that have been far too impressive! Magik having seen how certainly impressed we were with her self-description informed us that she had,

"Once seen a white cat and it looked very odd!" It turned out there was one that lived further down the road and, hopefully, was totally oblivious to Magik's slightly unkind opinion. I asked her to describe her life which was answered in poetic fashion, "Full of Angels with sun shining from all corners of the house". As Magik spends a lot of time in the room where Jacky is working, this we thought was very apt.

For this *Celebrity Pet Talking* book I devised some extra questions that differ from my normal line of chat. I asked Magik to describe Jacky and her answer was,

"A heart of gold, but tends to overstretch herself", and as for Jacky's best quality, "Thoughtful and forgiving" For anyone who knows Jacky, that I'm sure, would have pretty much been their sentiments too, as for the next answer, I would have placed a sound bet on them not guessing this one – 'If Jacky was not working as a writer, what other job do you think she would be good at?'

"A driving instructor!" was Magik's answer, loud and clear. She must have sensed my hesitation on passing that one over, so also informed me that Jacky was very methodical and calm, and would simply just tell them, 'Now, let's do that one again!' It turned out that Jacky had given both her daughters driving lessons before they started with their instructors, so Magik was, as usual, pretty correct.

Many other things were covered and when it came to Jacky asking Magik a question, she posed a very interesting one.

"Why is she here with me?" Magik immediately responded with,

"You didn't need me, but I am a beautiful accessory", coupled with a mention that she wore a diamante collar which really was 'so her'!" Then I heard another voice say,

"But I needed you to heal me", which came from Jacky's other cat, Tigger, who had been patiently waiting his turn.

So, for her last and very important question, which I devised for all the animals to answer, being, "What do you think your contribution to this book will say for animal communication?" In her words,

"To let people know it's lovely being a cat, and if we could read books, we'd read this one!!" (As I said, I never make anything up, and that would have been way beyond my imagination anyway!) I thanked Magik for talking to us and said that Tigger really needed this time now, and maybe he will explain about the 'being dropped' bit that you mentioned earlier.

Tigger was a stunning ginger and white cat, and quite a size, I might add. He was not fat, just a grand, big gentleman of a cat but lacked the boldness of his dear friend, Magik. This indeed was true and he was quick to show me a rather 'grabby' pair of hands, which I presumed must have been something to do with his start to life. Earlier I had ascertained that he was a rescue cat, but on questioning him I told Jacky that he did not come across to me as a cruelty case, in an abused beaten up kind of way. I carefully explained that it looked to me as if he had experienced some rather rough handling, and that is maybe relevant as to why he is so shy with strangers.

Jacky explained, he had actually been a feral kitten, and at sixteen weeks, he, his mother and the other siblings had been caught and taken to the rescue centre. Ah, this made perfect sense, because I do know from experience, that sometimes, (with a big suede glove on, I might add) rescuers just have to 'grab' them the best way they can to be able to get them to safety. This may well have been when he was dropped as it can be so frightening for them; they can put up a fearsome struggle and will sometimes slip through people's hands.

As you will have noted from Magik's 'milk-bar chat', they do remember things from a very tender age and this is often the cause of problems later on. We told Tigger that people who visit certainly did not want to grab him, and to try not to be so suspicious, he asked Jacky to use these words (a bonding key), 'It's okay, we only want to admire you'. This, I hope, will allay his fears, so at least he can sit, albeit at a distance, in the same room as visitors.

Talking of sitting, Tigger showed me a picture of him sitting very majestically in the bay window; complete with head tilted up to show the vision. Jacky laughed and said,

"Oh how funny, I am watching you, and you are doing the same actions!" I laughed too and said it is so funny how animals can get me to do the physical actions to go with the pictures. (On that note – you know when cats do that 'making puddings' as I call it, that paw kneading action, it is that is just such a lovely woozy, hypnotic feeling. I know this as, one day I was given the sensation to experience from a very kind and knowing cat who also informed me that it actually produces endorphins!). Tigger by now was in his stride and when I asked him to describe himself, his regal reply, complete with accent I might add was,

"Unashamedly good looking!!" Well, we all roared with laughter, and I made sure that Kim didn't miss that in her notes. Jacky informed us that everyone, even the vets tell him that! (A perfect example of an animal really taking on board what people say.)

Jacky asked me to ask him if there is anything he would like to make his life better. With that, he declared his favourite colour was blue – royal blue, and gave us clear instructions of wanting a squashy cushion in that colour. Jacky said she didn't have anything like that but she would get some material and make him one. Delighted with that result, and our peals of laughter, I'm sure, he then showed me a gold twisted cord, complete with tassel to adorn the edges of said cushion. I thought this was so funny, and very imaginative, and laughed even more when Jacky said he actually had that exact same cord on his present bed already!!

So with that sorted I checked if there was anything else, and he commented that the cat flap (well, what I presumed was a cat flap) was rather small for a big cat like him. Jacky said it wasn't the proper cat flap he was talking about, it was a hole that they had made at the back of the garage so Magik could get through to the back garden. It was really a tad too small for Tigger, although he did manage to squeeze himself through, with an 'octopus moving through a tube impression' but he then quickly announced that it didn't matter as they were moving anyway! This was actually fact, as Jacky is planning to move down to Cornwall (which I did know) where other members of her family are. I distinctly heard, "October." So I asked Jacky if she thought it would be around then.

"Oh, No," she replied, "we should be moving next month, definitely not as far away as that, that is another five months away. I laughed and said,

"Oh, well, let's hope I got that wrong then."

"Me too," said Jacky, "October is going to be so busy for me, I have got a new book coming out and lots of things happening." We moved on and Tigger decided to bring John, Jacky's husband, into the conversation by showing me him sitting very close to a man.

"He is my confidante, you know." I told Jacky this, and she said that she felt he was very close to John and did spend more time with him she thought, than with her. Although Jacky thinks of Tigger as her cat, he will often sit with John in the evenings and she teasingly call him a 'traitor!'. Tigger seemed to be more than happy to talk about things other than himself but then informed us that he knew where ever John was in the house due to this 'clunk clunk' noise which indicated the sounds of shoe heels to me. Well, Jacky's face was a picture, and she exclaimed,

"I am always telling him off for wearing shoes in the house!!" and I said,

"Well, even the cat is talking about it now! Tell you what, why don't I ask Tigger what his advice would be to try and get John to take his shoes off." So with that I posed the question and Tigger was very clever with his reply.

"He (John) is meticulous and dresses so beautifully (this being spot on) so, by wearing outdoor shoes in the house, he is really letting himself down!! I suggest you go and buy him a pair of soft Italian leather slip on shoes for the house, he might like to wear them." I said I hoped that might help, and as Tigger was 'in full swing' he went on to say, "I think he should be wearing glasses, you know". I said to Jacky I didn't take notice if John had glasses when we met him and she said,

"No, but he wears them for driving." Not satisfied with that answer, Tigger was still impressing upon me that he thought it was more than that. Jacky then pointed at their very large flat screen television, and said, "Actually he does struggle to see that clearly". Mmm, I go with Tigger on that one, and I am sure Jacky will let me know how John gets on with his eye-test!

"Oh, we have a visitor!" announced Jacky, but we knew straight away, not of the ordinary kind, but a spirit one. (If you have read any of Jacky's Angel books, you will know that Jacky has seen spirits since she was a child). "He is standing in the doorway, a tall man, dark hair…"

"That will be my Dad" I interrupted, "That doesn't surprise me. He died when I was seventeen and he still looks after me. He appears everywhere and I am delighted that he is sharing in our day." And with that, he disappeared.

And so for more questions for Tigger; Jacky wanted me to ask him about his health, to which I got the reply,

"I do throw up sometimes", (but to be honest most cats do) but I just pass over what I am told.

"Oh yes, he does" replied Jacky, "It's his own fault, you know. He is a thief!"

"You mean the cat's a food thief?" I replied incredulously. Jacky continued,

"Anything, and I mean anything! Curries, Chinese any leftovers that happen to be there," Jacky informed us. In between the giggles, I suggested that I maybe 'had a word' to explain what was making him sick, as I thought logically it may have been to do with his early days as a stray. I did my best, but he just 'smiled' at me (it is true by the way, the colouring on his face makes him look like he has that Cheshire cat smile) and responded in his very plum accent,

"I know. I am my own undoing!" So, I made no headway there. He was simply just a greedy boy and there was no more talk on the subject.

On to more personal things – asking Tigger his opinion of Jacky's best quality, and his answer,

"Looking after me and checking I am alright." As soon as the words had fallen from my lips, Jacky responded with,

"I heard that too!" I was delighted, and thought to myself, well if that isn't validation of my work, what is?! Having heard that, Tigger chimed in with,

"She is beautiful as well." (I think he hoped she would hear that one personally too!) As for different work, he stayed on the writing agenda, but said that she could write murder mysteries (we laughed about how that would be at the opposite end of the scale from Angel stories!) as Jacky apparently can write plots in her head, and spin them round to fit! Jacky then informed us that she had, in fact, had a short fictional story printed and was presently working on a novel, but nothing to do with murder she hastened to add.

As we drew to a close, I thanked him for talking to us and asked him,

"What was the last thing he wanted me to tell Jacky?"

"Please say - I love you and to stay kind and considerate because that's why people love you too." The emotion stirred in Jacky's face, yet again, as she told us, she had asked him that morning, that if he could try to say he loved her through me. Bless him, he did!

Time was ticking on and we had to leave, but not before I had my photo taken with Jacky, as did Kim. Also, I left with a signed picture, inscribed, 'To Jackie, thank you for your excellent reading, love Jacky Newcomb'. High praise indeed from a lady who works with top psychics/mediums, so is very used to hearing accurate information regarding people and their lives.

It was such a blessing having Jacky's help. Not only did she put me in contact with several people in this book but I now regard her as a friend. She has a font of knowledge regarding the publishing industry and so much more.

In my other books, which are complied of case stories of work that I have done and how an animal has transformed etc., they are adorned with illustrations from the very talented artist, Jacks Fennell. Her bespoke cartoons express and convey hilarious, cute and sometimes downright absurd things animals have told me, and their owners, about. I decided to commission a picture for Jacky and send it to her as a surprise as a thank you for all that she has done to help me with this project. She was thrilled with it and I am delighted to have permission from both of them to include it with this story here.

"Exquisite darling_exquisite"

Barrie John

Barrie, with his three pets - Milo the cat, Brandy the Miniature Poodle, and Azlan, who was a huge five-year-old Leonberger, lived about thirty odd miles from Jacky's house. It took us roughly an hour to get there, and having actually obeyed the sat nav it took us right to his house!

Barrie welcomed us at the door and we were directed straight to his reading room, which consisted of a beautiful rich brown Chesterfield settee and a wingback chair to match. Barrie made us coffee while we got ourselves organised.

Kim and I sat on the settee and Brandy, a sweet little boy, thought to be around twelve years old, gently greeted us. He is a black (well, a bit salt and peppered now) Poodle with those 'clouded glass' eyes that were giving away his age. (I made a mental note to check his sight with him later).

With Barrie now sitting in his chair, and in between sips of coffee, I started the chat with Brandy. Azlan was shut in the kitchen, having been openly deemed by Barrie to be rather boisterous and weighing a massive twelve stone so I readily agreed that I could do it from a distance and meet him at the end!

Whilst getting to know Brandy, Milo the cat made his appearance too. Brandy gave us an introduction about himself, which was,

"I am a happy chap, thoughtful and like to be people's friend." This was validated by Barrie, who totally understands how important validation is. Barrie is a medium, and a well known one at that. He has made many appearances on TV and radio, both here and abroad, and is sort after by many people who know of his genuine reputation. So, as opposed to me communicating with living animals like me, he talks to spirit people for their loved ones who want to hear from them again. I, at this point, do note that some people reading this book will not be into things like that which I have no problem with - we all have our own freedom of choice and beliefs.

I treat my work in a very grounded way and find that once people realise that what I am telling them I could not possibly guess, they have a change of heart. This also happens when sceptics (who I have no problem with either as I have been dubious about other things myself) go and see a genuine medium, they then, although they might not understand how it's done, will see how difficult it would be for someone to stand there and just guess accurate personal information. I admire mediums for getting up in front of an audience and doing what they do, they bring a lot of comfort and often a lot of humour with it. I have done demonstrations myself to raise money for a cancer charity, which sometimes put me under pressure, and the animals I were talking to were here living on earth!

Brandy then showed me a picture of being what I perceived to be shut in a cage, and an anxious feeling to accompany it. I carefully asked Barrie if he knew about this, but as I suspected, this was to do with his former home, hence the 'about' age. Barrie said that he had rescued him at about two years old, and that he was actually for Barrie's mum, but that situation was more than possible, so to please continue. Brandy showed me him looking bewildered, which I thought would have been how he was when Barrie got him.

This was so true, he had never really experienced much of the outside world and sadly, very shortly after, one day outside his new home, he bolted into the traffic and was very seriously injured. He survived, but told us that he screamed when he was run into, and amazingly, the incident had made think and, as he so deftly put it, 'brought life round to face him' making him realise that he never wanted to leave Barrie and his parents, so he took the line of caution after that. (Talk about a positive out of a negative!) Suddenly Brandy asked,

"Why is he (Barrie) not talking to you?" I laughed, and realised exactly what he meant, but then asked Barrie,

"Do your animals sit in with you when you are doing readings?"

"Oh yes," replied Barrie, "the people love it, it often puts them at their ease." Another little voice piped up,

"I hear things too!!" That was Milo, the cat, also twelve years old, black and very knowing and talkative, as you are about to find out. Barrie was laughing and told us that Milo always knew when someone was here for a reading, and promptly made himself at home in the room ready for it.

Conversation now hijacked by Milo, so I asked him to tell me something that Barrie would know, so we would be sure it was him he was talking to. With that, a very clear picture of a black cat, yawning, as wide as his jaws would go! How strange he should offer that I thought, but true to form, Milo was talking and that is exactly what he does when he is "bored and had enough" as he puts it. Barrie said, he goes one step further and very obviously turns his back on people, often on a windowsill for the true effect.

So, a joint conversation it was to be. Brandy was in the crook of Barrie's left arm, and now Milo was in his right one! After a few minutes, I just realised how gorgeous this was, and politely asked if I could possibly take a photo. Barrie agreed, and said, actually he could not remember the last time they had sat together on him. They were sitting so quietly so I delved in my bag, found my camera and snapped away. I got some gorgeous shots, one of which I chose and sent on to Barrie a few days later which I am sure he will treasure.

Brandy butted back in, showed me in the direction of his teeth and told me that he had been fed rubbish when he was small. I asked Barrie if his little dog had had many teeth problems, and he said that he only had about three left, as he, from a young age, had had major problems. I told him that according to Brandy, the people had fed him 'rubbish' so that was one questioned answered as to why they were so bad. Brandy showed me him being handed in mid-air like you hand a toddler to somebody else.

"Oh, that will be to my Dad. Mum died a few years ago, which is why he comes here to me but, at night time Dad comes and takes him back home." Brandy told us that he understood where people go when they pass over, and was quite matter of fact when he then informed us that sometimes there are other people (spirits) in the room too. Brandy went on to inform us,

"I am very special little dog, and very intuitive too!" As Barrie was nodding, I heard what I knew was a perfect imitation of Barrie's voice saying, "Come on, give me more," which Barrie confirmed is what he asks (silently from his mind) of spirit to give more information so the family/friend will be in no doubt that it is their loved one connecting for a chat.

Milo, the cat, interrupted again, by repeating that he is 'in' on the conversations too. I thought I would ask him, "What do you think Daddy does?" (Milo called him Daddy, so Daddy it was!)

"He tells people good things," and had his attempt at imitating people, by saying, "thank you, thank you, thank you!" which we knew was from the clients leaving after a reading. Whilst still nestled into Barrie's arm, he so sweetly informed me,

"There was a man (he gave me the vision of an elderly gentleman) who came here, and Daddy really helped him. He (the gent) was really surprised, but it made a big difference." I repeated this all to Barrie and said did it make any sense to him? Straight away he knew exactly who Milo was talking about, and told us that he went and personally visited the man at his home afterwards too, which is something he doesn't tend to do.

Milo held the conversation so I asked him to describe himself, but Barrie made us laugh with his suggestion of, "Maybe master of the house?" With chortling ensuing from us, he conceded with, "No, Daddy is, but I am a good second best!"

"So how do you describe yourself?" I asked, and with ease, he announced,

"Very knowing, but very welcoming at the same time."

"My turn, my turn," I could hear from our little Poodle friend, so I let him have his say too, and for his description of Barrie, (also referred to as Daddy) he replied,

"A big man with a very soft centre." We knew Brandy's self-description already, so I asked him,

"If Daddy wasn't doing this work, what do you think he could do instead?" Quick as a flash he replied,

"An interior designer," complete with a picture of beautiful long drapes. Barrie smiled; the long drapes were apparently in his sitting room and he admitted to having a keen eye for style. Still 'holding court', Brandy started talking about his own health issues of which, although mild, there were a few.

Suddenly Barrie announced,

"There you go, you missed it, Milo did his "I am bored now" yawn!" Milo then proceeded to make his way carefully off the chair and onto the windowsill, complete with his back for us to view! I quickly said,

"Okay, hang on Brandy, I will just finish Milo's chat and then I will come back to you," and he agreed to wait.

"Barrie, do you have any questions for him?"

"Yes, I do. Can you ask him what he thinks of Azlan?" (I was aware that Barrie kept the cat and dog apart, so I thought it was a good question to ask.)

"He's such a pain!" Milo told me without an ounce of hesitation.

"Oh, that was a bit harsh," I said, "can you expand on that?" he obliged with,

"I'm sorry, but he *is* boisterous *and* thoughtless!" Barrie said he was not surprised at his candid answer as Azlan is rough and just doesn't know when to leave him alone. Just then I heard another voice - a new voice,

"But I wouldn't hurt him, it is just fun you know!" "Ah, Azlan has been listening in and wants to add that he wouldn't hurt him and it is just fun?" I said, with a questioning tone (I'm always aware that I would never advocate for someone just to take it on my say-so that there would not be trouble, or worse) and Barrie said,

"So true, he has never hurt him, but is so boisterous and he will insist on trying to push him around. Milo is too old to be bothered with that, so I just keep them apart".

Just then, Brandy butted back in with a funny picture, and really making me think that he, a very small and delicate boy, was boss over Azlan. I put this to Barrie and this was the case. Apparently, if Azlan over steps the mark, Brandy growls and tells him off. Oh, what a picture that conjured up and especially as Brandy had only got about three teeth left. I asked Brandy,

"What do you say to him then?"

"Don't bother, and he listens!" I asked Azlan to wait his turn, we wouldn't be long, but Milo and Brandy have a few more things to say, and answer.

"Milo, before you finish, can you tell us what do you think is Barrie's best quality?" He replied,

"He puts things away where they should be so he doesn't waste time looking for things". Bearing in mind we were just in one room and had not seen the main house, but this was absolutely 'on the button', in fact, Barrie told us his philosophy is 'Everything has a place!'

I thanked him for talking to us and apologised if he got 'bored' at the end, but before he went, could he answer the crucial question regarding what he thought his contribution to this book would show? His final answer,

"It is proof that we can interact with people as we can with spirit." (I thought that was a very clever answer, as most people working in my field, or Barrie's, know that animals are 'open'. They can see and hear (clairvoyantly etc.) just like

Barrie and I can see, hear and know things, but to animals it is nothing unusual, they use telepathy everyday!)

Over to Brandy's last little bit. He mentioned his poor eyesight but was quick to inform us that he did not bump into things (true) and when he got to within six inches he could see them. He said,

"The medicine was making my tummy bigger". Barrie agreed, and it was an unfortunate side effect and he was aware of it. Barrie asked me to check if there was anything else, especially since Brandy was hit by a car when he was young. Quick as a flash, he showed me a line on his left pelvis.

"Did he crack his left pelvis?" I enquired.

"Yes, he did," Barrie answered.

"It knitted together pretty well considering," commented Brandy and did not pass any pain issue to me.

Now for the Barrie's 'best quality' question,

"He feeds me! No, really, joking apart - he makes people happy," was the reply and then commented to us what a good answer that was! I thanked Brandy for talking to us, and asked if there was anything else he would like to share with Barrie. He replied,

"I know I am truly loved, and even when I get pain, it is balanced out with love." (That was a reference to emotional pain, like when losing Barrie's mum). And for Brandy's contribution about animal communication - he said it was his chance to tell people,

"When we get old, and our eyesight is failing, we work it out, and just get on with it." I am guessing that could allay a lot of fears for pet owners wondering how their beloved animal is coping.

"Hello, I am the star of the show," was Azlan's opening introduction line to us! With Azlan still in the kitchen but relishing his turn, he informed me of the words Barrie said when he first saw him as a pup.

"When he chose me he just looked at me and said I was gorgeous!" With clear recognition of this moment, Barrie pointed out that the reason he remembered saying that was because he was actually the odd one out - rather weedy and not expected to grow like the others in the litter.

Azlan told us that Barrie was so pleased to get him home, and was like a kid with a new toy! Barrie laughed, and admitted he still is like that kid, as Azlan is so easy to wind up and they have such fun! Azlan then declared, "I am rather clumsy you know, and I have even knocked a few things down." Mind you, if you were to see the size of him, I think that would be fairly easy to do just turning round! Then to emphasise his stature, he showed me a lovely picture of him giving Barrie a 'bear hug' and Barrie is at least six foot tall!

Azlan, in a very straightforward fashion asked me if he was ever going to be a dad? I paused, as often animals are often not terribly clear on the girl/boy gender or if they have had 'that' operation, so I quickly asked Barrie if he had been neutered? And, yes, he had, but what I suspected was then confirmed by Barrie saying,

"He really had not got the gist of that!" Barrie said that he understood about this topic as quite a long time ago Azlan mistook a pram (an empty one I hasten to add) for something that might return his manly affection! On another occasion there was an 'encounter' with a bull mastiff that looked positively un-amused! I gave Azlan a quick biology lesson in the hope he will give up any further thoughts of fatherhood.

Azlan had us in fits of laughter with his views on life. He showed me that he really does not know how to 'fetch', coupled with the line,

"Hey, there is no need, Barrie just goes and gets it anyway!" We had to agree with his doggie logic on that one, but again he was rather missing the point! After lots more mirth and fun, Azlan-style, I asked Barrie if he had any questions for him. He asked the usual, is he happy etc., which we all knew would be a resounding – "Yes!" Also, Barrie wanted to know,

"What is his favourite food?" I put his to Azlan and was presented with a picture of a roast dinner, complete with dining plate!! My mind went into,

"Don't be silly, people don't feed their dogs roast dinners on plates, do they?" I asked the same question again and having got the same vision I suggested it to Barrie.

"Yes, exactly what I thought he would say. He gets a roast dinner, on a plate, every Sunday, complete with vegetables and mashed potato too!" Kim and I were amazed and Barrie went on to say,

"They all do, even Milo the cat!" A dog sitting down to Sunday lunch was pretty amazing, but a cat too?! Now that really is like being part of the family!

I moved on to the question of, 'What other job did he think Barrie could do?'

"Anything precise!" was Azlan's quick reply. Barrie thought that was a great answer, being a self-confessed perfectionist. Having heard Barrie's response, Azlan showed his theatrical side by saying,

"Ah, but do you think I would recommend you?" and after a short, but well-timed pause, he said, "Of course I would!"

Although Azlan was clearly enjoying himself, as were we, time was running on and I had to bring things to a close.

So, for the last question of what he thought his contribution to this project would do? And his answer,

"It will let everyone know that we animals are highly intelligent and that we all should have roast dinner on a Sunday!"

With our sides and faces aching with laughter, we got to meet 'Azlan the Lion' as Barrie calls him. He was huge, but very friendly and although I'd already taken a photo of Barrie with Brandy and Milo, I asked if I could have one of him, me and Azlan. This 'Lion' took some positioning believe you me!

When I got home and loaded them onto my computer to view and there above Barrie and I, was a very clear orb of light – yes, my Dad was with me there too.

I still keep in contact with Barrie and hope we meet up again sometime in the future. I thank him for taking part in this and I know that he, and his animals, enjoyed it as much as we did.

Having done a 250 mile round trip, Kim and I eventually got back in time to enjoy a well-deserved pub meal and enjoyed mulling over what we classed as a wonderful and enlightening day.

Sir Roy Strong

There are people in this life that say they are passionate about cats, well, Sir Roy Strong is certainly testament to that. This has to be defined by a quote of his, "I am afraid that no door is too sacred not to have a hole cut through it to facilitate the passage of these glorious creatures." And this from a man who lives in a house steeped in history and antiquities.

A true sceptic might think that I would 'cheat' and look up the internet for information on Celebrities so that I could pretend to give good information on a reading. Even if I had dreamt of doing such a thing it would be pretty futile anyway as usually there is so very little information about these people's pets, and definitely not what their pets 'say', but as anyone that knows me will vouch, my memory is rather poor. Chemotherapy might have saved my life and helped me with this gift, but I am sure it deleted many of my memory cells while it was at it!!

I did, as anyone would, research about Sir Roy as it would be ignorant of me not be to be furnished with information of exactly who anybody is and what he or she is known for. I immediately recognised him from *The Diets Time Forgot* television programme that was on a couple of years ago. I can now see why Sir Roy was so ideal for this series from his wonderful résumé, which reads from having been the Director of the Victoria and Albert Museum, and the National Tate Gallery, to a broadcaster and prolific writer - an obviously and extremely well read man.

Sir Roy lives in a beautiful location in Herefordshire which was only about an hour trip for me and Kim. I lived in Herefordshire for twelve years and know the area well. True to form, we left in good time and for this occasion I made sure that we were both 'formally' dressed in smart trousers and blouses, complete with court shoes. I knew from the TV programme that Sir Roy knew more about etiquette than most people, so I wanted to make sure we would not look out of place. Also, I have to add, I had never met anyone that had been knighted before, so that also came into the equation. But, as you will find out in the story, he is the most decent, unassuming man you could wish to meet, which was confirmed by one of his cats in a later conversation.

The heavens had opened that day and given the ground a good lashing with much needed rain, but just as the sun broke through, we saw the sign, The Laskett. This name is actually renowned in itself, as the Laskett Gardens are the largest private formal gardens to be created in England since 1945!

I drove up the sweeping drive to be met by a Jack Russell coming towards my car with haste and with no signs of stopping. I gently applied my brakes and then crept along slowly.

"Oh thank you so much for slowing down," said Fiona, who was actually Sir Roy's personal assistant. I smiled and said I didn't think her dog was going to move out of the way and that we were here to see Sir Roy.

I introduced myself and Kim. Fiona said,

"Yes, you are here to see the cats, aren't you?"

"Yes," was my reply, to which Fiona added,

"To talk to them I hear, very interesting." I breathed a sigh of relief, to be honest, as I wasn't totally sure if Sir Roy knew exactly what I was going to be doing because although he had previously thanked me for my 'charming' book, I had no idea if he had had time to read much or any of it.

"Sir Roy has been held up and is actually just finishing his lunch, would you like a quick tour of the gardens meanwhile?" Fiona enquired.

"Most definitely," I responded, as apart from the thought of the most magnificent sights and senses I was about to enjoy, I knew that there was a large memorial statue to one of Sir Roy's cats, namely, The Reverend Wenceslas Muff. (His picture, and a note about how he has been commemorated, adorned a card that Sir Roy had sent me in response to my first letter.)

As Fiona guided us round I have to say, it was so stunning and one garden seem to lead to another, then another and forever onwards. Kim remarked it was just like the story of the secret garden, full of surprises and wonder. Having seen not just one tomb but quite a few memorials Fiona commented that the gardens used to be denser with trees when Julia (Sir Roy's late wife) was here but over the last few years, the garden had been opened out more. I was aware that Julia, who was actually Dr. Julia, had passed away a few years previously. I said as much to Fiona, who responded beautifully with,

"Yes, but she is still here with the cats!" I was very relieved to hear her spiritual views and we had a lovely conversation confirming our thoughts that people, and animals, just 'move' on when their time comes, and one day we will be re-united.

"Ah, and here he is," Fiona said as she gestured down a garden path, which Sir Roy was coming up.

"Hello, and pleased to meet you," he said, and we formally shook hands. "Have you seen Muff's tomb?" he enquired. We said we had and he volunteered to show us more of the gardens himself. Kim smiled at me, as there we were in our 'formal' attire, and there was Sir Roy, dressed very casually complete with a pair of very modern trainers on his feet! Over the far side of the orchard we were shown a beautiful memorial for two of his cats, Souci and Larkin, and Sir Roy told us he had named Larkin after an obscure Jacobean painter. (That was about as far away from Pop 'Larkin' from *The Darling Buds of May* as you could get!) From the main garden we headed nearer to the house where there was another grand memorial complete with a very clever twist on the cat's actual colour. The engraving which ran up the length of this beautiful sweeping stone said, 'The Lady Torte-De-Shell.'

"Would you like to see some cat portraits?" Sir Roy asked, and with that offer we followed him into the house.

Incredible, this man's love of cats was so apparent. These portraits were works of art and integral to many of the pictures would be a cat, and sometimes even two. What a lovely thought, when the pictures are admired by generations to come, just like ones in galleries, the cats will all be part of it. The picture Sir Roy gave me for use in this book is one of the fabulous portraits that 'greet you' as you go from room to room. This one was of Sir Roy with Lettice, painted by Paul Brason. Sir Roy made us laugh when he said,

"Lettice got very cross, you know!" I am not surprised. Can you imagine how many hours it would have taken of Sir Roy's time, let alone his cats? Bless her, she does look very animated and beautiful, so I am sure she is proud of it now.

"So, what is the format, what are we to do?" Sir Roy asked as he ushered us to sit in a divinely furnished room. "I have told the cats you are here to interview them, but I do not know where they are!"

"I thought that might happen," I said, "But as I said on my email, if you have a picture of them, I shall 'link in' to them that way." Sir Roy handed me two pictures and I decided to speak to young Perkins first. I say young; he was three years old and a stunning tabby and white Maine Coon, with little white socks on his forepaws and longer ones on the back!

I gave an outline of how the communication worked and explained that it is just like talking to child. I said,

"They hear your response, so, for example, if he says proudly, 'I can climb a ten foot wall and he can' then…" but Sir Roy interrupted me with,

"Well he can't, they are indoor cats!" I smiled and thought, 'no point in asking them what they think of the gardens then', but thought I would just start and see how we went.

Having introduced myself to Perkins (what a splendid name!) he showed me a picture of himself fully stretched out, lounging somewhere and gave me the feeling that if someone entered the room, he would just lift his head, as if to say, a slow and purposeful, 'Yes?' I explained this as best possible and Sir Roy thought about it and I think agreed. Sir Roy then started to try to tell me things, to which I had to gently say,

"I can only repeat what he tells me, but if you have some questions for him, we can come to that later if you want." I told him about Perkins liking to hide under things and how Sir Roy acknowledges him, with a,

"Ah Perkins, there you are". This struck a chord so I carried on, and said that Perkins gave me a cheeky impression by saying,

"Yes, I am here" and to be honest he makes me feel like a cheeky little boy, rather like a naughty schoolboy.

"Yes, he is a cheeky boy," Sir Roy responded and also told us, "I have two names for him actually, and the other is Bouncer!" I quickly asked Perkins why, and, yes, he does use the furniture like a trampoline but hastily informed me that he does not cause any damage, and that he knows to 'shut his paws' so he doesn't scratch or scrape anything. I dearly hoped this was right, firstly, for the sake of the beautiful antique furniture adorning his 'playground' and secondly, I was not sure by Sir Roy's quiet reactions to what I was saying, and was wondering at that point, if he was rather unimpressed and just being polite. In actual fact, I was right and it was confirmed he didn't scratch or damage anything. Sir Roy said that 'Bouncer' was very apt for Perkins as he, 'bounced up onto things and bounced back off them again!' Phew! I told him lots more and we also discussed the time Perkins escaped outside and was frightened so cried to come back in. Also a funny one was when Perkins declared that cleaning himself, complete with picture of him bent double trying to clean his chest while on the edge of a piece of furniture, was a 'bit of a balancing act! Sir Roy laughed, and said he had seen him fall off, and often thought it was done with jovial intent, and I think he was probably right.

When Sir Roy commented that he was small for his breed, Perkins informed us straightaway that he was not delicate and showed me a demonstrative picture of him running and skidding along the corridors of the house. Sir Roy laughed and said he was like one of these 'hooded teenagers!!' I was surprised that when Perkins told us that he like to show his 'air of contentment', I had to declare, apart from the relaxed, once again stretched out demeanour, he was purring but, also doing a gentle wag of his tail too. Sir Roy nodded and smiled.

I thought I would ask my *Celebrity Pet Talking* questions instead and see where this led us, as the questions are designed to be more personal to their owners rather than what the cat gets up to on a daily basis. On asking what he thought was Sir Roy's best attribute? He said,

"Sir Roy was very open minded and thought it was good to try and experience many different things in life." Perkins also told me he thought that was a good attitude! Sir Roy agreed, and that is probably why I was sitting here! My work is a new experience to most people.

"What does Sir Roy do that amuses him?" When Sir Roy puts down a book, or suchlike, and then walks round looking for it, complete with the mutterings of, 'Oh, where is that blasted book?' And, the question, 'What do you think Sir Roy does as a job?'

"Catalogues things," was Perkins' short reply. That didn't sound terribly grand for someone who has been knighted, so I asked Sir Roy if he thought it applied to him in any respect. And yes, it did. Sir Roy organises things, which tends to be a matter of compiling and listing things, so, 'to catalogue' would be a fairly good descriptive verb.

Having known about the Forgotten Diet series, I asked Perkins,

"What other television show do you think Sir Roy could do?"

"One on architecture," was his clear reply, and added the reason why, "Because he has a very keen eye!" As I was telling Sir Roy Perkins' this answer, I was given a clear picture that I recognised but my memory failure set in (once again). I could see the dome, and even knew who had designed it, and turning to Kim said,

"Oh, what did Sir Christopher Wren design? You know, the one with the dome?" Kim shook her head, so I (bravely) said to Sir Roy, "I am sorry to ask you this, but what was the name of the building in London he designed?"

"St. Paul's Cathedral", came his reply,

"Of course," I said, feeling rather embarrassed that I had to ask.

"Good Lord, how very psychic of you!" Sir Roy exclaimed. "The reason I got held up from meeting you was because I was just finishing sending an email to someone about that very building!!" Well, you know how your jaw drops? Mine actually snapped shut! Kim and I looked at each other, Sir Roy nodded in agreement, and then I thanked Perkins for his sheer accuracy and proof that what I was doing was for real!

To finish off, I asked Perkins to describe his breed as I knew very little about them and as Sir Roy was obviously besotted with them I thought it would be of interest.

"Very individual, and know what we want." Was his answer, and, "Very, very," was Sir Roy's. The final one I asked of Perkins,

"What did he want people to know from his contribution about animal communication?' His statement,

"Even though I don't go outside, we accept our lot, and it is a very beautiful lot at that!"

Sir Roy nipped out to take a phone call (incidentally from the phone that made an annoying shrill sound according to Perkins!) and, now feeling relaxed thanks to an architect's work from the 1600s, I picked up the picture of the beautiful Lettice. I tuned in with her and she instantly told me she was like the Queen of the house! And, with attitude and accent to suit, gave me the impression that Perkins had to wait his turn, and wait his turn he should! We were still laughing at this as Sir Roy returned and when I repeated it, he said,

"Absolutely!"

Lettice, who has been in many portraits, asked me to ask if when her long tortoiseshell tresses were combed, could they be done gently? Sir Roy said that she didn't need to be combed nearly as much as Perkins, but she is a very large girl so they had to be careful.

"In proportion, in proportion!" Lettice retorted, having heard this 'offensive' description. I repeated her words to Sir Roy. He thought for a moment and said,

"Well, she is large!" The, 'In proportion' was clearly repeated again, which I duly did (again) then laughed and said to him,

"I can't believe this, but I think your cat is trying to tell you off!!" Just as Sir Roy was smiling, she quickly went on to the softer, loving side of things. Lettice showed me her coming up Sir Roy's left side and really nuzzling into his neck and with the feeling of heat to go with it. He gestured to us her coming up his body, left side was the usual, and yes, she did push into his neck and stay there.

"Wonderful man, wonderful man" was clearly heard so I told him and said I would ask her why she said it. She eloquently informed me her reason was, "Because he has taught so many. He's shown such patience as he really wanted to pass his knowledge on to others." 'Oh, how lovely' I thought as Sir Roy acknowledged it as true. What a lovely man whose company to be in.

Lettice showed me copious amounts of pens and pencils, (I was sure I could see an old-fashioned fountain pen, but Sir Roy could not place it) and I wondered what this was relevant to. He explained that he actually had three offices in his house. 'Gosh, who thinks you might slow down when you get into your seventies?' I thought to myself, 'Definitely not this gentleman!'

Lettice then showed me that she likes to 'shadow' him, but not in a constantly at your side or on your lap way. She showed me being at a doorway, for example, to watch him from a distance. This was her to a tee. What she would do was seek him out, and then recline on a piece of furniture often near to an entrance so that she could see all that was going on, not just in the room he was working. Having listened to us discuss it, she volunteered,

"It is nice being a cat!"

"And why?" I asked.

"We get what we want, to do what we want, and when we want!" That sounded very much like Perkins' description of them knowing their own minds. On the subject of Perkins, I thought it would be nice to ask what she thought of him. After all, she was aged ten and him, a young pip-squeak by comparison. With a complete air of superiority, she gave me a picture of Perkins sidling up to her, and repeated her words of,

"There is no point in sidling up to me, no, Perkins, no!" Sir Roy's face lit up with mirth as he said,

"Oh yes, she does keep him in his place, but quite rightly so!"

Sir Roy then gently asked, "I wonder if she remembers my wife?" Fortunately due to the earlier conversation with Fiona about Julia going to Heaven, I was more relaxed to ask about this. As soon as Sir Roy had said that, Lettice showed me a very delicate looking fine bone china bell, complete with the ping like someone would do to distinguish one from another. I told Sir Roy what she was showing as an association and he said that Julia had a great interest in fine china. Lettice then volunteered that,

"Julia was needed elsewhere to help others." She went on to point out that Julia was so generous of heart in her life, and would strive to help others, and that she is still doing that now even in spirit. This resonated with Sir Roy and I was honoured to pass Lettice's beautiful thoughts over to him.

On to Sir Roy's best quality described by the lovely Lettice.

"He likes people to treat him just like a normal person, and does not expect any preferential treatment. This way people can be themselves around him."

"Wouldn't have it any other way," was his concise reply. I have to admit, having spent an hour in his company, and in such palatial surroundings, complete with chandelier above our heads - he was gracious, warm and very welcoming. At that point, 'Queen' Lettice appeared in the doorway.

"Ah, here she is," Sir Roy exclaimed delightedly, to which she lay down on a rug, rolled over and 'batted' her big green eyes at him.

"Look at me Daddy, look at me," I could clearly hear ringing in my ears, at the same time as Sir Roy was gesturing and saying how beautiful she was. I did note however, she was purring and doing the 'slow tail wag', the same as Perkins had shown me! (We didn't get to meet Perkins 'in person', as he was hiding somewhere, and it would have taken an age to find him!) Then she showed me Sir Roy stroking her under her chin, which is usually accompanied by those same 'beautiful' words. He recognised that and I commented that now he knows she really *does* understand what he says to her! Lettice went on to tell me that she 'exudes affection and is very personable', which Sir Roy said he totally understood. I asked why she thought she was in Sir Roy's life (I believe that animals find you, or are chosen for you) and she said,

"To bring love into his life and to bring warmth and light to his life especially in the winter." "That is true," Sir Roy stated, "she sits on my lap in winter but not in the summer!"

I asked her to finish – "What would she like to say for the book?" And her words were,

"We're not just a cat, we are part of people's lives, and that is very important to know – thank you!" I couldn't have put it better if I had tried, but I wouldn't, the animals do a far better job! I was prompted to ask one more question of her which I thought was important.

"How would you describe yourself to your Daddy?" And her encapsulating reply was…

"His!"

I thanked Sir Roy for his time and gave our thanks also to Fiona for her guided tour and hospitality.

Driving back home along roads that I had driven so many times before, suddenly I had a 'forget the diet, I need chocolate' moment. Kim, amazingly doesn't like chocolate, but opted for some new type of pickle flavoured biscuits at the first shop we encountered. Before I delved into my chocolate Kim offered me one to try, which to be honest was mouth-watering.

"Oh, why does everything that tastes so good, have to be so bad?" I moaned.

"Oh, just pretend you are eating lettuce," was Kim's quick reply. We both laughed as it dawned on her what she had said - same name, different spelling! Maybe I could use Lettice's, 'In proportion' saying and forget the diet!

Melissa Porter

With the wonders of technology I was able to hold a 'face-to-face' communication with Melissa and her King Charles Cavalier Spaniel, Hugo. Melissa, who we know here in the UK for her TV presenting skills on various property and lifestyle programs like, BBC's *Escape to the Country*, *To Buy or Not to Buy* and *Get a New Life* which was based on her own property buying experiences. Melissa, at this time was in America where she was living, but was travelling back and forth between there and Cheshire, here in England. The reason she comes back to Cheshire is to her parents' home, which is where the lovely Hugo still lives.

The technology for this chat was by webcam via Skype, which is a very clever telephone service through the internet. I do many face-to-face calls like this, as it is just like talking to someone sitting in front of you, which makes the chat even more expressive and animated. So here was a conversation with Melissa in Connecticut, her dog in Cheshire, and me in Shropshire!

With everything sorted out Melissa called me, although slightly earlier than arranged, as she had to get to an appointment. She is a very busy lady, and actually we had been trying to co-ordinate this call for several months. With webcams switched on, we said our greetings and then Bob, who was note-taking for me, ducked down and waved into the camera to say 'Hi' to Melissa.

"Gosh, is he Italian?" she asked?

"No... just well tanned," was my reply, and laughed to myself thinking how exotic to be married to an Italian with that olive skin and natural sense of style they are renowned for. It turned out that Melissa's father, Aldo, was Italian so hence the thought. Sally, our now pretty–well-known collie, as about every newspaper/magazine article that I have been in, her photo has appeared too, followed us into the office. So Bob thought it fit that she should wave to a celebrity too so he lifted her up for Melissa to see! Having got to know Hugo during this communication, and had he been with Melissa at that time, I am sure that he would have insisted on being admired in this way too!

With a quick explanation like I usually do summarizing this as like talking to a child I told her that Hugo came across as loving and very sweet as when asked to say something about himself,

"I am a pet to have and to hold!" was his reply.

"That sounds almost like a marriage to me!" I said, but then he gave me the replay of him running along the floor to her open arms, saying, "Mummy, Mummy, Mummy", which clearly demonstrated their bond. This, as I thought, was his greeting when Melissa had returned for a visit. Melissa smiled and said she did do that to greet him and that was his response.

Hugo declared, in a rather 'upper class' way, that he was lazy, and if lounging in his basket, he would get up, but only if it pleased him at that time!

"That's so right," said Melissa, "My father says Hugo thinks he is master of the house!" Later in the conversation Hugo did admit to that by telling us he was,

"Masterful, but not bossy!" Hugo then gave me a picture of him being up on something, I was guessing a chair/settee or suchlike and looking out of a window at a wonderful colourful view. Melissa immediately recognised this and said that she knew that Hugo got up on the back of one of the large settees, although he was not supposed to. Hugo said, with that 'behind the hand', (or paw should I say?) effect, that,

"They didn't really mind." Melissa said that from that vantage point he had a clear view of the garden, complete with waterfall.

"Very nice," I said, but hang on, let's ask about the garden from a dog's point of view. Following the pictures of the varieties of colours and of what seemed to flow from one thing into the next, I carefully said it didn't come across to me as a very formal garden.

"Formal?" said Melissa laughingly, "You are right, it is anything but; Italian chintz gardening is how I would describe it! It is just like Pandora's Box - full of surprises, simply a 'mish-mash' of everything."

"Oh, how funny," I said, and explained that it was only days earlier I had visited Sir Roy Strong whose formal gardens were renowned and very much of the Victorian classic design. So this was from one extreme to the other, but both very beautiful in their own way.

Whilst we were on the subject of home life with her parents, Melissa asked me to see what Hugo would have to say about her father. I was given the picture of someone that seemed to do most things at speed (or impatience), coupled with a remark that he didn't shut cupboard doors very quietly! I put this across as tactfully as I could muster, and again Melissa laughed and said that her Dad, being Italian, was very like that. I know Italians do hold a reputation for being a bit hot headed, but as with everyone, these generalisations do not cover everybody. Hugo was quick to say that it did not bother him, he had a, 'whatever' attitude and just walks away. Talking of walking, Hugo said that he did enjoy his walks, but when he had had enough, he had had enough! I said I felt like he just came to a 'stop' and that would be it for that walk.

"Oh, that would be right," Melissa said, and went on to explain to me that recently whilst she was walking him with her parents in a park, he had somehow managed to tug the extending lead out of her hand and then made haste across the grass. He ignored their calls for him to stop, and only did so when he was sat at their car door! Melissa said that she reckoned that was as clear as you could get of, 'I have had enough now – thank you!' I don't suppose Melissa could run terribly fast at this point as she was heavily pregnant and due to give birth in a few months.

The reason the pregnancy came up was because, although it was 10 o'clock in the morning (3pm over here), Melissa kept yawning! She apologised and explained that it was not because she was bored, quite the opposite in fact, but that she was getting so very little sleep as could not get comfortable when lying down. She said her boyfriend described it as, 'like trying to sleep in a wave machine!'

"A boy!" I clearly heard, and thought quickly to myself, I don't want to say the wrong thing here. So I asked her if she knew what she was having.

"Oh yes, a boy!" I then told her that is what I am sure Hugo had said to me and, with that, I mentioned that surely it must be difficult to fly so late on. Melissa said you can fly up to thirty four weeks and she would be flying back to Britain next week anyway. She said the whole pregnancy, staying in the US/visas etc. was a sort of 'flying by the seat of your pants' thing, and they were working things out as they went along. I was sure I heard,

"It could have been worse, it could have been twins!" Now a braver person might have said it 'as it is' but I thought I would be cautious as you do not know what might have happened in the pregnancy, or whether in fact, I had got it totally wrong. So I said,

"Although we know you are just having one baby, were twins in the family? "Yes," she replied, "At first they thought I might be having twins!!" I then told her what I thought Hugo had said, but she understood my caution and was clearly surprised that her dog knew about that. Melissa said that Hugo had taken to putting his paws on her ever-expanding tummy, and yet he had never put his feet on her like that before. We had the 'You would be amazed how much animals do know' conversation. But, if you think of it, there are so many cases now written about how an animal picked up on someone's cancer, others that know when someone is going to pass to spirit and many more things that we often can't explain. But, as I say, 'Why question it, just marvel in the fact that they can!'

Melissa wanted to check why Hugo got grumpy when she asked him to move over when he is sharing her bed. It turned out, as she had thought, to be just a 'grumpy old man' thing, objecting with a, 'Do I have to?' Well, he is nearly nine, so maybe he thinks he is entitled to be. She said his routine is always the same – at night time, at first, he will always go and lie under the dressing table in her parents' bedroom, but the second her father sets the alarm, he gets up and goes into her room. With that, Hugo showed me a picture of lots of glass ornaments, cut crystal items, complete with a light sprinkling of dust!! I had to ask Melissa if her Mum had lots of ornate glass things there, and sure enough she did. I braved it, and said,

"I don't know how, but Hugo is showing me dust on them, would you think that's correct?"

"Oh yeah," laughed Melissa, "My mum is a junk fiend. I went there and did a 'de-clutter' recently."

"Oh, there are loads more," a little voice from, you-know-who announced. Melissa acknowledged his remark,

"Oh, I know, it's only the tip of the iceberg!" Bob, or should I say 'Roberto' was writing away 'ten to the dozen' on my left hand side but still able to join in the laughter too.

"I have been feeling the heat," Hugo told me which, considering the unusually hot weather we had been having, didn't seem out of the norm to mention.

"It's probably also because he is overweight too," Melissa added. "Do you know, he had spaghetti bolognaise the other night and on another, he had the end of the fish and chips!" 'Mmm, no surprise about his weight then,' I thought. So for fun, I said I would ask Hugo what his favourite food was, as 'fish and chips' is said to be a British person's favourite. With no hesitation whatsoever,

"Steak!" was his concise reply. I passed it over to Melissa with the same lack of hesitation, and yes, he does get steak, and not just any old steak – fillet steak!! Melissa informed me that her Mum buys it for him, and her mum, Mary, being the soft-hearted lady that she is, does spoil him but he is just so adorable she can't resist. On hearing Melissa talk about her Mum, Hugo gave me a picture of who I presumed to be Mary straightening pictures. I hesitated slightly, as this did not fit with the accumulating junk images, but Melissa confirmed that her mum does, in fact, keep re-positioning things around the house on a regular basis.

On a personal note, Hugo was keen to let me know that he was very proud of Melissa (his Mummy) and said that she had done very well, and showed great integrity as, he thought, she only does things because she thinks they are right to do, not just because, 'it would be handy' as he put it. Whilst we were on the subject of best attributes etc., although what he said really covered that, but to answer it as a direct question, his answer,

"Honesty!" For my next one,

"What does she do that amuses you?" I asked.

"Doing her hair in the mirror, like - 'yep, that's done', and then goes back minutes later and checks it again! That doesn't make any sense to me," he declared. Animals know so much more than we realise, but beauty and our little idiosyncrasies are probably not worth losing their beauty sleep over!

Knowing Melissa is a TV presenter, I asked Hugo for an alternative job he thought she would be good at. He presented me a picture of what looked like someone doing some sort of needlecraft and that type of painstaking work of attaching tiny beads etc. Melissa does crochet, and also said that she understood what he was showing me as she really likes to pay attention to detail, and, unlike me, she has the patience to do such fiddly things. So, maybe a career in fashion design/creativity for the future? If so, please remember, you read it here first!

Something that Melissa wanted to discuss was the fact that she knew he really disliked being put in kennels, but, as her parents do also need to travel (especially in October to visit the new baby) it was a necessity. I asked him his feelings. He had already told me that when Melissa leaves him at home with her parents, he does the 'sad eyes', but only because he didn't want her to think he was being unfaithful. That was nice to know, but regarding the kennels, that was entirely different. He told us that he would rather not go anywhere - he liked it at home where he 'had got his feet under the table!' (Truly, that was straight from his canine mouth!)

We had a quick reminisce of my story of the clairvoyant's dog from my *Animal Insight* book who wanted to be greeted with roast chicken when collected from kennels. This would make it seem far more tolerable, and amazingly, it worked! We decided to try the same thing with Hugo, and he obliged by showing me a picture of treats (namely biscuits - well, anything edible) being hidden under his blanket at the kennels, so a surprise for when he got there. I didn't know if this was possible to arrange, but as it turned out, Melissa worked for them when she was age fourteen and had kept in contact with them ever since. She knew that the kennels went to extra lengths to keep the dogs happy, so this would be no problem, and if they could hide some for him during his stay, that would be great too. Let's hope it makes things better for him. He did admit that he still eats while he is there, so that proves he is not that sad. Melissa said it was actually like 'Dog fit camp', as he is on portion control and plenty of exercise to help him lose a few pounds whilst he was there! He heard that, but did not comment, which was just 'so Hugo!'

Hugo said in his serious way,

"Please tell her that I understand about life and that she has to go away. Please tell her I do not feel 'torn' and that she should not too." Ah bless him, what a wonderful little chap.

I asked Hugo for a statement he wished to make using this animal communication platform so I could put it in the book. He told me,

"That animals rationalise things the same as people do." He went on to give the example of the fiery Italian nature that Melissa's Dad has, saying,

"It is just the way he is, it is not personal to me, and so why should it be a problem?" Well put, I thought - we should not have to tiptoe around animals just because they can hear, see and feel like we do, but just treat them with respect and understanding as we would a another person. After all, some animals are louder and brasher than others, but it takes all sorts to make a world, and whatever breed we are, or they are, we are all individuals. But one thing that animals do achieve far better than we humans is how to show unconditional love. As he had shown us - it is accepting the whole person for what they are and loving them just the same!

Melissa was a joy to talk to (she is a friend of Jacky Newcomb so I wouldn't have expected anything else) and I appreciated her honesty when she said that she really was surprised that animals do think in this way and basically do have cognitive thoughts. So, the next time she lifts his ears to make him look like a rabbit, she will know that he adores that and finds it so funny, and how does Melissa know? Because he told us so! I hope I have brought something more into her life, and Hugo's too, which is my plan for this book to do for animals everywhere; well, everywhere that my work can reach.

With the call over, and Saturday horse racing beckoning for Bob's attention, my 'Italian Roberto' disappeared but fortunately left me with a very detailed set of notes for this story.

William Roache MBE

Sometimes dreams come true and this was most definitely one for me. Not only did I get the chance to talk to William's three Jack Russell terriers but also went to his house in person to do so.

I believe there is no such thing as coincidence and here follows an example of that. During a conversation with a friend of mine, Helen, whose horse's story was featured in my first book, I told her about my idea of writing this one to help spread the word about animal communication. I knew that she had been to a wedding of a member of the *Coronation Street* cast and, as William is known to be lovely and spiritual, said wouldn't it be superb if I could get a book to him personally. Then, as if by 'magic', it turned out that the actress was coming to stay with Helen that very weekend! The actress very kindly passed my book on to William and within a week he had called me. He said that he loved what I did and how wonderful that I could show people how truly magnificent and sentient animals really are and he would do what he could to help me.

This visit didn't take place for over a year as 2010 was a huge year for *Coronation Street* with its 50th year anniversary. William, aka Ken Barlow, is the only member left of the original cast so he was extremely busy with interviews and commitments. I have to say, it was well worth the wait as we had such a fantastic time (I say we, as Kim, as usual was writing for me) and what joy we had meeting not just William and the dogs, but also his daughter Verity.

On a crisp sunny day at the end of February 2011, Kim and I set off for the two-hour drive to William's house in Cheshire. Once again we allowed ourselves plenty of time and, with the aid of our map and sat nav, we reached close to our destination with a half hour to spare. We decided to search for a pub/café for a coffee and have a quick check of our hair and make-up. The first place we found was not open so we travelled on and then spotted a sign for *The Frozen Mop*! Well, I have to admit we laughed and laughed - we were in a very affluent area and wondered how on earth a pub had gained such a name. Undeterred, we drove up, checked they were open, and parked the car. Still chortling to ourselves, we entered unsure of what we would find, and wow, what a lovely upmarket place it was! It was complete with sumptuous settees, marble floors and although empty still had that ambient atmosphere. We ordered our coffees and I couldn't resist asking how the place got such a name.

"This used to be a farmhouse many moons ago," the young man explained, "and when the farmer used to go to market - apparently his wife used to leave a mop outside to let other men know she was alone and they could call."

"Oh, how funny!" we enthused as he continued,

"But, on one winter's day, she put the mop out and it froze solid and she could not move it to get it back inside. Her husband came home and later one of her gentlemen callers appeared and all hell broke loose!!" I remarked what an amusing tale it was and as I was up here visiting someone about writing a book could I possibly include this too? He very kindly agreed that he thought it would be no problem at all.

So, with our coffees finished and our appearances checked, we set off to find William's house, and, in spite of our best navigational efforts, I still had to phone him and get the final instructions.

William greeted us so warmly, invited us into his beautiful house and put us at our ease. Although we could hear the dogs they were still in the kitchen and William settled us in and even made us coffee! He is as people say - down to earth, very genuine and a lovely, warm man. He explained that Verity would be here any minute and would I mind waiting until she had arrived, as she was also really excited to hear what the dogs had to say. This was no problem at all; Kim and I were happy gazing at all the beautiful family pictures and some of William meeting the Queen. The décor was breathless and, as he explained, was all the work of his wonderful, dearly departed wife, Sara. It was so touching to hear William repeatedly say, "Sara, my wife" (as in the present tense) because as he and I, and so many people now know, that although people leave this physical earth they are still living elsewhere but as a spiritual being.

Having finished our coffees, it was time to meet the dogs in person. I had already tuned to each of them before the visit and written down some notes. Out of the kitchen they bounded and greeted us with great enthusiasm. Little Poppy, who had told me herself that she was beautiful, ran up with her tail wagging and greeted us like long lost friends. She, the mere baby of the pack at five years old, was closely followed by the boys, Harry and Oliver, ten and eleven, respectively. They were all related but looked so very different. Poppy was a very small little girl, with the cutest little tan and white face and a white body. Harry was the usual Jack Russell size and stature, black and white with spots flecking through his coat. As for Oliver, he was really large by comparison, was tri-coloured and had the most amazing large ears that looked like they would billow in the wind like sails on a yacht. He also was the most vocal of the bunch, barking and running back and forth, which William immediately commented on and said he would like me to speak to him about this noisy behaviour.

With perfect timing, they heard Verity arriving and dashed off to the other side of the house to greet her. Verity quickly put the goodies in the fridge that she had bought for lunch then came and sat down with us.

I explained how I worked although they had a pretty good idea from my book. We did wonder, however, if having the three dogs together with us would cause a distraction whilst I was trying to talk to one at a time. We decided to play it by ear and see what happened. I had my record sheets with the photos printed up complete with my 'tune in' notes and Kim, as ever, with her pen at the ready.

I said that I thought we could start with Poppy as by this time she had made herself at home beside Verity and seemed totally settled looking out of the window. I explained that I talk to their subconscious so we were not likely to see any interaction but occasionally an animal would, which is very special when they do.

So, with everyone settled, I repeated what Poppy had told me when I asked her to tell me about herself.

"I am very beautiful, they tell me that!" With a big smile from William and a gasp from Verity as she declared,

"We, do, we do!"

"I can be a bit bossy towards the boys," and showed me 'the look' she had perfected to get her message across. This was also well received with confirming nods.

"I have to watch my weight as I can put it on quite easily!"

With that comment Verity burst out laughing and told me that she is always saying to her that she can't have too much to eat for that very reason.

"So precious, so precious," truly were the words often said to Poppy by Verity, so it was so nice for me to validate that Poppy was really understanding and appreciating those special words.

I could see by their smiles and reactions that I was definitely tuned in with Poppy and that we were going to have such a lovely communication. Poppy declared that she was impatient and didn't like to wait but also that she could ignore people if she happened to be 'doing her own thing'. Poppy also said as she was small, she felt she had to assert her authority!

"Doesn't she just," replied William and I could see that he was finding it very amusing that she was describing her actions as he had perceived them to be. Poppy gave me the sound of laughter and expressed what a happy home she lived in, full of frivolity and fun.

"I am a little girl but I won't be having any little girls myself," she said. My logical brain immediately thought that meant she had been spayed and I said that with the comment. However, actually, as William explained, she had not been neutered, but because she was such a small dog, they had decided they would not risk her having any puppies and pointed out that the boys had been 'done' so there would be no problem there. I could see that William and Verity were quite amazed by the fact that Poppy had obviously listened to a discussion about it and seemingly accepted it, but also that she was passing this information to me.

After expressing how much she was loved and adored being cuddled I asked her if there was anything she wanted to ask/say to William.

"Yeah, Dad. What's with all the books here there and everywhere?" Complete with the knowledge that he seems to start one book, and then go to another and sometimes never getting back to the original. This was met with such laughter with Verity nodding and saying,

"Yes, Daddy, you do, you do!" With that, Poppy placed herself right in front of William and begged with her paws going up and down.

"Paws, Daddy, paws," she was saying and William obligingly leant forward and touched her paws. I think that is as close to a doggy-handshake as one could get, bless her. I asked if she had any advice for Verity and she was quick to reply,

"Bold, Verity, bold! Bold is beautiful!" This we assumed was to do with Verity's design work and Verity did say that she tended to work with pastels but lately had changed direction and was pushing into the 'bolder' realms. Then, as if to give her real clarification, Poppy said,

"The colours of the rainbow are the most natural you'll ever get." And I suppose when you think about it, 'splashed' together can create a very dramatic and bold effect.

On to some of the celeb questions, I asked her to describe William, her 'Dad' as she calls him.

"Honourable and genuine, those two words sum him up," she replied concisely, and I think most of the British nation would agree with her. She then added, "He is soft and doesn't mind people knowing," which I thought was lovely and to be honest,

William is known to be such a caring and spiritual man and really does talk from the heart on such matters. Previously, even though William had not met me personally, during a phone call he said he thought what I was doing was brilliant and that he was happy to help me to make a difference for the animals out there. (He also very kindly gave me a lovely foreword for my *Animal Insight* book). So yes, Poppy, you certainly do know your 'Dad' - us humans could not have put it better ourselves!

For the question, 'What do you think he does when he goes to work?' her answer,

"Cause trouble and says sorry a lot!!" William laughed, and we all agreed that really did seem like his character Ken Barlow to a tee, and just for fun, Poppy gave me her impression of his wife Deidre saying, 'Oh, Ken!' in that drawn out and exasperated way. I have to admit, I tried to do an impression of it but I don't even think Anne Kirkbride, who had played his long-suffering wife for countless years, would have recognised it! Anyway, I just repeated what Poppy gave me – well, that is my excuse and I am sticking to it!

I asked the one... 'If he wasn't an actor what could he be?' She thought about it and led me to believe that he could paint and I got the impression of a watercolour. Then just as I was going to impart this piece of wisdom, she informed me,

"But the problem with that is, he probably wouldn't finish it before moving onto something else!"

I smiled and passed this on as I perceived it to mean and William gasped, and pointed at the door, saying

"Oh my goodness, there is a half finished painting in there that I started two years ago!! Well done, Poppy, and you, that is amazing!" I was touched by his compliment.

For fun, I had devised some questions for advice for various family soap characters and we decided Peter Barlow, Ken's son, would be Poppy's choice. So what advice could she give to Peter?

"Tell him to say what he thinks. Stop sitting around like everything is rosy in the garden. He just sits back and waits until everything gets out of control and then tries to sort it out." Well, that truly summed him up we all agreed, but then told Poppy it was a great idea but actually it would ruin a lot of the story lines! She also informed us that he (Peter) does have respect for his father, Ken, but just doesn't tell him that. William smiled and pointed out there was the very occasional moment where they do have one of their good 'father and son' chats but they are a rarity.

Verity asked if they could ask Poppy some questions which of course I was delighted to do.

We covered if she was happy (this being the most popular question I hear from all loving owners) which we decided was very obvious from the onset. One very valid question was to check that she didn't feel like she was deprived by not having masses of long walks and also being left at home whilst they were out working.

"Most definitely not!" was her emphatic reply, and with that she showed me her, and the boys, running round and round the garden and also informed us that smells and mousing were just as entertaining as any walk could be. She was absolutely fine about being at home and that they amuse themselves. Poppy gave me the urge to smile, and I pointed this out that she just made me feel like smiling – she was one very happy little dog.

Verity wanted to know what Poppy thought of London as she had taken her there a couple of times. As soon as London was mentioned, I heard something familiar but could not get the words out correctly.

Celebrity Pet Talking

"Metrop..Metro.. Pollis of the world" I struggled to say,

So turned to Kim (not for the first time either) and asked her if she knew what I was trying to say. She clearly said,

"The Metropolis of the World".

"Ah, got it" I said with some relief and Poppy then interjected that she wouldn't want to live there but it does make her feel important being there. Verity said, "Oh, I totally agree with that. You can see by the way she walks down the road like, 'Oh yes, it's me folks!' With that, I was given a picture of another dog dressed up in an outfit and said I presumed she must have seen one like that. Verity immediately asked if Poppy wanted to be dressed up too?

"No thanks, a pretty collar is enough for me," she responded. "Oh, she has a diamante one that she wears," Verity told us and we smiled at the thought of this little girl with such a dainty sparkly collar on. We talked with Poppy about Lucy the cat that sadly had gone to Heaven just a week before my visit. Poppy offered me the age, eighteen, (which she was) and informed us Lucy was, 'With the other cats', which I took as meaning in Heaven with others that had lived here too. William was pleased to hear that and said they had had many cats over the years so it was lovely to hear that they were now re-united.

As many of the people reading this will know, Sara, William's wife, passed to spirit very quickly and unexpectedly at the age of fifty eight. It was such a great shock but at least William and the family knew that this was not the end of 'life' as we know it and one day they will be re-united too. What I hadn't until recently realised was that this happened on the same day as my birthday, so, when I was celebrating surviving yet another year, tragically Sara's life here on Earth was finishing. Before the visit I did wonder if there would be any questions asked regarding Sara and the animals, so it was no surprise when Verity asked if Poppy ever saw Mummy? Poppy showed me a loving picture complete with words,

"Oh, my darling dog," and something like, "you are safe, you are okay," which I felt was Sara reassuring her from the spirit world that she would be okay without her. Verity felt the phrase 'Oh, my darling dog' would be very like something her mother would say and as soon as she said that I was given the feeling that in life, if Sara entered a room, she would just light the place up and people would gravitate towards her. William smiled in recognition and to be honest, he doesn't need me or Poppy to let him know that Sara is around, as Poppy says,

"We are never alone." To have such faith and belief in what has been proven a million times does not make losing someone any easier, it just makes it slightly more bearable.

Another question that got covered was what she thought of meeting dogs she didn't know. She immediately said she felt rather defensive, overwhelmed and intimidated by them, which is exactly what William had thought himself. As the other two boys still had to have their turn I drew Poppy's conversation to a close (or so I thought) and asked her what her contribution to the book would show. She told us that it is nice for a dog to watch life flowing along and following what is happening in people's lives. I thought that was very apt as I have learned through being an animal psychic that they know so much more than just what is happening in their presence, so it was lovely to hear it expressed by her.

We moved on to Harry's chat and I read out my pre-communication findings. His opening line was a classic...

"I am kinda like the director!" Complete with the visual and beckoning, "Come here and look at this, come here." Well this was met with tumultuous laughter from William and Verity and I was given the reason as to that remark. William explained that they actually used to call Harry 'The Brain' as he used to know where all the doors were and try to guide people through them. If you didn't use the nearest one, he went to the next and the next and so forth like he was showing you the way out. And actually, when Kim and I did make a trip to find a bathroom, sure enough, Harry was on 'directing' duty. I read out some more communication, one which was,

"You think it - I know it!" which again summed him up as a very clever cookie indeed. Again, we knew I was tuned in, and on asking what he wanted to say he told us,

"If I were a person, I would wear a waistcoat!" We laughed and reckoned that he had either been listening to Poppy's chat about not wanting to be dressed up or wanted to add more to his 'directors' persona. Harry informed us that he might look old but he is in good physical shape and that he likes good food, 'really good food' was repeated for emphasis.

"Ah, a little food connoisseur, are we?" asked William jokingly.

Harry then went way back in time and told me he thought that to get him as a pup really was an 'on the spur of the moment' decision.

"Yes," Verity agreed, "He was. Mummy suddenly decided to get me a puppy for my birthday, so she quickly located a breeder and that is how we got him." (It always amazes me how these animals remember things from such a very young age and such a long time ago too). He said he was not an over-demanding chap and just fits in, sitting back watching what is happening. To be honest, they both said that he was quite self-assured, and was the cool one of the trio and not demanding in any way.

Suddenly Poppy interrupted with,

"I'm not, I'm not either!" and started doing her really 'Miss Cute' look.

"Oh, are you going to smile for us, Poppy?" Verity asked, and with that, Poppy pulled her lips back to make a doggie smile. Oh, how we all laughed and then she did it again and again, delighted with her efforts at amusing the human species.

"Oh, no wonder I said I felt like I wanted to smile earlier during our chat, she really was trying to let me know that she knew how to smile!" As funny and adorable as she was being I had to explain that it was Harry's talking time so we would go back over to him.

"I can fall asleep in an instant," declared Harry, no doubt relieved to have his turn back again. With that rather strange statement (I can only repeat what I hear) William looked rather quizzical about this. Having thought about it for a few seconds he remarked that in fact he might well do so and they would watch out for it and we were all quite amused by what funny/odd things they want to share with us.

He now had his commanding position lying on the settee with Verity and she just happened to brush one of his feet with her hand. He quickly turned round at her with a look of, "Oy, don't touch my feet!"

"Jackie, can you please ask him about that. Why does he not like his feet being touched?" I put the question to him and got a very simple answer – it gives him a horrible, not ticklish but similar, sensation which he really does not like, hence the 'Get off' reaction. He did chew his feet and lick his legs slightly but was quick to assure us he was not lame, there were no scabs and there was nothing the matter with him. These comments were swiftly followed by an inference that he was none too keen on going to the vets – point taken!

His nickname is 'Boo' which he had no problem with being called, in fact, he said you could say it close to his face, like saying it in a fun way and that would create much tail wagging. He then volunteered another 'oddity',

"I am like a builder, always wanting to do something!" I asked for further information to accompany this and he gave me the impression of moving something to one place, then going and getting another to do the same. Well this left me quite confused which I freely admitted.

"Oh, I know exactly what that is," said William, "we used to call him 'The Toy Master' as he would go and collect toys one by one and place them in front of you. Actually, come to think of it, there are not so many toys here now so I think Verity we should maybe go and get some more." What a lovely picture this conjured up of this industrious little lad working away.

By this time, Harry had jumped off the settee and was now lying at my feet. Having listened to Poppy's chat, he gently told us that he had found it difficult when they lost Sara as he used to spend his 'quiet time' with her. William said that as she used to often be home in the daytime and the dogs adored being with her so that could have been quite possible. William put forward the same question about other people's dogs and Harry really wasn't fussed about trying to socialise. He said he would rather keep back and not get involved but apparently joined in with the barking anyway!

"Oh, look," said William, he has just done that 'instant sleep' thing - he was wide-awake a second ago! And with that, whilst Harry was lying on his side, his one back leg started to move in a 'running' fashion. We started to laugh and I suggested he move his front leg too, and he did! Then he stopped that and then seemed to manage to get both back legs going at the same time so, amidst our laughter, I had the insight to ask him what he was doing.

His reply, "I am cycling!!!" Well, this was getting hilarious and he seemed to be having great fun (although seemingly asleep I have to say) showing that he could amuse people just like Poppy could.

With our sides aching at the absurdity of the whole interactive 'exercising' I moved onto the celeb questions. He told me that William's best quality was that he was appreciative of things that people do for him, especially if someone is doing a hard task, like a gardener digging the garden for him for example. As for another job - he thought that William would make a wonderful host at elite functions as he really knows how to make people feel comfortable and not left out.

I asked Harry for his opinion of William's screen wife, Deidre, and this was his summary,

"She has been very misguided in the past but she does love Ken and would defend him at every corner. (I think that is a good example – as in many relationships, you may sometimes say unkind things to your partner but don't dare have anybody else say anything bad about them!)

Before his chat finished Verity had one very quick question.

"We leave the television on when we are out, does he like it?"Adding, "It *is* on the style channel." Well, with a pause from Harry he delivered his answer with a good hint of irony,

"Does she think we watch it?" We burst out laughing thinking, 'Mmm, maybe an interesting choice for Verity and her type of work but for dogs?' Anyway, he conceded that it made a welcome noise in the background and was okay with him.

So, after having such a lovely conversation, Harry gave us his answer as to what he thought his contribution to the world of animal communication showed.

"It proves that we can all live in unison and still be different characters." What a brilliant reply and just as we were congratulating him on his wisdom, he threw us one last remark, "and also... we can pretend to be asleep!!" What a little monkey!! He really did have the last laugh on us. No wonder William says he will never look on these dogs in quite the same way ever again.

Working as an animal psychic, I love the fact that I constantly am able to add another dimension into the beautiful relationship that people have with their animals. And, to be able to do it for someone such as William Roache, makes me feel honoured.

Last, but not least, it was time for Oliver to have his say. I got his sheet out and read off what he had told me about himself earlier too.

"I am an attention seeker" and he showed me that he liked to recline along the edge of the settee. The second remark I knew to be correct, as he had been doing this whilst we were there, and as for the attention seeking,

"Absolutely!" was sung out in chorus by William and Verity.

William went on to say that he thought Oliver was nervous, but Oliver who was listening intently was quick to come back with,

"I am not nervous, just hypersensitive." This being relayed with a certain emphasis, I might add.

Then he delivered a knockout line,

"Okay, I admit it - I scream like a girl!!" I burst out laughing while trying to deliver his words.

"Oh, yes, he most certainly does," came the retort from Verity and with that William went back to something he had asked if I could address when I met the dogs initially – Oliver's barking when people come into the house. Although he did stop after a while William wanted to know why he seemed upset. I had to say I didn't feel he was upset and told him that at the beginning of our visit whilst Oliver was barking, I am sure I heard him say,

"I'm funny," just before he launched himself onto my lap. (Verity even remarked later on, that it was incredible that Oliver had decided to curl himself up behind me 'as, to be honest, he never does that with strangers, it is a family only thing'). Oliver pointed out that his tail would be wagging whilst he was barking and so he didn't think he was exhibiting fear, just excitement.

"Yes, yes," Verity whooped, "I have been Oliver's champion defender for years as I have always thought it was a form of excitable behaviour and I was right!!" One nil to Verity! He also went to lengths to point out that if he was afraid of something, he would cower (which apparently he does if he gets a fright) and he certainly does not do this when barking at the door or visitors. The barking at the door bit we tried to address. William wondered if he was afraid of the doorbell by his loud reaction. Again no, in fact, he thought the postman was exciting as he brings things to the house and also pointed out that it was only nice people that came there anyway. The main reason for barking on hearing people at the door, we were informed, was quite simply,

"That people need to know we are here." We couldn't argue with that one, they were most certainly doing their job. William did say the problem was that he could not hear people on the intercom for the barking, and not just Oliver but all three. Oliver suggested William get another answering device in another room, so he can tell the people, "The dogs are barking, so I will go to the other intercom to talk to you!" (Apparently they had one upstairs, but I would think that would be rather inconvenient for the everyday purpose.) I left that answer with him and in William's words,

"So he is not going to co-operate, is he?!" We began to realise that Oliver had his own mind and he definitely wanted to - tell it, and do it, in his own way. I thought the chances of discussing what he didn't were rather low. I summed this up by saying,

"If I were a betting person, then I think Peter (Ken's son in 'The Street' who owns the betting shop) would be very pleased to see me as I would be just giving him money!!"

As for Oliver's summing up on the subject, he informed us that, 'William sometimes puts a little too much thought into things!' This is from the dog that admits that he is at the bottom of the doggie pecking order and he knows they feel sorry for him! Oliver does not feel sorry for himself, he says in actual fact, it is fine, as he gets pity, so hence more attention. He then made me feel like clapping my hands as children do to each other in the playground. I did my best to put this one over and Verity, quick as a flash, told us that she does 'high fives' with him, which he seemed immensely proud of, I have to say.

Verity asked me if I thought Oliver had 'special powers' as he seemed different and maybe more psychically connected than the others. On hearing this, he immediately started to impress upon me to tell Verity that within a year her new venture will have 'taken wings and flown'. She was delighted to hear this and I said obviously I (and Oliver) could be wrong but actually already some of the things from this book have turned out to be just as the animals had predicted. So, I wished her well and said when she was highly successful, remember where she heard it first!

Oliver also imparted some very sensible advice, which I myself will also heed – 'Be selective, not impulsive'. Verity thought that was so clever and admitted that she could be impulsive at times. I suggested she print the words up, and whenever making an important decision, just run them through her head first, courtesy of their beloved dog. Oliver then told me,

"I like this," and 'this' was, bizarrely, the sound and feel of rustling leaves!! This was a new one on me but it made me feel as if he was a very sensual dog. Verity was delighted to hear this and exclaimed,

"See, I told you he was special. I see him taking notice of things." This then led me onto Verity and how she is very connected spiritually (Spirit, my guide in this case, likes to tell if people hear and see clairvoyantly etc.) and then we had a chat about the type of healing that she has just been studying. She is very in tune, especially with this dog who told me that he could not have lived with a nervous owner. William said how true that statement was. Apparently the breeder said she knew she had to be very careful to home this sensitive little pup with the right family. William and his family were delighted to have him and, suffice to say, I think he has taken full advantage of their kindness and understanding! (I remarked how wonderful that the breeder was a so intuitive breeder and William agreed).

"About Oliver and other dogs," William broached.

"Just don't even try," was Oliver's response. We had got the gist by now but I still asked him to clarify what his barking was about. He admitted it was quite an hysterical, "Keep away, just keep away!" effort. We did have a discussion about how to handle the worry it was causing William about the reactions of the three terriers on a walk if they saw another dog. We set a plan into action, that instead of getting worried/panicky, simply put into practice – all dogs on the left hand side and let's walk straight on by. I assured all three that they were safe and that William and Verity would never let any harm come to them.

I do hope this helps as it is hard when you have three to contain on leads especially if they are jumping up and down barking. William said he was pleased to find out (apart from with stranger's dogs) that Oliver was actually not of a nervous disposition but just displays over-excitable behaviour and he would see it like that from now on.

We shared some lovely spiritual things from memories of musical boxes to different spirits that the animals notice from time to time in the house. One that did tickle us was a cat that was climbing the curtains and William did recall one that did just that. Believe you me; if you saw the luxurious drapes in their house, I think that really would be one step too far!

We decided that we would let Oliver base his celeb answers around Verity (well according to him she will soar as a designer, so one day she may well be a household name too) so here they are:

Verity's best quality was,

"She would give someone her last penny and not ask for it back."

If she was to do a different job what could it be? And in true Oliver style, he chose something he thought she *shouldn't* do by giving us this lovely reply,

"Not a secretary, she couldn't even spell organised!!" Fortunately, Verity laughed as she knew he was just having fun at her expense but admitted her spelling truly wasn't her forte.

The advice question for Oliver goes to Tracy Barlow, William's 'Street' family's wayward daughter,

"Tell her - if she keeps treating people in the way that she does, she will get her comeuppance, and actually, that goes for everybody." I thought this dog was very special and maybe does have a deeper understanding than most, like such things as Karma that is present in our human world.

And having now acknowledged Oliver's 'special powers' he brought us straight back down to earth with his answer for what his contribution to the book was,

"Some dogs you can't tell what to do!!" Thanks Oliver!

After the dog chats we had some lunch and it was so delightful to be able to listen to the wisdom that William has learned over the years and hearing how there are so many people out there trying to make a difference in so many ways. I know that readers, through these dog chats, will be so pleased to have had a glimpse into the life of a very special man that has graced our screens for decades.

Words cannot express what a fabulous day this was! The dogs were so amazing; all with different ways and ideas, they were a joy to communicate with. And as for Verity and William - they certainly made a dream come true for me. This will most certainly help change the life of countless animals and that will be a dream come true for the animal kingdom too - and I would like to take this opportunity to thank them both on their behalf.

With smiles on our faces like two Cheshire cats, Kim and I said our goodbyes and set off on our journey home. Funnily enough, we found that throughout the two-hour trip we seemed to be taking a keen interest in the names of every pub we drove past. Not one came near *The Frozen Mop* though – it won with a clean sweep!

Jenny Smedley

Having read one of Jenny's books, *Pet's have Souls Too*, I knew that there would be a very deep connection between Jenny and her dog KC. Once again, this was an introduction through Jacky Newcomb who knew Jenny well.

Jenny is an amazingly interesting lady and has an array of talents from TV presenting and being a best-selling author to someone who also writes songs! In a way, her life mirrors mine, and many other people's lives too. This I mean by us suddenly reaching a turning point and now doing things that we had never even dared dream of let alone be living the reality.

I set off on my travels with Bob as this time he would be my note-taker. We were to be staying with friends near Bath, as Jenny lives in Somerset which is not that far from there. This gave us the perfect opportunity to catch up with them too, as it had been a few years since we had seen them, and as we all know, time just seems to fly by, and for some reason - the older we get, the faster it goes!

Also with us was Sally our dog, who would be staying with us in their house, complete with two cats! Our friends, Wayne and Sara (Wayne is a horse dentist like Bob) were actually a huge influence to us regarding animal communication.

They told us about their experiences with Julie Dicker who, alas died a few years ago, but had done many communications with their horses. They had repeated so many personal examples of showing the truth that animals really can 'talk'. So thanks to them, we used to recommend Julie to many of our dental clients, and heard lots of irrefutable evidence for ourselves. Roll on a few years, and it is now me that is doing the communicating for Wayne and Sara and some of his dental clients too. The journey took us nearly three hours, but we arrived safely and then went out for a bite to eat. We chatted into the night catching up on all the news and I was really pleased to hear that more and more of his horse clients are beginning to think of animal communication as a very useful way to find answers for any problems their horses may be having. And as for Sally, she found the cats as totally fascinating as they did her.

It was approximately an hour drive to Somerset from Bath, so I had arranged to be at Jenny's for eleven o'clock. We set off with plenty of time in hand, so we could take in the beautiful countryside on our way. Eventually we came to Jenny's country lane and as we wended our way round it, amazingly we spotted her house without any of our usual detours. A gorgeous white bungalow nestled in the countryside, with the birds chirping and a black Springador (Labrador cross Spaniel) looking out of a large window at us as we opened the front gate.

Jenny greeted us, and introduced her husband, Tony, and showed us to her sitting room. We sat down and gazed out of the large french doors and down the garden which meets the edge of a wood. There was a flurry of activity on the numerous bird feeding centres and Jenny commented that sometimes Ashley the peacock, makes an appearance there too. (He wasn't their peacock but lived in the vicinity and was a delightful adornment to their patio when he made his visit.)

Celebrity Pet Talking

There was no sign of KC; she seemed to be keeping out of the way. Jenny seemed a little concerned and asked us to sit down and quickly explained that KC is actually rather wary of people so could we please be quite quiet and let her come to us.

"No problem," we agreed, and having a rescue Collie we were well used to assuming the non-threatening persona.

With a little persuasion, KC eventually entered the sitting room to join us. She kept a slight distance, weighed us up and then came forward to me. I let her sniff me and she seemed happy with that and moved over to Bob, who by this time had his book out ready to write.

I said aloud that I had come here to see her and that she looked far better than her photo portrayed. She jumped up on the settee, sat and looked at us for a few more minutes and then came over and greeted us like old friends, and even positioned herself just perfectly for her back to be scratched! With 'doggie introductions' over, she got back onto a settee facing us and glued her beautiful amber eyes on me. It was so strange, and Jenny was quite taken aback, for KC was sitting there so quietly which was really not like her at all. KC then seemed to know why I was there and just looked at me as if to say, 'Please start!'

Jenny knows all about animal communication so I did not need to explain anything, so I asked KC to show/tell me something to make sure we were 'connected'. KC presented me with an image of her running and skidding to a stop. This made Jenny nod and laugh as she pointed out the bank in the garden which drops down providing perfect inertia for KC to skip down for her 'meet and greet' of animals from the adjacent wood. Amazingly, many have got used to her and she has just become part of their lives too.

"I am beautiful!" KC announced with pride.

"Batty, more like," was Jenny's rhetorical reply. I laughed and said, I would ask KC why she thought Jenny would say such a thing. KC obliged with a picture of very active back and forth behaviour coupled with a clear sense of excitement. (This hyperactivity was clearly not apparent to me as she was sitting there so quietly.)

"Oh yes," Jenny replied, "She just keeps coming back and forth, back and forth. She is so persistent; she just adores playing and the attention that goes with it."

At that point, KC leant into Jenny and started to lick her hand, and, not just a little brush of her tongue – with real zest and focused attention. "That's a point," said Jenny, "Can you ask her why she does this/what does it mean to her?" "By all means," I replied and got a very straight forward answer,

"Because she's mine!" No arguments there!! Jenny's husband, Tony, excused himself and said he was heading off to the office but would be back soon. With that I heard an odd 'grinding/whirring' sound. KC seemed to want me to mention it, so I asked if they knew what it was, did they have anything that sounded faulty that she was hearing? With blank faces, neither recognised what I was talking about.

On the subject of hearing, KC told us that she has actually got what she describes as 'over-sensitive' hearing. Jenny again, knew all about this. I asked KC to explain more. She said that the high pitch was really acute and that she hears noises far away, and sometimes they scare her. To be honest, there is not a lot Jenny could do about that, but just to re-assure her as she normally does. KC was 'on a roll' now and listed another fear – cars! Jenny had asked me to try and find out what was her problem with them. KC showed me very clearly her 'swerving' away from any passing car, which is what she did. Her explanation was, that cars invade her space and importantly that neither she, Jenny or Tony have any control over the vehicle. This was a valid point, the driver is in control, and why should she trust them? I chatted to her and asked if she had ever been 'knocked' by a car, which was 'No' and showed me an uphill lane that the cars seem to come close to her. I pointed out that she was totally safe and that she would always be on the inside of whoever was leading her, and that as no car had ever hit her, I thought that should be proof enough that they will not. I gave some reassuring words that KC had chosen to be used when she is being walked to 'prick' her subconscious.

Having been given the view of the 'uphill lane', this turned out to be on the way to her favourite walk. She made us laugh, declaring that sometimes she does get tired on a walk, but only the uphill bit, as when they get up to the top, she is suddenly rejuvenated and runs round seeking out rabbit holes and anything else of interest.

We covered previous problems with her stomach, following KC's remark,

"They are very careful what they feed me you know!" She then indicated me to her right shoulder. I asked Jenny if she knew of a problem there, and sure enough, she has intermittent lameness on that leg. Jenny, at this point seemed quite taken aback and then was very complimentary about the clarity of my information. She declared,

"I cannot believe you got that straightaway, and, you can quote me on that!" So thanks Jenny for such high praise, and from someone so knowledgeable on the subject of animal communication, so quoted it here I have! As Jenny didn't really know how this shoulder problem had occurred, I sought to find out. KC showed me her, and very much a youngster at the time, as if she has fallen down over something and overstretched that leg as she tried to save herself. She said it was not painful, just niggled her sometimes, but didn't like it to be pulled far forward. Jenny thought that sounded feasible as she came from a farm and were running about amongst all sorts of things when she went to buy her. We assured her that they, nor the vet, would ever pull it far forward again.

Tony came back into the room and Jenny remarked how quiet KC still was.

"This is so unlike her!" Jenny expressed,

"And I can vouch for that," added Tony. Then I heard it, KC gave me a sound like a dog purring!!

'Mmm, cats purr,' I thought, 'not dogs,' but as strange as it sounded, I mentioned it to them.

"Oh yes, she really does purr, it is a deep contented sound as she snoozes away!" "KC butts back in,

"I do it deliberately, and by the way, I am loving this, (she meant the communication) and true, I wouldn't normally sit still at all!" We had definitely established how happy and what a very deep relationship she had with Jenny, and not forgetting Tony either, who KC described as, 'Very intelligent, but soft as putty!'

For her description of Jenny, 'Amazing - she can do ten different things at once!' That I could quite believe, as Jenny does so many diverse things, she must have one heck of a busy mind. KC did give us a giggle, after giving her owner such praise, then informed us that, to her amusement, Jenny goes in rooms and forgets what she went for, and then has to retrace her thought pattern.

For the question of, if she was doing this work… KC's answer showed me doing intricate drawings! I tried to describe this to Jenny, and said to be honest it almost looked like mechanical pictures, sort of like wheel cogs and suchlike.

"Oh my goodness!" Jenny exclaimed. "I had a friend round yesterday who I am helping illustrate a CD cover, and guess what was in the picture? The moon and stars, complete with a few interlocking wheels!" We were all quite astounded how accurately KC had managed to pick that up and pass it on to me.

KC's offer of advice for Jenny raised a wry smile from Tony. KC's words,

"You have an answer machine - let it do its job!" (Apparently Jenny is the same as me - I too cannot resist answering the phone even if I happen to be in the middle of dinner etc.!)

KC was so adorable and was definitely the centre of Jenny and Tony's world, which was also confirmed by the mention of not wanting the dynamics changed in the household. And just to make sure that they got the message, another dog might push her around, and she would really not like that!

So for KC's final question about what does she think her contribution to this book would show people? Her answer,

"We live and breathe like you, we really *are* like you!" Jenny immediately declared,

"I spend my life telling people that!"

"Me too!" I responded.

With the communication finished, (and sadly no show from Ashley the peacock!) we sat and chatted about things in general and Jenny gave me good advice about how to get more people involved and gave me some lovely suggestions of who I could contact. She took me to her office so she could show me on her computer where to do more research, and as I entered, I heard the 'whirring/grinding' noise. I laughed and pointed it out, and Jenny shouted through to Tony,

"We have found the noise - it is part of the computer that's making it!" Well done KC, I now realise it was nothing to do with being faulty, it was her very clever way of showing me that she understood where Tony was going, when he mentioned going to the office.

It was wonderful to meet another author who cares so much about the animal kingdom. Jenny was kind enough to write about my visit in her latest book, *Pets are Forever…*

"Recently we had a visit from Animal Communicator, Jackie Weaver. She was collecting material for her new book, *Celebrity Pet Talking*, and wanted to do a reading with KC to put in it. It was a remarkable experience. Jackie was able to describe KC's favourite walk, the exact terms of endearment I use on a daily basis, and pinpoint precisely the seat of KC's previous lameness, but all of those things, to the sceptic, could I suppose be extremely good guesses, so when Jackie came up with the next item I was very pleased, because I defy anyone to doubt it. She asked KC if I ever did anything that had impressed her. And if there was anything I did she thought I was good at. KC 'told' her in thoughts that she'd been quite impressed watching me take a lot of trouble in drawing some specific shapes and details on something she described as two circles that looked a bit like a piece of machinery, all the while accompanied by a quiet 'buzzy' noise. What Jackie did not know, could not possibly know, is that the day before I'd spent a couple of hours on the computer designing a CD cover for my good friend, Madeleine Walker (Jackie does not know her either). The design was based around a double circle, with various intricate, symmetrical shapes such as hearts, stars and moons around it and in it. It did take a lot of time and effort as it was the first time I'd attempted such a thing. KC had sat and watched the whole time, and listened to the constant 'buzz' of my computer's whirring brain. To me this message was indisputable proof that Jackie was able to communicate with my dog.'

With Jenny's visit over, we said our goodbyes and headed back to Sara and Wayne's house but stopped on the way to give Sally a well-deserved walk in the beautiful surroundings. I mentioned at the beginning that Sally was mesmerised by the cats, and I have to say she was as good as gold. For two days, she walked round the cat food, having been told it was not hers - it belonged to the cats. I was very impressed, because as inviting as it was just sitting there on the floor asking to be eaten, she didn't touch it. One of the cats kept doing that, 'I will saunter up and down here, just to see what you will do', and bless Sally, she just watched it intently at a distance.

The next morning whilst finishing breakfast at the dining table, the doorbell rang. As Sara answered it, the caller's large Labrador shot through the gap and came tearing flat-out into the kitchen. Very quickly he was swiftly manoeuvred back outside, but not without having devoured some of the cat food on his way past! With that momentary excitement over and done with, we proceeded to take our bags out to the car. As I came back in, there was Sally licking her lips, standing by two beautifully clean and polished bowls now devoid of any cat food. Although her face was showing her guilt, her tail was doing the deliberate slow wag as if to say,

"Well, if it was good enough for him, it was good enough for me!" I agreed with her chain of thought, so gave her a big hug and thanked her for being so well behaved in someone else's house. I also told her I was immensely proud of her for not chasing the cats and they would have been extremely grateful for that. As I had said, she was fascinated by them and when we got Stanley, our little tabby boy who adorns this cover, about a year later, she then become 'cat nanny'.

She follows him everywhere she can, often with her nose just off his tail. He doesn't care one iota, in fact, he takes great delight in chasing *her* up the field! It is hilarious to watch. It's so lovely to see two species living side by side in such harmony, and if you don't think they are communicating, you couldn't be more wrong!

One thing that makes Bob laugh to this day was my advice to Stanley to heed whilst out on his wanders.

I told him that should he be approached by an unfriendly cat, not to get into a fight but simply say, "I've got a big dog!" and then make his way back home, pronto!

Kim Thomson

I have stayed in touch with some of the people in this book and they know I am there for their animals should they need me. Once such person is Jenny Seagrove who called me to say she had passed my details to her friend Kim, (also living in London), whose little dog was ill.

At the time of me writing this (2011) you would probably associate Kim with the Yorkshire Dales, rather than London. She played the fantastic part of Faye Lamb whose story lines were full of twists and intrigue and she was even suspected of murder! The incredible story (a first for a soap opera, I think) was when Faye appeared in *Emmerdale* having tracked down her husband, Mark, who was now bigamously married. He was living a deceitful new life with Natasha Wylde played by the lovely Amanda Donohue. I think any male viewers would have been secretly congratulating him on having managed to marry two gorgeous women and for them to fight over him in spite of what he had done! In the end he paid the ultimate price - he lost his own life!

Kim contacted me the same day and sent through details and a picture of Sheba. Instantly I thought of those cute, wispy, cuddly toy dogs you can buy for children, and adults like me who admit to having several cuddly animal toys. She was eight-years-old and a gorgeous, rough-coated Jack Russell with an expression of 'I'm so cute!' Kim had 'inherited' her from a landlady from Los Angeles who had passed away. So, here was me talking to a dog from LA and telling her owner that I am going to LA myself later in the year! Of all the places in the world...

I organised to do this by phone that day, as I knew from Jenny that Sheba had been to the vets and that Kim was obviously very concerned. Apparently Sheba was doing this odd shaking thing and seemed very anxious about what was happening to her. She was now being treated for pancreatitis, which is inflammation of the pancreas and an extremely painful condition.

Jenny, as I mentioned in her story is very intuitive and as it turns out, does Reiki (energy healing) so had been to visit Kim to try to help Sheba. The reason I came into the equation was that Jenny, having listened to the background and symptoms, was not sure that it was pancreatitis. I can never ignore veterinary advice but I can do my job and pass on what the animal tells me, which in turn, can be put forward to the vet.

(Most vets are not open to what we communicators do; I can't blame them; they studied for seven years to qualify for a start, and what we do does tend to 'fly in the face of science' anyway. So I, with the help of the animal, work out how to suggest or point things out casually to the vet.)

That same evening I phoned Kim and, like most of the celebrities in this book, she had not experienced animal communication before. I started off in my usual way,

"I am very cute and watch everything," Sheba had told me and Kim agreed saying that she is very 'attentive'. I had to say my 'I don't diagnose...' spiel, but that she was making me feel rather odd. It was that shaky feeling I described that you feel when your sugar levels have got rather depleted and you get that very uneasy trembling sensation. Kim knew what I meant and said she thought that described what it looked like. I had to say, although I was feeling slightly nauseous, I felt it was from fear of not knowing what was happening rather than stomach pain but stressed I couldn't go against what the vets had said. I suggested to Sheba that we chat about nicer things in her life but would cover how she was feeling if she wanted to now or later on. She took the latter option.

Sheba made me feel like she is a sensitive little girl and when groomed this would have to be done with much care. Kim immediately recognised this and said,

"Oh, yes! For a dog that is so brave in some ways but not in others, you are right. A silly thing like - if she suddenly finds a leaf or a twig had attached itself to her hair, now that is a performance!" I heard a 'shriek.' You know the dramatic doggie kind and said,

"Does she sometimes let a shriek out with it?"

"Oh, yes, she does and comes running like, 'help me, help me!'" Kim was laughing and I thought this was so adorable it is just like a child running to its mum.

"I am a bit of a 'stay at home girl'" Sheba told me. I took this as meaning that she tends to prefer to stay at home rather than romping about in the parks etc. I passed this over to Kim and she said,

"No, she loves exercise; she does lots!"

"Oh, I don't know why I got that then," I replied.

"Oh, but," said Kim, "I know what this is about; I have got an injury so I have not been able to exercise like I normally do, so she is limited to the dog walker at the moment."

"Ah, that makes sense." I replied. "What has happened to you?"

"I do kick boxing and have torn a hip joint."

"Wow!" was my immediate response, quickly explaining that that was in regard to her doing kick boxing but a 'big ouch' for the injury. Kim said it is most painful, even just gentle walking aggravates it. I suggested that maybe Jenny could do some of her Reiki on it! Kim laughed and thought that was not such a bad idea.

Sheba then passed me a picture of herself with a truly defined waist (like a model!!) and this was so right. Kim said Sheba was a very fit little dog and still very shapely for her age. Sheba made us laugh showing us her on a walk scooting behind trees and darting back and forth.

"I am not a nuisance," she declared.

"Absolutely not!" was Kim's emphatic reply, "she is such a good girl." With that though, I was given a picture of what looked like a very young Sheba chewing some form of book complete with the look of 'Oops, I shouldn't be doing this, should I?' I said this to Kim and although she could not recall the book incident she said that Sheba is always chewing things, still!

"I don't do the expensive stuff," Sheba immediately informed me. I repeated this and said that I thought she didn't chew her good furniture and suchlike.

"Oh, no, just her own toys so it is not a problem; she gets such fun out of doing it and I then I just give her some more." (Phew! Kim having had a lengthy acting career spanning back to the days of *The Life and Loves of a She-Devil* and before, I am sure she would have accrued many beautiful things).

Sheba made out like she could 'beckon' Kim.

"Oh, she does," responded Kim.

"And she falls for it every time," replied a cheeky Sheba. She hastily added that she understood about 'her time and place' so I suggested that when people visited that she was not a dog that kept pestering people for attention. This was right; what a well mannered little dog. Kim went on to say that even when she takes her into a shop, she is so good. I was given this most funny picture: it looked like someone that had a dog tucked under their left arm but more like you would have a handbag not a real dog, most strange. I did my best to explain what I thought I was seeing but Kim immediately said that Sheba didn't like being picked up so she didn't do it. I could not fathom this out but as I got the same picture repeated I thought maybe this was Sheba watching other people shopping complete with an 'inert handbag style dog' under their left arm. I said to Kim to look out for it and smile to herself if she spots the 'doggie-bag' shopper in the future. (I bet she does!)

Sheba then gave me a very odd audible sensation like she could hear static, crackles and such like. I suggested that she was maybe hyper-sensitive hearing wise.

"Oh, yes, absolutely!" was Kim's emphatic reply, "she reacts at such odd things, I have often thought that myself. One thing that drives her to distraction is the sound of rain lashing down on the road so I have to pick her up. Ah yes, so I do pick her up but probably only on these occasions as I have to try and get her further away from the noise on the ground." Sheba was making me feel stressed and I told Kim I would relate this to her feeling like someone with tinnitus – when the rain was hitting the ground, it was a resounding echo in her ever-so sensitive ears. During this discussion Sheba interrupted with something so funny, from a dog…

"I don't cross my eyes though!" I laughed and told Kim what a comical thing to say and quickly tried to fathom it out. I am sure she was describing what some people do when a noise or something else is of extreme aggravation; they scrunch their faces and often the eyes are averted in a direction – like that 'fingernails down the blackboard' reaction. How funny that a dog notices something like that. We as people can move our face so much for expression; animals are really restricted on that front. But, as I say in life, every negative has a positive and so this one would be the lack of needing botox and facelifts!!

Talking about noise - Jenny had mentioned to me that when she was at Kim's house, whilst trying to do the healing on Sheba, there was such a racket going on next door due to building work. This also came up in the conversation with Kim and I got the impression of one of the long rubble chutes and the thundering sound every time they launched masonry and whatever else down it. Kim said that there was one, it was right beside her house and poor Sheba was finding it very distressing. In fact, Kim was worrying about how Sheba felt when she had to leave her at home by herself. True enough, Sheba was finding it extremely annoying. I checked with her and normal everyday noises like the phone, ping of the microwave etc. were fine - the problem was, these noises were loud and inconsistent so she was finding it hard to ignore them.

Kim was doing what I often suggest to owners, to leave something with a constant noise on, like a radio in the background. Kim said she left the TV on all the time for her. I wonder if Sheba pays as little attention to the actual programme like William Roache's dogs and their 'style channel'! Funnily enough, just as I have written this I realised they were Jack Russells too! (I just love synchronicities.) I also mentioned (although I never advocate anyone to give an animal anything, that is for vets and other trained people) that lots of people use homeopathics with good effect. There are ones that work for nervous children so maybe worth looking into. We also set up a bonding key for her which she offered as,

"They are just working – don't worry about them." I thought that showed us that Sheba had indeed understood and I know that Kim will keep telling her. I do hope it does the trick.

With that Sheba brought us round to her illness and symptoms. She did what I term as the 'jigsaw' effect which is putting all the pieces forward in the hope that they will form a picture and also give guidance for the vet. Although for the last few days she was on one of those vet-formulated, tinned dog foods - these were all her indications:

"I am not fed a rich diet and that over the years has not changed." True.

"I have not lost my appetite." True.

"My water content is the same." True. (Her thespian version of 'I am not drinking more than I normally do').

"Angio rhythms." This was a combination of words I did not recognise but very carefully mentioned (so as not to cause any worry) what I had heard, and maybe this was indicating to do with the rhythm of the heart. I asked if Kim was aware of anything regarding Sheba's heart and it turned out that Sheba did have a heart murmur. I said to please bear in mind that I could be wrong, I am just repeating what I heard and there might just be a change in her murmur that is causing this odd sensation.

"You can palpate my body and it is not sore." The vet had pressed her tummy and all around there with no reaction.

"This can occur in the middle of the night but by 8a.m. I am back to normal as if nothing had happened." This had been the case for all previous bouts of this complaint and Kim volunteered that Sheba had vomited once on a previous occasion. (The impression I was getting from Sheba was that these shaking episodes could occur with many months apart which was correct. There was no pattern, nor an obvious reason behind it.) This time however, she was, as she put it, 'just not her normal self' the next day, hence the worry and vets treatment etc. True.

I expressed my thoughts to Kim that I felt it didn't seem to sound like pancreatitis, ably defined by Sheba saying,

"It just doesn't stack up!" I spend my life saying, 'I could be wrong' as I cannot go against a vet's diagnosis but, if it was reassuring to know, that I was certainly not being passed any serious discomfort either. We would have wait to hear the test results tomorrow but at least Kim had a good outline of information to pass to the vet should it be needed.

Sheba moved us swiftly back off the subject of her physical symptoms by showing me a leather Chesterfield couch and said,

"Now that *is* nice!" I asked Kim if she had one and she told me she didn't! I was rather perplexed but was given the same clear picture and even ventured the colour green to Kim. Still a 'no'! I started to laugh and said I had no idea what she was showing, maybe it was from somewhere you had been or go to, but one sure thing is, you wouldn't see it in the Dingle's house. (*Emmerdale* watchers will understand that – The Dingle family are top of the list of suspects should anything disappear or a bit of poaching had become apparent, and also have that ever increasing family of 'long lost relatives!')

"I know about fireworks," Sheba declared but not in a frightened way so I passed it over the way I got it and Kim said,

"Oh, yes. It was the July 4th celebrations on Monday and people were letting off fireworks." I know some dogs absolutely detest fireworks and find them extremely scary but Sheba made me feel like she had coped with situation. Kim agreed and said that she thought she was getting better about them. As soon as Kim had agreed with that Sheba gave me a picture of a jar with round treats in it. These Kim instantly recognised and said that she takes some on walks with her so I reckon a little girl wanted some for 'coping' and being very brave.

I won't go into the fireworks debate as I feel so strongly about them but animals seem to be of no priority to councils and the likes. I am not a kill-joy but I think it should be agreed upon that just ONE day for each year should be set and that would be the only legal day people can use fireworks. Dog owners, then being aware of the said date, can take the necessary precautions (give their animals sedatives as many do) and then that is it over for another year. That way we would avoid this fear that so many animals have to suffer on so many occasions and the sad stories of animals that have run off in terror never to be seen again. Maybe this 'one day a year' will be implemented when people realise that animals are not just dumb, unfeeling creatures – this book I hope will go a long way to help with that.

Talking of being stressed, Kim wanted to check that Sheba had not been stressed by Kim going away to Yorkshire all the time, which I think was the main reason Kim left the show. (I have learned so much from doing this book – we, as members of the public, think their lifestyle is full of glitz and glamour, award ceremonies and the like. Yes, there is that side of it, but they have to travel about so much, work all hours God sends and often not see their families until weekends. It can be a very tough and demanding lifestyle and they are also expected to look 'perfect' all the time!).

Sheba said to me,

"It was okay - travelled home on Fridays." I took this to mean that Kim came back home to London and Sheba at the weekends. I was nearly right; yes, Kim did travel home on a Friday but with Sheba, not to her, as Sheba used to go to Yorkshire all the time with Kim!

"I could have had a part," volunteered Sheba, "I could have just sat in a corner like I belonged there." Kim laughed and said that would have been funny and, as she was so well behaved, it could have been quite possible.

"Did all the travelling about stress her?" Kim enquired. "I feel that this illness may have occurred because she was going back and forth."

"Certainly not!" came Sheba's emphatic reply and she proceeded to tell me how she loved it and all the people there. To try and clear this point up and let Kim know that none of this was of her making, she said,

"Just think of it this way – say you had taken me for a walk and I had hurt myself, you wouldn't have thought, 'Oh, I just wish I hadn't taken her there.' It really is just one of those things."

"Oh, my goodness!" exclaimed Kim. "She *did* cut her foot on a walk up there. It was a really nasty cut and she had to wear a little boot until it healed." So, as Sheba said, it was just one of those things. She still went on plenty of walks whilst she was up there which she wouldn't have missed for the world.

Sheba then presented me with this funny picture of her with dripping wet hair around her muzzle. Kim laughed and told me,

"Sheba is obsessed with water, absolutely obsessed. Every day, without fail, I have to get the hose out so she can bite and attack the water spurting out the end of it. She is so hilarious."

Kim and I arranged that we would chat on webcam Skype the next day and see what Sheba's vet tests had yielded and do the celebrity questions then.

I thanked Sheba for talking to us and what would she like to say until we resume the chat tomorrow.

"I am one in a million, cute, funny but know how to behave!" Kim said that truly summed her up, thanked me for my help, so until tomorrow.

The next day, with our webcams on this time, we resumed our conversation. I was mighty relieved to hear that Sheba's results for pancreatitis had come up as negative. I was relieved for her and Kim but also for myself – In this type of work, any communicator will tell you that to say things, especially about any medical condition, takes a huge leap of faith. I take my work very seriously as things like this are of the utmost importance to the animal and their owner. I know we cannot be expected to be right 100 percent of the time, just like vets can't, but I hope that most of the time I do steer people in the right direction.

I am very fortunate that I have a vet friend who I can contact and ask her advice. Sometimes I get given information that I have not got enough medical knowledge to quite understand what they are showing me. This lovely vet, whose horses I chat to, will invariably know exactly what I am describing and then give me information to pass on to the owner. In this case, she was also under the impression that my 'jigsaw pieces' didn't seem like gastritis and regarding the words 'angio rhythm' maybe an ECG might be helpful.

As I tuned back into Sheba for this quick chat I laughed as I was explaining to her that I was going to be asking questions like, "What is Kim's best quality?"

"Loving me," was her instant reply before I had even got started! I said I would remember and note it down. I also felt she was feeling brighter although complaining that the small portions of food were merely 'staving off her hunger'. Kim confirmed both and told Sheba not to worry as she would soon be back onto a normal diet. The first thing I told Kim was the quality answer and she laughed saying,

"I put a lot of love into her, so I think that is right!" I asked Sheba if we could possibly have another offering that wasn't about her.

"Organising!" This was coupled with pictures of people in various rooms and Kim seeming to be aware of what each and every person would be doing, and giving the impression that she would be a lady that could 'keep many plates spinning at once'. I put this across as best as I could and Kim said she thought that was quite apt and would enjoy the directing side of the things.

"Good at multi-tasking," I volunteered but then realised that most film directors seem to be men! We had a good giggle about the men and multi-tasking point!

Another good point about Kim was,

"She looks pretty and changes her voice."

"Glad she appreciates it" said Kim

"So do many others!" replied Sheba and went on to inform us that Kim likes to get things correct but is not pushy with it.

Having been aware that Sheba went with Kim to the different locations I thought I would ask what it is like to be an actresses' dog.

"Variety is the spice of life!" I was most clearly informed.

"Oh, I am so glad to hear that," replied Kim, "so many people say that dogs like routine. So she is happy coming with me wherever I go?" In reply,

"I could be an acting dog!" volunteered Sheba and went on to give me her rendition of what she thought would be good – I could see her on a settee and every time an actor went to sit down she would move to where they would want to sit, so they would have to quickly stand back up again. She was chortling away showing this and thought it would have been a rather comical effect. I agreed and told Kim about her acting debut offer.

"That would be just like her; I go to sit down and she gets under my feet, she is always 'just there' when you are trying to do something." I thought this was so lovely that Sheba thought it would be good to watch, as did Kim. Just as we were moving off the subject she added

"And I could be called Moira!" This name meant nothing to me but thought it was quite a random offer all the same. (I freely admit I have very little time so tend catch up with the soaps as and when I can. However, this made perfect sense to Kim as in *Emmerdale* there is a character called Moira. She is played by Natalie Robb, a great friend of Kim's who is Scottish, as are both Kim and I.

I loved the synchronicity about this as I remember Natalie from my days living in Scotland watching her in the long running series, *Take the High Road*. Apart from being an avid watcher I knew the place it was filmed; a little village called

Luss on the banks of Loch Lomond – and where do you think I grew up? Drymen, within five miles of Loch Lomond!

I think Kim was quite amazed that Sheba had picked up on the name and with that Sheba informed us,

"I am highly intelligent, switched on and know what is going on! Lots of people know me and everybody loves me!" This was absolutely true and how nice that she knew how much people cared about her.

Kim knows that I am here should there be any more worries with Sheba and I appreciate her letting me share all this in the book. For Sheba's final question about her contribution,

"Love your owner; they will love you whatever you are like!" Well put, Sheba. Kim thought that was adorable, as did I.

Tony Stockwell

Anybody reading this who is into mediumship will know Tony's name; he is to spiritualism what David Attenborough is to nature - a joy to listen to, very accurate, but most of all, a very unassuming person. For those of you who have not been fortunate to share in this spiritual knowledge, Tony is a one of the UK's most highly regarded mediums. Apart from his television shows (some even covered psychic detective work which was absolute compelling viewing!), he does live shows all over the world linking people with friends and relatives that have passed over. You might think that this would be all doom and gloom but it is most definitely not. The venue or TV studio is often filled with laughter as spirits like to remind us of the funny times, just as if we would recount a tale to a long lost friend.

As I have said, Tony is renowned in his field and we as the public are blessed as he still teaches people about mediumship - some people are excellent at what they do but struggle to teach others; however, Tony can do both and I was lucky enough to attend one of his workshops. Although I do not want to work as a medium I learned a lot and, as everyone says, he is such a charming and funny man, and I thoroughly enjoyed the course.

Whilst there, I took the opportunity to ask him if he would be willing to join in with this book and, if so, I thought it would be fitting to talk to one of his animals in spirit as well as a present day pet. This I thought would be a great opportunity to show people that their pets really do 'live' on, just somewhere else. He smiled and said he would be delighted and to contact Stuart, his partner and manager, who would organise it with me.

Stuart and I had spoken several times and I knew that he also wanted to hear what the animals had to say. We eventually managed to find a date and time when Tony could fit this in and arranged to do it via webcam. (Again, I was acutely aware of taking up someone's free time so doing it this way was at least still 'face to face' and as usual, I had Kim note-taking beside me. She was pleased to see Tony again as she had also attended one of his workshops several years ago.) Tony and Stuart had chosen two of their terriers – Archie, an eight-year-old Border, and Madonna, their little Toy Yorkshire who is now in spirit. (I was also given a photograph of their other dog as a back-up should I fail to manage to contact Madonna. As with spirit people, you hope they will come through although there are no guarantees; but given the opportunity, I think most spirits do tend to take it.)

In this book I have been honest about the few times I found myself getting slightly nervous, and this was one of them! I am well aware that there are animal psychics out there who have been doing this a lot longer than I have and was sure that Tony would have heard animal communication done many times before. But, I was guided to do this project, as hard as it might be, so, like anything worthwhile, you have to step up to the challenge and try your best. In my everyday work I don't have such pressure but this time I was about to read for someone who is 'Master' of his trade. I hoped I would be able deliver and that he would enjoy the experience with me talking to his animals for him. He brings so much happiness and love to others, I was delighted to try and do the same for him.

So, with webcams on, I started with Archie and repeated some of the information I had been told by him when I had tuned into him prior to the call. Having asked Archie to tell me about himself this was his reply,

"Very astute; you can't fool me, if you say five minutes and are longer, I know!" Tony burst out laughing and told me that they always tell him that as they go out of the door! Archie also let me know that he was very good at getting them to come and pet him when he wanted it. I also said that I thought he was a bit of an attention seeker although Tony pointed out that Archie didn't jump on them for fuss or attention but that he would usually manage to entice them to him! I gulped slightly thinking I was maybe going to be way off the mark with the next bit as Archie had shown me being stroked round the back of his ears and kissed on his head. I described the picture I was given and was relieved to hear,

"Oh, yes, that is correct, we do do that," from Tony and then Stuart commented about how much Archie loved his ears being massaged.

"I do love attention!" chipped in Archie and I told them that Archie thought they would say how very cute he was which raised a big smile from them both!

Tony and Stuart knew I was connected with Archie so I asked what else Archie wanted to say. With that, I could see a very random picture; Archie seemed to have his head in a wastepaper basket! I laughed out loud and told them I had been given this rather odd picture but…

"Oh, yes, he certainly does that," replied Tony, "he has this thing for chewing gum wrappers and loves to get them back out!!" Archie went on to impress upon me that he was of 'good stature'; very well put together with big strong shoulders. Tony said, "That's correct," and quick as a flash, Archie responded with,

"No... that is absolutely true!" We all laughed at his self-assurance and, bearing in mind the photograph I had was only of Archie's head, I was pleased to be 'correct' or 'absolutely true', either statement was good enough for me!

Onward from Archie then informing us that he was, 'his own man', Archie showed me him lying on a squashy cushion bed. This Tony recognised and with that Archie mimicked them saying,

"Ah, look at him, he so cute." Then proceeded to lie there wagging his tail with an air of, "Attention, please. Come over and give me some." Stuart laughed and said,

"Yeah, that would be right."

I asked Archie to tell me about Tony, and he said,

"He is generous of heart and gives a lot." Stuart nodded in agreement and then Archie made me laugh; he said, clear as a bell, complete with graphics to match, "Spirit people just plonk themselves on the settee you know, but I don't mind!" I was laughing at his nonchalant manner and thought it was just as well it was a medium I was talking to. This comment reminded me of when I went to Jacky Newcomb's house and my Dad's spirit made a fleeting appearance there. It is something so natural and comforting to think that loved ones do watch over you and sometimes like to show you they are there with you. I also recalled Tony's workshop where he mentioned inviting the spirit to come and sit beside him for a chat - so it is definitely working, well according to his dog anyway! I asked Archie where he thought he fitted in the household.

"I am not the boss, I am there to make them laugh." Tony agreed and said that he did make them laugh and thought that Archie wouldn't want to be a boss. I said I felt that too, as although Archie came across self-assured it was without any arrogance combined with it. Archie then threw me a strange line,

"Bling is good and doesn't make dogs look stupid!" I had to laugh and asked if Tony had any idea what this meant? (That colloquialism has now even made its way into the dictionary and apparently means: flashy, ostentatious, and glitzy!) Tony said that Archie didn't have any bling; he just had an ordinary collar and lead. I was really wishing Archie had not told me this line as nobody was quite sure what he meant. I felt I had to justify the comment so I asked him to explain further. He said,

"Tony has a good eye for beautiful things." So now even more perplexed, I just repeated it. Fortunately, Stuart immediately commented that Tony appreciated good art, so I suggested that maybe Archie would like a more 'interesting' collar to go with his excellent physique, and left it at that - but, Archie being Archie, chimed in with, "It would add to my cuteness!"

As Tony knows, when you are given information, you cannot change it; you can only repeat what you get and just do your best to convey it as clearly as possible. This happened on the next bit of information Archie offered, he kept showing me what looked like a row of lots of smart trousers. I didn't know what Archie was trying to show me so asked Tony if he had lots and lots of pairs of trousers? (What this would mean to a dog I was not sure but I could only say what I could see!) However, Tony shook his head and said he didn't think he had an unusually large amount. Tony suggested that this was maybe about the rather vast quantity of suits he owned but, there again, they tended to stay on the tour bus. We were now all rather puzzled. Archie bless him, who was now making me wish he had just agreed and said, "Oh yeah, I just wanted to show you he had lots of suits," and let me off the hook, but no such luck. Animals (and spirits) will often repeat themselves until they get over what they are trying to convey and once again Archie went on to show a picture which clearly seemed to be him looking up at said row of trousers. So, I put it to Tony again asking if he had many that were perhaps up on a rail?

"Oh, I know what this is," said Tony, "he is really nosey, and if you open a wardrobe door, he is straight in there searching about to see if there is anything of interest for him."

"Ah," I remarked, "that was just his way of trying to show me an interaction with you – thanks for sharing that one with us Archie!" It would have been much easier had he said, "I am so nosey that if someone opens a wardrobe door I am straight in there to see what I can find!" but this work is often not totally straight forward.

If you have ever watched a medium giving information you may have noticed that sometimes they have to repeat things several times until suddenly the recipient registers what is being referred to. This takes a lot of nerve to do, especially in front of a live audience, but if mediums feel that the information is right, they will persist with what they are hearing or perceiving until they get the confirmation.

I thought I would go on to my celebrity questions and see what Archie would give us.

"How would you describe Tony?" was the first one.

"Generous of heart totally encapsulates it," was Archie's emphatic reply. That received a knowing nod from Stuart once again.

"What do you think Tony does when he goes to work?"

"He makes people feel very comfortable, and points a lot!!" I laughed and said I could understand the comfortable bit, but the pointing? We think this was a reference to Tony being on stage when he gestures to an area where he thinks the spirit is trying to link to a particular member of the audience. (Years ago I often tried to fathom out how a medium 'just knows' where they should be to talk to someone until I actually found myself doing this on a course - I was amazed how spirit guided me so that I 'just knew'. People simply expect mediums to be right but the process is incredible when you actually stop to think about it.) On to my next question,

"If Tony wasn't doing the work he does, what do you think he could do?" With that I saw, and heard, someone looking at very smart menswear and instantly being able to look and say something like, 'Oh yeah, that tie goes with that, and that goes with that. Oh, that is nice. Very smart. Perfect.' So I suggested this to Tony saying that he had a great eye so could have maybe worked in haute couture? Tony shook his head and Stuart laughed saying,

"Tony has no interest in clothes; I get all his suits and shirts etc. for him!" Tony smiled and nodded in agreement so it seemed that as either I, or Archie, had got our wires crossed. I asked Archie again, this time very clearly, if I could have a message for Tony please, and this was his splendid reply.

"Undoubtedly you have changed people's lives but it hasn't changed you." Stuart nodded and Tony acknowledged this. I thought this was such a lovely thing to say and, to be honest, if you met Tony you would understand this statement; he really is like one of us but exceptionally talented at what he does but without any hint of arrogance. He makes mediumship look so easy, yet still filled with genuine compassion, and has done so much to show people how wonderful and normal working with spirit can be. We have a lot to thank him for and much to aspire to. When I asked Archie what his contribution for the book should say, he emphasised all of this by saying,

"To let people know that even if you do become famous, you don't need to change." I think that is great advice for so many people. Everyone who is famous had to start somewhere and I think it is so important for them to remain grounded and remember the people who helped get them there. After all, without their loyalty and belief in them, they probably wouldn't be where they are today.

Tony was happy with Archie's chat and I thanked Archie for talking to us. Tony went on to tell Kim and I about Archie's self assured personality. Having taken Archie to the usual training and socialising classes the dog trainer had actually remarked that she had never met one quite like him! Archie never challenged or looked subservient to another dog there – he just walked round socially with confidence. Apparently she'd remarked, 'That he simply seemed to be so very comfortable in his own skin that it seemed he didn't feel the need to make the effort one way or another!'

I said that is exactly how he came across to me during the reading and that life seemed very easy and comfortable for him. I asked the lovely Archie if he wanted to add anything to the conversation, and he replied,

"As I said earlier, I am my own man!"

We moved onto to Madonna who again I'd asked to connect with prior to the actual reading, to tell me about herself. (When I do spirit readings, I do them much the way I do readings for animals on Earth as they are still living, just living somewhere else.)

Madonna passed me a cute picture of her watching somebody working at a desk and it seemed as if she was sitting on the desk watching them! This was slightly off the mark as Tony did not recall her actually sitting on a desk but said that whenever he was sitting there writing etc. she would always be in the room with him. (I felt that maybe she had some vantage point where she would get up and watch at the same level, hence my 'on the actual desk' impression.) She gave me a feeling of a 'queasy gut' and coupled this with the words about being careful what they fed her.

"Oh yes," said Tony, "she had colitis. That is correct." (Colitis is inflammation of the digestive gut similar to irritable bowel syndrome in people.) Poor little girl, it can be such an uncomfortable condition to have but with good management, it is fairly controllable. I also said that she made me feel like her passing was from her body getting old, losing weight and just simply giving up on her. Tony confirmed that was the case. She shared with me a very caring picture as if someone laying something gently onto her body. I could not see clearly what it was but asked Tony if he had lain something on her body, a cover/flower or suchlike? Tony immediate responded with a 'No', as sadly they were both out of the country when she went to the vets to be put to sleep. She insisted on showing me the same touching picture again. I felt that she really wanted to show them that it had all been very peaceful and that somebody had been gentle and thoughtful with her body and maybe they had even given her body a final gentle stroke? Whatever it was, I thank the nurse or vet for their compassion and hope that it was good for Tony and Stuart to hear that as it must have been dreadfully hard not being there for one they loved so dearly. She then went on to say,

"I was truly adored and they said that they would never find another like me!" I passed this over word for word and immediately Tony nodded and said that was exactly right and that is why they now have Border Terriers.

I went on to share a picture of her looking so cute perched on a cushion like a little doll, which was confirmed. I then distinctly heard,

"Put me close to his face," with a visual of her being cuddled in close. I said,

"She is asking me to put her close to your face. Did you used to hold her there?"

"Err, no really, more on my chest I would say." Again Madonna gave me the very same picture. This felt like another 'Archie and the trousers' moment but this time she coupled the words, "My Baby" to the vision too. I put this to Tony asking if he used to call her that and he confirmed that he did. I took this as a moment of her asking to be held close to feel him and hear those words again.

Madonna moved on saying that she was not a yappy Yorkie like some can be.

"No, she wasn't at all," was Tony's reply which, to be honest, I thought was a great validation of the truth as a high percentage of these little ones can be very yappy!

Madonna showed me visions of her running to different parts of the house and burying herself in a duvet or the like. I actually thought this was like a game of hide–and-seek but Tony made us laugh with the explanation - she loved to go and hide her dog chews all over the house and they were often to be found in the oddest of places. Bless her for sharing that cute little game with us.

I asked Madonna what she thought was special about her, and her reply,

"I was very loyal and not needy."

"Absolutely true," enthused Tony, "she was loyal and actually very independent." I smiled to myself thinking how Archie was full of self confidence and now here was this tiny toy breed full of self worth too – what a delightful home they have given to these animals. With that, Madonna shared with us her delight when Tony connects with a spirit animal in a reading or on a show for someone. She told me,

"I watch him, it is so exciting. I just love it."

"I just love bringing through people's pets too, it is lovely to do." Tony told us, and I felt like little Madonna was rubbing her paws with glee and very proud of what he was doing - such a lovely feeling.

I thanked Madonna for connecting with us for this and asked her,

"As a spirit connection for this book what would you like to say to the readers?" And this was her wonderful reply.

"Although we have passed over, we never go away, we always live on in spirit. I want everyone to know – there is peace, no suffering and it is *not* the end." She then said,

"Give them a kiss for me." Oh bless her! I was delighted to pass that on.

You might be thinking, 'As Tony works with spirit every day, then surely he could have got the information from Madonna himself?' And yes, he can ask her whatever he wanted, whenever he wanted but, there are endless things to say and memories to go with them. I hope that he enjoyed hearing her messages through me with the information that she wanted me to share with him. It really is just like having a conversation but we all differ in the way we converse and what someone feels important to say at that time.

An example of this was when Madonna wanted to let them both know that she had had a fantastic life with them, and was never lonely even when they were away. She said that somebody was always giving her love and attention and to thank them for that. Tony nodded and said that she never went to kennels, she always went to family and so they knew that she would be loved and cared for until they came home. Her not being lonely would have been a fact Tony would have known but I am sure it was as lovely for him to hear her thanks as it was for her to thank them.

Before we finished I asked her if she had anything she would like to share with us? She said she thought it was important to make people smile as, 'Smiling is really what makes the world go round!' I agree with her sentiment entirely. The world is a tough place, life is hard work but a simple smile can lift your heart and help your day.

Madonna was the only spirit animal I was doing for this book so this was my one and only opportunity to show people, without doubt, that animals do pass to spirit the same as people do. She came through for us loud and clear and I hope hearing about her will help ease many people's hearts.

I adore the work I do and have had great fun doing everything to put this book together. This was a challenge but such an honour to do this for Tony. I can't thank him and Stuart enough for setting aside the time for me to talk to their animals.

When researching for people to take part in this project I was told that Tony was an animal lover and having chatted with his animals I know this to be so very true. He has such a huge following so his contribution to this book will go a long way to spreading the word not just about communication with animals on this earthly plain but also about the ones that have gone before us and that, one day, without doubt, we shall meet again.

Paul McKenna

On a typical dank British day in late August 20I0 I was to chat to Paul who had moved to the sunnier climbs of Los Angeles. Although I was very excited about doing the reading, I have to admit to being rather nervous in anticipation but I am sure many other people would have been in my shoes too. In the UK I think you would struggle to find someone that doesn't know who he is. Funnily enough I got the connection to him through a longstanding Californian client of mine, Nicola McFarland, who described him as 'an extremely interesting man that has the most amazing results!'

A couple of years ago Nicola gave me a wonderful testimonial for my website having chatted to her pony Scampy, who actually has had a small feature in both of my books. Through her I landed up chatting to Luke Branquinho, the 'Two-time World Champion Steer Wrestler', well, to him and his horse to be precise, and not long after I did a reading for her boyfriend, Buster, a steer wrestler also. These cowboys canter along, at rapid speed I might add, and then launch themselves off their horses to attempt to catch the steer by its neck/horns and restrain it the way they do out on the prairies and, all in the fastest time possible.

I checked with the horses and they didn't seem to mind, and no, before you even think it, I haven't asked the steers for their comments! They're mad if you ask me, but for Luke to become world champion twice is a real achievement as it had never been done before. After the last call with Buster, and Nicola having originally told me that my reading was far more accurate than any she had had in the US, it turned out that she was friends with Clare Staples who shared a house with Paul and their two gorgeous Great Danes. She was actually his girlfriend a few years back but now she is Paul's manager as he has moved over there, and is very rapidly becoming as well known over there as he is here.

Clare had organised everything and we were doing it via webcam on Skype. She contacted me half an hour before the call just to check we were still on (wouldn't have missed it for the world!) and I said jokingly that as I was a bit nervous, was there any chance Paul could hypnotise me first! With the cameras on we started the call but to be honest I could hardly see a thing. The light behind Clare was blinding and funnily enough the light looked rather strange on my end picture too, but I assure you it had nothing to do with sunshine this end - 'sunshine' what's that?! With me straining to see them on the screen, I heard Clare calling Paul and then saying,

"Poor girl, she looks petrified!!" I had to laugh, I was nervous, but not that bad, but the camera was obviously doing me no favours with its rather odd ghostly white skin effect. With camera's fixed (or so we thought) Paul's face appeared and so did his dog Bentley.

As there were two Great Danes, Mr Big and Bentley, it was decided that Paul would be with Bentley, aged 2½ years, and Clare, with Mr Big, now aged 8 years old. These dogs were huge and cue Bentley from the left as with a swift 'lurch' he tried to launch himself into full view on the settee with Paul!

Celebrity Pet Talking

"That's the first thing Bentley showed me!" I exclaimed, and Bentley added that he knew he was big but it is good fun! I quickly told Paul that Bentley's opening line to me was,

"I am really funny and I like my presence to be known!"

"That's him alright," Paul laughed and then disappeared momentarily off camera as Bentley threw himself back down.

Then a conversation about the weather ensued, how very British! (Clare is also British too). We somehow touched on the subject of global warming which was quite surreal as here was I with two famous faces looking through the screen at me but this put me at ease which I did appreciate.

Although Paul is a hypnotist, on a daily basis I am sure that he makes people feel comfortable with any conversation they are going to have with him. He has astounding results from stopping people smoking to weight loss and overcoming fears, which he clearly demonstrates on magnificent TV shows showing just how quick and slick his key to people's minds can be.

We let Bentley take the lead in the chat and he made us laugh as he really came across like a naughty schoolboy admitting that he really didn't look where he was going! I felt he really didn't quite get the gist that he was 'enormous' but thanked Paul for letting him have his freedom. Paul totally understood the 'freedom' bit and went on to explain that an ex-girlfriend was an animal behaviourist and she was more disciplined with Bentley and, although Paul understood where she was coming from, (she had at least a dozen dogs, and although in a house we can usually cope with one joker, to have twelve jokers would be complete chaos) Paul was more lax with him and didn't mind his 'in your face' attitude. I said that Bentley didn't seem to think before he acted, he just 'blundered in' and without a care in the world!

"Oh yes," replied Paul, "even snakes he will run up to with an 'Oh yeah, what have we here?' attitude and he will even chase the coyotes too!" On the subject of large animals Clare wanted to know what he thought of the horses. His reply,

"They smell!" They laughed and so did I and Bob, being an ex-jockey, who was scribbling furiously beside me.

We chatted some more but Paul said he really did have a concern and hoped I could help him with it.

"It is about his foot," he said. "He has had such persistent trouble with it and, having had course upon course of antibiotics which didn't work, as a last resort the vets recommended they amputate the toe, which they have. Bentley was indicating to me that is was his right front foot Paul was talking about, so I checked this with Paul and showed him where on the foot I was talking about by aid of the webcam and me pointing on my right hand to indicate the spot.

"That is right," Paul replied and then carried on. That tickled me, as it seemed so normal to Paul that I, across the Atlantic, could just point out the exact foot and area by reading Bentley's mind. Mind you, I work to the subconscious in my way and Paul does in his, so I guess it seemed normal. (Clare did however tell me later that Paul was really impressed. Apart from me pointing out the correct foot, but also the exact toe too! High praise indeed and from such a well respected person - his thoughts are very much appreciated by me.)

The problem was Bentley kept licking it as he had done before the operation and if he wasn't careful he was going to make it sore and weepy once again. I asked Bentley why he was doing it and he explained that there was a bit of a 'tingling' sensation which was encouraging him to do it. It certainly wasn't sore but at present, he had not got used to the feeling so was drawn to it.

Paul said that he had been doing 'tapping' on him. This is a method that involves tapping on certain areas of the body (often the forehead) and on acupressure points and it can have amazing results. Paul asked me to ask Bentley whether it was having any effect. Bentley's reply,

"It keeps my mind off it!" I am not sure if that was the reply Paul expected but he thought it was positive and would continue as he felt it was making a difference. (He had actually done it on a friend's cat and they were amazed at the result. He also knew someone that did it professionally so would seek his help for Bentley if need be. I did my usual and asked if there were some words that Bentley could give me for Paul or Clare to say to him to prick his sub-conscious to remind him that if he continued licking that more vets visits would likely be in the offing. And having told me that he was good at the vets but could not wait to get home I thought it would be sensible to 'lean on this'. His words were,

"If you keep doing that you'll have to go back to the vets." As soon as I had said the words to Paul, Bentley showed me a distraction thing Paul did with his hands, so I suggested he combine it at the same time. Paul said he would give it a go.

Then the wonderful technology started to fail, my webcam picture went a bright yellow shade, but worse, I was getting all my words repeated back through my speaker to me. (Unbelievable, I use this often for my foreign work and never have a problem. The one time… grrr!) So we decided to cut off and start again and as all seemed to be okay we carried on.

As all loving owners do, Paul wanted to know if Bentley was happy. On being asked, this was his reply,

"Oh yes, I get to act the buffoon!"

"Oh that is so right," Paul stated, "he is a buffoon."

"But, a gentle one," Bentley added. Paul expressed how much he adored him and said he wouldn't change him for the world. Bentley also said he loved the way Paul would often say, 'My boy, my boy, my boy' to him, which he loved to hear. I knew that Paul was touched by hearing this term of endearment being repeated and acknowledged by his 'boy'. It is so lovely for me to be able to share these things with animal's owners, and from that point in time, every time their owners use that phrase they really *do* know how special those actual words are.

"I have another question," said Paul. "What does he think of Mr Big?" (Mr Big is Clare's dog).

"He can be rather aloof, you know," was his quick retort.

"Absolutely!" Paul chortled and Clare, who was in the background throughout, said,

"That is so right, that is him. He is just like a cat sometimes – nose up with an air of 'Err yes" said with a rather plum accent!" I had to quickly point out that having tuned into Mr Big earlier that his introductory line to me was,

"I am the most inoffensive dog you would ever wish to meet. I am soft and gentle and just lovely!" That rendition was met with a,

"Oh, that is so him. Oh Mr Big!" by a very enthusiastic Clare who called him to come and take his turn in the proceedings. Webcam crashed again! That was it, I had had enough. It is hard enough listening carefully to what the animal's voices say in my head without hearing my own voice coming back at me every time I spoke. I decided to use the phone so called them and we switched the internet gadgets off!

Paul was short of time so I cracked on with the celebrity questions that I thought suited this chat.

"If Paul wasn't a hypnotist, what other job do you think he could do?" Bentley decided to answer in 'Bentley' style saying what Paul *couldn't* be,

"A mechanic," came his reply complete with picture of someone looking very blankly at a car engine. I passed this to Paul also saying I don't know whether you are one of these people that know nothing about engines? And he made us laugh by saying,

"I don't know about that, but I wouldn't want to get my hands dirty anyway!" Fair comment, good answer!

"What do you think Paul is doing when he hypnotises someone?"

"He suppresses part of the brain that is overactive."

I think I can see where he is coming from as Paul does remove people's fears, so I guess that is suppression of something that is overactive.

Bentley says his chance during this communication is to let the world know,

"That although we are big, we're as gentle as lambs!"

I rounded off the conversation by thanking him for chatting and he wanted me to tell Paul on his behalf that,

"I want for nothing, my life is full of love and excitement." Definitely one very happy and contented dog!

I was most grateful to Paul for taking part and I know that his participation will go a long way to show people that animal communication is real. After all he is a hugely successful man, so he had no need to do this but he wanted to, and it will make a difference and I thank him for that.

Clare Staples

As you read from the previous story, it was through Clare's organising that I did the chat with Paul and Bentley. With Clare, we have the gorgeous, (but sometimes aloof according to Bentley) Mr Big. So aptly named, yes I know all Great Danes are big, but in the photo they sent to me, he was sitting with his backside on a couch on a splendid looking terrace complete with all four feet still touching the floor.

As I have also explained previously, my client, Nicola, passed my information to Clare and Paul, and although I knew she was Paul's manager, I found out that she is English, an ex-model, and a stunning one at that, and in America she has a huge following and is a very popular lady. I also found out that she had written a book, *Everything I know about men I learnt from my dog*! Excellent, very apt, so I designed some questions on that theme, but from Mr Big's point of view.

Mr Big was as gentlemanly as he had described and was so soft and affectionate towards Clare. He was actually very different from his housemate, Bentley, as Mr Big was quite reserved and not 'gung ho' like his friend. Although saying that, when the doorbell rings, Mr Big is straight up and barks loudly to inform of his presence, whereas Bentley would just stay lying on the settee, like, 'Oh yeah, door!' I took the opportunity to ask Bentley why he was so 'not bothered' and his reply,

"It's never for us is it?!" You couldn't argue with that logic and that answer certainly tickled Clare and Paul.

Mr Big was coming across as 'very grand' and informed us,

"If I were a person, I would wear top hat and tails!"

"Oh, that is Mr Big to a tee!" exclaimed Clare, truly delighted that he spoke just as she thought he would. He really was the most 'inoffensive' dog as he had described himself and they told me that they actually call him David Niven! This, which I did not say at the time as I am not one to ruin the moment, immediately reminded me of the most silly film starring David Niven which was called *The Brain*. (This was a film from the 70's that was ludicrously funny with David Niven playing part of someone with such a 'super-dense' brain that he couldn't hold his own head up! He had to lean 'nonchalantly' by pillars etc. with his arm crooked to support his head hiding this 'heavy' fact from passers-by.) With that thought quickly pushed out of my mind I totally got the 'David Niven' name, as David was known to be a gentleman onscreen, and off.

Mr Big gave me a very tender picture of Clare swishing her long blond hair back and round her neck as she leant forward to give him one of her many kisses. He described this as endearing, and I would too.

I decided to ask him about horses as the question had been asked of Bentley. He was quite vague and said that he didn't think they were the safest of things! Clare said that he had met horses ages ago but seem scared so she hasn't taken him to see her own horses. She did note, however, that she is sure he knows when she has been with them as on her return he really sniffs and sniffs her. Ah, this validates what Bentley said, maybe to a dog horses really do smell!

Big (as he is affectionately called) chatted away and was just adorable and spoke in such a very 'educated' way that I commented so.

"That's because he is a posh dog, as he originally came from Kensington!" Clare told me. He liked that comment and gave me the feeling of pride.

Clare suggested we ask him what he thought of Bentley. Without hesitation he said,

"He has no manners! I would step aside, *he* would just push through!"

"Absolutely right!" declared Clare, "that is just what it is like. If the door is open Bentley is through it regardless of who happens to be in the way!" I suggested we ask Big if he had any suggestions to help with Bentley's lack of care.

"Tell him he is rude, I don't think he will like that!" was his instant reply.

"We do, we do," proclaimed Clare, "I say those exact words to Big." She then gave me a rendition of it, "Oh, he so rude, so rude!" I noted that obviously it doesn't bother Bentley after all but did suggest that she explain to him, like you would a child, that Big is much older than him, an elderly gentleman in fact, and to treat him with a bit of respect and care. This I hoped might make Bentley think, as Big did comment that Bentley does sometimes barge into him and he would rather he didn't.

Physically for his age (eight years is quite senior for this breed of dog) he is doing well but on mentioning his health he did give me the impression of being tight in his backend/pelvis area. I asked if he looked like that when he walked and Clare said he did. I felt this was not an arthritis problem (he is on glucosomine already) but I felt that he would maybe benefit from a chiropractor or a massage person as maybe at some point he might have tweaked the lower part of his back, just like we people can do. Clare said she would look into it and this would probably cover another reason why he was a bit grumpier than normal. It could be an old age thing, but if he is a bit uncomfortable it wouldn't help.

Clare also said that she wondered if Big had not forgiven her for getting Bentley. He dismissed that immediately by telling us that he knew she would never do anything to hurt him. He just found Bentley boisterous so tried to avoid being bumped about by him. Another question was, "Why does he not sleep on my bed anymore?" He told me he had grown out of it. This actually made sense as I suggested he had not done it for a long time and Clare confirmed that. He also wanted to point out, as did Bentley - it does get very hot so they seek the cool to lie on. We covered much more, like him not wanting to walk so far, and could he possibly have some quiet walks with her alone. Oh, how sweet, that is genuine quiet 'together time'. There is such a special bond between them and he was just a delight to talk to, as was Clare.

As I mentioned at the beginning Clare has written a book so here are the questions that I thought Mr Big would like to answer. So, from me to him...

"What is the best way for a man to get a woman?"

"Give her a box of chocolates. If that doesn't do the trick get her a bigger box. And keep going until she gives in!" A simplistic view, but I reckon he thinks that maybe men give up too early and maybe a bit more effort might change a girl's mind.

"What is the best way to keep a woman?"

"Keep attentive and say sorry!" I kid you not, that was really his reply. Mmm, I think he does understand a lot about that species we call 'men'!

"What would be the best thing a man could do for a woman?"

"Blindfold her and then whisk her away on a plane to a table that he had already booked for dinner." Us girls totally agreed (although I did say when he started off with the blindfold I was a bit worried), but we noted his suggestion and I told Bob to go buy a plane!

"What is the worst thing a man can do?"

"Forget her name!" I think that has to be a top of the list answer, clever dog. Well, I have to say, I had the most delightful time talking to Clare and Paul and two very different dogs. When animals are so obviously different it validates the work genuine animal communicators do, we just can't guess these things. I take pride in the fact that at the end of the call that Paul and Clare thanked me and remarked that I was spot on and very accurate with what I had told them.

I thank Clare for being so lovely and open and sharing her time with me. And, as usual, for the last question I asked the darling Mr Big, what did he want as his contribution to the book to be? And his reply, in true Mr Big fashion,

"We are highly intelligent and would wear top hat and tails if we could!" Bless him.

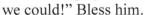

Sara Crowe

As I have said, in this world we have to take chances and follow our dreams, doing this book was certainly one of mine. Many years ago some ladies from a Women's Institute (W.I.) decided to do a rather risqué calendar in aid of charity. The whole idea had come about as one of their friends had developed leukaemia and they wanted to do something positive to help. They'd hit upon the idea of raising eyebrows in order to raise money for *Leukaemia Research*. (This is a close one to my heart as my cancer was lymphoma which is now linked into the same charity.)

This type of calendar format has now been copied again and again but these ladies were thought to be very daring at that time. For each month a different W.I. lady would pose naked but with her modesty hidden by various means. The one that always springs to my mind was of the 'two iced buns' strategically placed! As you can imagine, in their type of social circles, there was much controversy about what these W.I. ladies were doing and hence the film *Calendar Girls* was born. It is an extremely funny yet also poignant film to watch and being based on a true story makes it all the more interesting.

So, you think those ladies were brave to have their photographs taken and published in a calendar and actresses to repeat the performance for a film? Well, how about doing it live on stage? That is exactly what Sara, along with other actresses, did in front of audiences when the film was cast as a play for London's West End. (It received rave reviews and apparently *Calendar Girls* has become the most successful play to ever tour the UK and has grossed more at the box office than the smash hit film.)

Although Sara is recognised more for her theatre work, and has received a clutch of prestigious awards at that, she has graced our television and films screens too. Sara is a friend of Jenny Seagrove, who also does a lot of theatre work, and that is how Sara became involved with my project.

Unlike Jenny, Sara had not experienced anything regarding animal communication, or similar, and I gathered that she was slightly sceptical that this was possible. However, I guess she decided that if Jenny said it was true then how intriguing it would be to hear about her dog, Ada.

Sara had sent me a fantastic picture of Ada, a slightly long-haired, crossbred dog, lying on the grass with a Frisbee resting on her back! She was a stunning, dark, burnished copper colour, looked to be of a medium to large size and, if I was to hazard a guess, maybe a Collie cross Labrador.

Sara was to be appearing at the Severn Theatre in Shrewsbury as she was starring in the stage version of *Lark Rise to Candleford*. This was excellent news for me as not only would I get to meet her but also watch the show. I love costume dramas, so this was right up my street!

Sara suggested we meet prior to the show as she thought there would be enough time for us to talk to Ada and for her to get ready to go on stage too. So I drove to Shrewsbury, picked

Kim up and we got ourselves settled in the theatre's upstairs lounge.

Sara duly arrived and joined us at a table in a quiet area and I introduced Kim to her as my official note-taker. I knew that time was of the essence and so I gave her a brief outline of exactly what we would be doing. I handed Sara back her photograph and told her that Ada had said of herself,

"I am what you would describe as genuinely sweet." She continued with, "although I don't do many things wrong, I *do* know when I do!" This introduction was completed with,

"I am good looking and people have even remarked on it!"

Sara looked genuinely moved and said that she would agree with that and that many a time people have commented how what a good looking dog Ada is. I remarked how wonderful that animals can truly understand what people say, and just think the next time someone says something about Ada - you will smile to yourself knowing how much that means to her.

Ada was coming across to me with such a lovely light energy that I even said to Sara that her dog just made me feel like smiling.

Ada continued by saying,

"I might be good looking but I don't mind getting dirty!" Sara laughed out loud and told me that was true but also that Ada certainly didn't like being washed after she got dirty! (Oh dear, now there's a doggie dilemma!)

It was clear to see that Sara truly adored her dog and that they had a very close bond. Sara said it was so hard leaving her at home and she missed her dearly. Ada piped up saying,

"I miss her too, but missing someone makes the re-union even sweeter." So eloquently put and she was absolutely right. Ada showed me her looking up at what seemed to be a shelf. She was giving me the feeling of something of importance so I asked Sara if this would be a bookshelf or similar?

"No, it isn't," she laughed, "it is the titbit cupboard which she stares at adoringly until I give her a treat!" Ada was quick to follow the food theme declaring,

"I am not a greedy dog but I *do* like the 'nice stuff'." I repeated this to Sara adding,

"I am pretty sure that this about chicken, is that at the top of her list?"

Sara burst out laughing and explained,

"It most certainly is, she adores it!" Sara continued, "she has daily medication and will not take it in anything other than chicken. I have tried hiding it in other foods and failed, so it's definitely a case of - chicken and her meds' or, no meds' at all!" I love hearing things like this, a classic example of 'who is really in charge?' Our Sally is very good at gently persuading us that her idea is actually the best especially when we are relaxed sitting watching TV. She casually presents us with a toy and, sure enough, in the end, one of us will throw it for her. Sara said that she thought Ada was so clever as she definitely knows the difference between a teddy bear and a ball and when asked to get either, she rarely gets it wrong!

The next statement I thought was so cute coming from a dog,

"I am a generous soul and don't get jealous if someone makes a fuss of Sara!"

We thought this was very funny and sweet, bless her. What did come up, however, was that this did not apply to other dogs. Sara told us that, in the past, Ada had gone for another dog that had approached and this had then turned into a no-win situation - Sara would get worried should she see another dog and, in turn, Ada would then want to protect her and the whole thing got tense. (This is surprisingly common). I could hear the emphatic words,

"I don't bite other dogs."

I could only repeat it although I am very aware that some animals (just like some children) will not admit bad things even if they are guilty of them.

"No, she has not actually bitten one but is not good when they come up close."

Ada gave us her reasoning for this behaviour, which was that some dogs don't have manners which she didn't like and, according to her, neither did Sara. I could see where she was coming from - I agree some dogs can be pushy and ignorant and, unfortunately, some owners just let them do as they please. To conclude, Ada informed us quite succinctly that,

"I don't think I am overtly aggressive, I just like them to go away and am perfectly fine with our own company."

Sara shared with us that as much as she loves having Ada with her, her husband loves having Ada at home with him too. That is why she was at home with him now. Having heard this, Ada said,

"Please tell her not to worry about me," and gave me the impression that Sara phoned home every night to check she was okay anyway. Sara said this was the case and glad that she was aware of it. (I bet Sara is the same as me. My first question on a call home is how are the animals and then my husband!) Ada made me think that when Sara leaves home that Ada would be fine and wag her tail as if she was okay about it. I said this to Sara and she told me in her gentle but comical way,

"No, she usually gets in her bed in a huff!"

I was surprised and checked again but Ada made me feel as if she was fine about the whole thing. I quickly asked Sara what her husband said about Ada's behaviour once she had left the house.

"Oh, yes, she is fine once I am gone!" We laughed and remarked how they can sulk and make us feel bad, again just like children. I felt by this point that Sara was pleased that she had chosen to join in and Ada was certainly making the most of it. On Sara's behalf, I explained to Ada that whenever possible and the venue was suitable, Ada would accompany Sara as she adored having her with her. Sara got me to check with Ada that she wasn't feeling too old for all this travelling now. This took me slightly aback and I said,

"But she is not old, seven is not old."

"She is thirteen." Sarah responded.

"Gosh, I have no idea where I got seven from (for some reason that is what I had written on my sheet) but, to be honest, she really has not come across to me like an elderly dog."

"Oh no, she really doesn't," Sara informed us, "You would never guess looking at her and when she is on the move you could hardly tell. However, she does have a touch of arthritis so could you check with her about that and please ask if her paw hurts as she had a toe removed."

(Unbelievable – having already chatted to Paul McKenna's Great Dane that also had a toe amputated, and here is another one in the same book! How incredible!)

"Osteo...?" was the word I heard and repeated it to Sara.

"Yes, Ostoemyelitis is what she had. Once there is infection in a bone apparently it is notoriously difficult to treat." I nodded in agreement. She said what a hard decision it was to have Ada's toe removed, but as we all know, infection can spread so she made a very hard, but informed decision. Sara had left nothing to chance, but sadly, sometimes these things just happen. (I know this from my veterinary work and impress upon anyone reading this to never ignore any lumps or bumps. Often they turn out to be nothing to worry about and are treatable or can be surgically removed. Bone infection, however, is a huge problem and can affect any bone in the body, not just the little ones.) Sara said that although Ada had bounced back quickly the vets think it may have caused a bit of arthritis in her foot.

Sara said Ada was on a small amount of pain relief and wanted to know if she was comfortable. Ada seemed fine and Sara was of the same opinion as me, the least amount of conventional drugs one can use the better. We talked about the benefits of alternative medicine, magnets etc. and how some of these can be used in conjunction with traditional medicine to with great effect. I said not to worry as I was sure the low quantity she was on would not be doing her any harm anyway.

Having listened to all that, Ada changed the subject completely and offered up a picture representing Sara acting with a cast, complete with an old-fashioned costume. I had no idea from which play obviously, but realised this was her way of showing us that she knew what Sara does when she is working. (Had it been a wedding dress, this would have been far simpler as Sara played the first bride in *Four Weddings and a Funeral*.) They quite often do this to show me things relevant to their owners. Sometimes I will be shown a pile of books indicating that someone is studying and so forth. Owners love to hear that the animals really do know what is going on in their lives, just like Sara wants to know what is going on in Ada's.

"I know I am to her, the most precious girl in the world, and I am glad that she knows that I do know that." Slightly long-winded but we got the gist, and this, once again had an image attached, which I thought seemed to be Sara sniffing her?

"Oh, yes, I do," enthused Sara, "she smells like chocolate brownies!" Ah, what a heart-warming comparison. While writing this sweet comparison, my mind was instantly cast back to those Philadelphia advertisements that Sara was in. Her part was to play a dippy secretary and offer rather odd concoctions to go with this cream cheese, complete with the catchphrase, 'Lovely. Well, *it is* my birthday!' I bet most of you dear lady readers, if asked, would have to admit to having imitated those words, complete with Sara's high pitched and innocent voice – I most certainly did!

"I am not a barky dog," Ada volunteered.

"No, she isn't," replied Sara, "Only when she does it as a trick."

"As a trick?" I enquired when I clearly heard 'speak'. "I can hear 'speak', so you ask her to speak?"

"Yes, I do." Sara enthused. "She is so good at it; she can do this deep rumbling one that sounds like a fierce 'Rottie' - enough to scare off any would-be burglar! It's a far more impressive bark than you would hear from a soppy Labrador-Collie, or, a 'lolly' as I call her.

"A 'lolly'! I have not heard that one before," I laughed.

"Or sometimes a 'collieador'," Sara added, "She was a 'collieador' when she used to jump fences - a very agile girl!"

There are so many clever crossbreed names now but that's definitely two new ones on me!" I said I would far rather have a crossbred dog. Apart from seeming to have far less physical problems than pedigree ones, their natures are often so wonderful as have not been tainted by the inter-breeding that, appallingly, goes on. Our Sally is a rescue dog and again I would always try to give an unwanted dog a home and there are so many desperately seeking them. This conversation prompted Sara to share a little tale with me – Ada also was an unwanted dog although a three-month-old puppy at the time. When she was handed in to the RSPCA centre she had a note with her saying, 'Please look after this dog.' Ah, this was just like in Paddington Bear. Well, Ada has been such a lucky girl and apart from all the love she gets, Sara knows that chicken to Ada is what marmalade sandwiches are to Paddington Bear!

So, with the clock ticking, still with her celebrity questions to do, Ada gave us Sara's alternative career.

"Without a doubt – a painter!" was her instant reply. She was spot on; Sara does do paintings when she has the time. She repeated that she thought Sara was 'adorable.' As for her contribution to the book,

"Even if an animal is thirteen, they are not necessarily old."

With the chat finished Sara left to get ready for the show. She was so kind to give me this time, especially as she was not really sure what a communication with Ada would entail. Once again, I had such pleasure giving a reading and being able to share in their relationship for a short time.

Within half an hour, Kim and I were watching Sara on stage. The play was quite different from the television series and we found it extremely entertaining. It was filled with much laughter and some sadness, complete with lots of singing too. To quote what was written at the top of the billing for *Lark Rise to Candleford* - 'One of those rare theatrical occasions with a genuine healing quality.' I hope that in some way my visit and meeting with Sarah will have had some of that same quality. I am sure I have helped allay her worries when it is not possible for Ada to be with her. They have such a close bond and how lovely for Sara to hear that Ada truly feels so precious and loved.

Anna Forrester

Whilst talking to someone about my ideas and plans for this book, she volunteered Anna's name saying she thought she might be interested and an ideal person at that.

"Did you watch the series, *Wildest Dreams*?" she asked excitedly. I had to admit that I hadn't. "Well, it was a fabulous programme filmed in Africa. There were about a dozen contestants who had to compete doing all sorts of things regarding filming and watching wildlife and she won it!"

"Who won it?" I enquired trying to decipher her words amidst her enthusiasm.

"Anna Forrester did! She used to work at Banham Zoo, and I know someone that used to work there too! Anna was amazing and the winner was to get a contract with the BBC - I bet she'd be interested." She obviously loves animals so this had to be worth a try. So with emails sent and various calls Anna was tracked down (please excuse the pun!) and was, indeed, very interested.

When I made contact with Anna, she was working abroad at the time and said that she would get in touch on her return to

Britain. During our emailing, I realised that I had forgotten to ask what type of animals she had. She replied,

"I have two very friendly female rats named Harley and Danicka who run around my house and I would be intrigued to hear what they have to say for themselves!" I have to admit that I was certainly taken by surprise. Firstly, I had absolutely no experience of pet rats, (apart from in a vets surgery) and secondly, I sure as heck had never spoken to one! I remember though, when I was veterinary nursing, I had seen many a person get very emotional over their sickly rat and had heard that they did in fact make great pets. I wrote back telling her,

"They will be the first rats I have ever done! I have chatted to guinea pigs and rabbits, but never rats. So, cool, what fun!" We left it at that and I promised to post my *Animal Insight* book to let her read about what I do. Then I waited to hear from her after her trip.

I obviously took the opportunity to look up *Wildest Dreams* on the internet and find out what it was about. I gathered that the contestants were filmed in various African locations and it seemed to be a bit like an animal version of *The Apprentice*. I didn't delve too deep (it is far nicer for me to hear it first hand and maybe through someone's animal) but I did watch a lovely video of her flying a hawk which struck a chord with me. Apart from previously working as an animal trainer, Anna was an accomplished falconer which is an art which I truly admire. I know the birds are trained to come back to you, but at the end of the day, they are totally free whilst flying so it is still their choice.

I have had some experience of birds of prey myself as, about a year ago, I was delighted to have been invited to spend a day at a falconry. I had some very interesting chats with various birds there and it was incredible what I learned from them, I was totally amazed. People use the expression 'bird-brained' as a derogatory term for "stupidity" which has to be the most inaccurate analogy ever! (You only have to think about the feats birds achieve with migration – imagine a person getting in a plane with no compass, or suchlike, and finding their way to somewhere like Canada, as geese do!) I was staggered that birds were able to tell me about the different ways they flew and even about their own weight! I had no idea until that day that as they are demonstration birds, they are weighed every day because they need to be at an optimum weight to fly. I have to admit, the saying 'bird-brained' would have been more applicable to me that day due to my knowledge (well lack of, to be precise) concerning metric and imperial measures!

It was whilst chatting to a Harris hawk, who was happily sitting on my forearm that the subject was brought up about being weighed as she volunteered that her weight was two-and-a-half! Two and a half what, I wondered? Her handler then explained the relevance to Bob and me. (My husband, Bob, was my cameraman that day.) I listened and when I understood more about it, bearing in mind this was being filmed, I turned to her and asked,

"Is that two and a half kilos or two and a half pounds?" Well, Bob erupted with laughter, and said,

"Jackie, if she was two and a half kilos, I hardly think you would be able to hold her on your wrist!" To put this into perspective, it would be the equivalent of my balancing the weight of a large oven ready chicken on my wrist! Point taken.

Apart from the hawks, there were various breeds of falcons and owls and as those birds had also chatted away merrily to me, I had no reason to doubt that Anna's rats would chat any the less. After all, I knew they were house pets, so I was looking forward to this challenge.

Anna was now based with the BBC in Bristol since winning *Wildest Dreams*. She had won a dream job in the BBC's famous Natural History Unit there. My hope was to combine her visit with that of Jenny Smedley who lives in Somerset, which is in the same part of the country. I suggested the date and it was perfect as she could do it that day after she had finished work.

Bob and I were staying down in Bath – so, after coming back from Jenny's, we took our time going up to Bristol. We navigated our way through Bristol (one heck of a big and busy city) and managed to get parked very near to her house. The area was very reminiscent of a scene from my favourite film, *Oliver*, when he sang, "Who will buy my sweet red roses?" Here was a similar scene with long rows of Georgian houses either side of the road complete with their central gardens enclosed by park railings.

We had our dog, Sally, with us so had a quick trip into one of these gardens in case Sally needed to do 'her business' before we went into the house. (I had mentioned to Anna previously about taking a detour to drop Sally off at our friends first as I was rather concerned about leaving her in a parked car in a big city. Anna said it wouldn't be a problem if Sally came into the house and it would be nice to meet her too. I thought Sally might show a little bit of a keen interest in the rats, but as Sally is so well behaved I wasn't worried. Also, as Anna knew we were bringing our dog I was sure they would not be running about loose anyway.

Anna looked just as she had on the video clip I had seen: pretty, with long wavy strawberry blonde hair and a genuinely warm smile. She was young (twenty, I think) and was sharing the ground-floor apartment with someone else. We went to her part of the house complete with a huge cage for the rats in the adjoining corridor. I (and Sally!) caught a glimpse of one of them as we went past but didn't know which one it was.

Fortunately, they did look very individual - Danicka was completely white and Harley had a lot of black on her.

With a cup of tea in hand, Sally sitting quietly beside me and Bob ready to take notes, I checked with Anna that she still hadn't experienced anything to do with animal communication. She said she hadn't but, having read my book, was looking forward to her pets giving an account of themselves. I said that, to be honest, I had no idea what a rat would want to talk about so let's see what came up. We started with Danicka, usually called Danni, and I concentrated on her and invited her to tell me about herself.

She immediately gave me a picture of her teetering on an edge of something, but very confident as if she wouldn't actually fall off. She informed me that she had a great sense of smell, was ticklish and liked to play-fight. Anna's eyes widened and she said,

"Yes. Yes, that is her. I watch her in the cage doing her balancing act and she doesn't fall and yes, I know she is ticklish." This was great. I knew I was tuned in, and with the right rat too. Danni went on to tell me that she sometimes got seeds stuck in her teeth! I had no idea if they would be fed seeds or not but Anna assured me that she did feed them seeds as it is part of a rat's diet. I then heard Danni saying,

"Me first, me first!" I repeated it and suggested that maybe Danni was the boss over Harley?

"Yes, she is," Anna confirmed and, with that, I was given a very sweet picture of Anna lying down and Danni burying herself into Anna's lovely thick hair.

"I am so cute," volunteered Danni.

"Oh, she is very cute indeed, and yes, she does burrow herself into my hair when I am lying on my bed."

I asked Anna if she had some questions she would like me to ask Danni. She came up with a good one.

"Is there anything that I do, or she finds annoying?" I didn't even need to pose the question - Danni immediately gave me this very odd sound, like a repeated mechanical sound. Very strange. I did my best to repeat the sound and asked Anna if she had any idea what Danni was trying to convey?

"Oh, my goodness!" she exclaimed. "I do. It is my alarm clock!"

"Your alarm clock?" I questioned. "It didn't sound much like an alarm clock to me."

"That is because it is a barking one," she giggled and immediately fetched it and gestured towards the cage saying that she would stop using it and get a 'more normal' one. This whole thing tickled me and what made me laugh even more was when Anna wrote a little testimonial for my website, at the end she said,

'I have now discovered that my pet rats hold a high and very loving opinion of me, even if they do get annoyed at my novelty alarm in the mornings!'

Anna got me to check that Danni didn't feel cooped-up when they were in their cage. Any fears she had were dispelled when Danni said they were fine and amused themselves climbing up and jumping off things. She then passed me this sound which I felt was a noise Anna would make to her. I did my best to imitate it and was chuffed that Anna immediately recognised it and said that when she does that, they come running! Wow, apart from being able to relay the sound correctly, I was amazed that the rats came when called, just like a dog. Well, some dogs, that is!

For my first celebrity question, I asked Danni what she thought Anna did best when working at the zoo.

"Being polite, and saying please and thank you." This we reckoned was about Anna dealing with the public. How lovely to hear of a youngster with such good manners! Sadly, standards in this day and age seems to have slipped somewhat. On asking,

"Where do you think Anna will be in ten years?"

"Not in the UK!" was Danni's clear and concise reply. Anna smiled and I said I would push further to see if she could expand on that.

"Australia – Anna has an affinity with Australia!" she told me confidently. I smiled and told Anna exactly what she had said.

"Oh, yes," she smiled, "I have relatives over there." I thought this was incredible information from her rat and this example really goes to show that whatever pet you have, they do get information from your mind (like I do with animals and a psychic can get from a person's mind) so can know so much more than most owners ever realise.

I went on to ask Danni what her thoughts were regarding Anna winning the *Wildest Dreams* competition. She straightforwardly told us that,

"Anna didn't think she would win as there were stronger personalities there." Anna nodded and said that was the case. I asked if Danni had any advice for Anna and she simply said,

"Be bold, brave and believe in yourself and you won't go wrong!" Excellent advice, I couldn't have put it better myself. Danni went on to tell us many more little things about her life and then answered my question,

"What do you think your chat will show people about animal communication?"

"We might be small, but we have big voices!" was the excellent reply from her. I thanked her and moved on to chatting to her friend, Harley. (One thing I found quite confusing was that these two pets who were both girls both seemed to have boyish sounding names!")

"I am not as forward as Danni," she began but seemed to think she was the better acrobat by declaring, "I have amazing balance too! I can even turn over upside-down and not fall off!" She went on to give me this little snuffle sound.

Anna said that I was correct and the snuffling sound was like a little choo-choo train going about! Harley complained that Danni pushes her out of the food but assured me that they got on well as they like to cuddle up close. Anna smiled and said that I was right and I told Danni to try to be more thoughtful about the food - there would always be plenty so there was no need.

"I am a little bugger for hiding under things but I am not stupid!" was a wonderful line from her and, I promise you, that was exactly as she said it! Anna laughed and told us that Harley was definitely the one that does that and she has to be cautious where she stands as she never knows what Harley has hidden under.

A thoughtful question from Anna was; as she has moved so many times, what did they think about it? I was assured that they didn't find it stressful and Harley said that they had never stopped eating because of it. In fact,

"It is a bit of an adventure for us to go to different places too!" That made us laugh; she was giving us the impression that they were following Anna's lifestyle, just on a smaller scale though!

For a celebrity question, I asked her to tell us what she thought Anna's good traits were.

"If Anna doesn't understand something, she will ask rather than bodging along not really knowing what she is doing."

This met with approval from Anna who said that is how she is. Sometimes (especially if you are in a group situation) it can be awkward to ask someone to repeat, or show you something once again should you not understand it the first time - but better that than a catastrophe further down the line. In Anna's work, she is dealing with wild animals and that can be fraught with danger. To know exactly what you are doing is paramount as after all, it is not just your own life you could be endangering but those of the others around you.

I have to say, although I did not see *Wildest Dreams*, I am so pleased on several accounts that Anna was the winner. Having met her and listened to her attributes through her pets, to me, she seems a great choice as an ambassador for people working with the animals in the public eye. If somebody else in the series had won it; firstly, they might not have wanted to join in with my project, or, secondly, they might have wanted to but had no pet. (I have talked to some lovely people in the media but, unfortunately, they did not have an animal, so couldn't take part).

As the whole series was about finding out more about animals this has given me a huge opportunity to show somebody about animal communication and that there is even more to animals than meets the eye. I am sure that this 'rat chat' will have left a lasting impression with Anna, which is lovely and also wonderful for the world of animals.

So, for the 'where in ten years?' question, this was Harley's suggestion,

"Having people working for her instead!" She went on to point out that Anna is optimistic and that is a good thing. I asked Harley for her advice offering.

"Do drive – it's not that bad!" I was a bit flummoxed by this, as I would have thought this up-and-coming young lady surely would drive, so I asked her if she actually didn't drive and said that she didn't. I repeated what I had been told and, with that, she gasped,

"Oh, my goodness, I can't believe this! All my friends keep saying I should learn but for some reason I keep trying to put it off." Up pops Harley's little voice saying,

"Er, hello – it is not like swimming with sharks!" Anna burst out laughing, as did Bob and I, because, true enough, Anna had actually swum with sharks on the show. Wow, hats off to her, I would have been petrified. (Before you think I could ask 'mister shark' to kindly swim away – it is not *that* easy! Remember, we work to the subconscious and hope it transfers to the conscious.) Anna told us lots more that they had had to do and I was wishing I had seen the series. What a great idea, and sorry, Lord Sugar, but it sounded far more riveting than your 'best man gets the job' show.

So, with some encouragement for Anna and her driving lessons (you never know, she might have passed her test by the time this goes to print) I finished the chat in my usual way and Harley's book contribution was,

"If we are only rats - how do we know all this?!"

What a perfect line to finish off a perfect day! I wished Anna the best of luck with all her endeavours and know we will be seeing a lot more of her on our screens in the future. Never in my 'wildest dreams' did I think I would be chatting to two rats for this book! I have to say, it was a fabulous experience and was a joy to do.

Toby Balding OBE

If you are into the horse-racing world you will know who Toby is. Apart from being a renowned horse trainer, having achieved over 2000 winners comprising of: two Grand Nationals, two Champion Hurdles and The Cheltenham Gold cup to name but a few. This trip also had a personal connection to it as well. Bob, as I mentioned previously is an ex-jockey, actually rode for Toby for the last twelve years of his riding career. I have heard so many tales of fun and laughter and many a betting coups. Although Toby was primarily a National Hunt (jumping) trainer he also trained some for flat-racing too. Bob rode on the flat for him and apparently the comment, 'Oh, those flat-jockeys' was often uttered when things didn't go according to plan.

Several years ago Bob and I attended a celebratory party for Toby's career as he had decided to retire and hand over the reins to his son-in-law to continue - no pun intended! It was a fabulous event and what truly impacted upon me, which I hadn't realised until then, was that Toby was very influential in the careers of most of the top National Hunt jockeys still riding today! Several of them made speeches thanking him for giving them a chance, the wonderful opportunities that had let them ride to glory and the loyalty he had shown them. It was heart-warming to see that they held him in such high regard and have never forgotten the 'leg-up' he so unselfishly had given them.

Talking of loyalty to his jockeys, Bob reminded me of such an occasion - Bob was riding a horse at Salisbury racecourse and whilst riding the finish and looking like a 'sure thing', his horse suddenly veered across in front of another but still managed to be first past the post. This was definitely a case for a steward's enquiry so thus giving a tentative wait for all concerned; especially the betting folks to see if they had won or lost their money. Toby met Bob as he came off the track and in racing words, 'bollocked' him for careless riding and fumed that he would more than likely get disqualified and have cost them the race... Toby having said what he felt, it was over and done with and he left Bob to go and get weighed in. Whilst waiting to hear the outcome of the enquiry Toby was standing in an area filled with race-goers and overheard someone saying,

"That Bob Weaver, bloody useless jockey – what was he thinking...?" With that Toby instantly turned round and said in no uncertain terms,

"Don't you speak about my jockey like that – he is a bloody good jockey!!" The reason that Bob became privy to this was because another jockey was standing nearby too. He thought this was hilarious and came back into the weighing room to tell Bob what he had seen and heard. This made Bob smile and, just as well, as he did get disqualified that day but, as they say, 'That's racing and you are only as good as your last ride!'

In 2010 we had a phone call from Toby informing us of the sad news that one of his prevalent owners and close friend, Bridget Swire, had passed away. Bob rode her first ever winner for Toby and throughout the partnership Toby trained countless winners for her and they had shared many fabulous racing days. A commemorative service had been organised so Bob, along with many jockeys and owners, were invited to come and pay their respects. I stayed at home to look after the animals but suddenly thought that Toby might be interested in being in this book as I knew he adored his horses and dogs but was not certain of his views. Bob went and duly took one of my books and a letter to give Toby on my behalf. As you can imagine, occasions such as these are sad but a great opportunity for many racing people to get together as it is an industry that is spread far and wide and there are many true and lasting friendships formed.

In between Toby's party and this memorial we were aware of the desperately sad news that Toby's lovely wife, Caroline (Caro as everyone called her), had passed away due to cancer. Bob took the opportunity to pass on our condolences and explained what had happened with me and, apart from the animal side of this project that I was trying to give encouragement and hope to others too. Toby said he was indeed very interested and would be in touch.

As you might have gathered this book took some time in the making and I practiced the art of patience. (Having spent so much time in hospital I honed the skill and as I say, 'Why do you think they call us 'patients?') Whilst making some headway with suitable months to fit round busy schedules we then heard the dreadful news that Toby had suffered a stroke and a severe one at that. We followed the news and updates and we were very relieved to hear he was on the mend but with an uphill battle ahead of him. If anyone could battle and win, Toby is your man. To add insult to injury, he had been due to go to Buckingham Palace to receive his OBE for services to racing. That was on hold for a while but a great day for Toby to look forward to. (We had a laugh later amidst the dog chats, as I said for the sake of my book, he had to get to the palace before this was published as so far I had a Sir and an MBE, so his OBE was now of even more importance than ever!)

Approximately six months later I had arranged to go and meet Alex Hua Tian who was the youngest ever event rider to compete in the Olympics. He rode for his country, China, and although now recognised for his excellent riding skills, is now also a goodwill sports ambassador for China here in Britain and at that time was based near Basingstoke. I checked the map and realised that his yard was within half an hour of Toby's so thought I would phone his son, Gerald, and see if Toby was up to visitors and if so I would love to combine it and bring him some cheer! Toby most certainly was and thanks to Gerald, it was all arranged.

We arrived in Kimpton, Hampshire with half an hour to spare so Bob took me on a tour to show me Fyfield House – the original training yard that had spawned so many top jockeys and where all the old gallops had been. We drove around the lanes where so many wonderful, and famous, horses had walked and trotted; conditioning their legs and hearts for the incredible work they would have to do. Bob took me to the gallops where all Toby's jockeys had learnt to 'sit a horse' as, at a certain bend Caro's little terrier, Weenie, would make its appearance causing horses to jink left or right or do a quick body-swerve. So, when you see some of the top jockeys staying on-board a horse when most of us would have been fired into the next county, it is worth remembering the mischievous efforts put in by one little terrier!

When we arrived, Gerald welcomed us, as did a little terrier by the name of Mojo. Toby was just finishing his lunch and stood up to greet us. He looked fantastic and had the same lovely broad smile – our hearts sung that such a lovely man had bounced back. He said he was delighted that we had at last managed to get together but, sadly, one of the dogs had died a few months previously, presumed to have eaten some form of poison. We all sat down at the table which was slightly away from a lot of young children having a bit of a party. Fortunately they were about to depart down the garden to the swimming pool – phew! I am usually organised for these visits with photos or at least some information of who I am going to chat with. I had absolutely nothing so I was just going to do whatever came up with Bob on note-taking duty once again.

Toby said that he would love me to chat to Mojo (as did Gerald, as he was originally Gerald's dog) and Mungo who was the yard's guard dog who would have seen a thing or two. I asked their ages and whilst getting Mungo's I kept getting the vision of a wagging tail. I thought this would be far removed from a characteristic guard dog but mentioned it anyway.

"Oh, yes, that is Mungo, he welcomed everybody."

"Oh, right." I replied, "I am not getting the feeling of a typical guard dog but we will find out later." I suggested we start with Mojo who I knew from Gerald had seen quite a bit of life, as at one point Gerald had been involved with a circus! Mojo was nine years old and a light tan colour with a greying muzzle who was now sitting on Gerald's lap at the end of the table. The children were still milling around, but Toby had finished his lunch and we were also joined by the lady who was helping him with cognitive therapies and suchlike.

In my 'minds-eye' I was immediately presented with a picture of Mojo sitting very erect and important like he was 'top dog' but not in an arrogant way. Toby smiled when I said that Mojo was making me feel very grand and important. Gerald said,

"Oh, yes, he is No.1 around here." I added that Mojo was coming across as confident with people and, as I told them that, Mojo stated,

"I cause less trouble than anyone else!"

"Yes, I would agree with that but could you ask him why he is disobedient then?"

"I am not disobedient – I just don't come back when called!" Mojo replied in a funny, but slightly sarcastic way. He quickly told me about his strong bladder and that he could 'really hold on' as if this was of serious importance. I asked Gerald if he knew about the relevance of this and he laughed and pointed to a puppy that was sound asleep on a settee. Mojo was very pleased with himself for having told on another canine resident, but we explained that the odd accident was to be expected as she was still very young. He seemed happy that he had informed us regardless.

Mojo was not getting away with skirting the obedience question but, to be honest, he really didn't seem worried and told us he had not been hit by a car! I did try to explain but realised I was getting nowhere fast! Toby was listening quietly and then Gerald mentioned about the show with him riding a motorbike with Mojo sitting in front of him. Gerald commented,

"Oh, we even put a ruff around his neck and I am sure he thought it was beneath him."

"No, I didn't mind," replied Mojo, "it was similar to a dog wearing a bow-tie; people would notice that and they *did* notice me." He gave me the feeling of sheer enjoyment and then said the 'bike riding' happened really by accident and showed me him jumping up onto the bike himself, and seemed more than happy to join in. Gerald, who is a fanatic motorbike rider, agreed that it all just seemed to happen and so in the end, Mojo landed up with a little party piece of his own. This was many years ago and now Mojo leads a more sedate life and, by his own admission, sleeps a lot. This was apparently in the bottom of one of Toby's cupboards that he had decided to take up residence of.

We covered many other things like why does he bark incessantly at a buzzing bee and, a most annoying thing he does, bark during the night. This reason was established by the picture of several eyes appearing in the dark – foxes!

Toby started to tell us how amazing Mojo had been since he had come home from the hospital.

"He never left my side. He was never like that before, it is incredible; he just seemed to know and wanted to be with me." I said I would ask Mojo himself.

"I didn't want him to have fear." Was Mojo's answer explaining why he thought having a constant companion would help. I could see Toby (and Gerald) were touched and I said that I hear this again and again from animals who really want to help and give love and reassurance just a like a person would do. I also said that I thought it was wonderful for this little dog to hear how much Toby appreciates this too. Mojo went on to say quite categorically that this stroke was just a warning and, also, that Toby had a very strong heart. I simply passed it over as said and hoped that this was indeed correct.

We covered so much more but we did eventually get to the celebrity questions.

'If he wasn't a racehorse trainer…'

"A driving instructor," was Mojo's reply. I immediately said I had already heard this answer for another person, but that is what he said and I can't change it. I decided to ask why. He told us that Toby was very clear in his instruction and people would learn very quickly what was right, and what was wrong. I guess that teaching people how to race-ride would have maybe had a similar set of instructions but with driving, brakes usually are a certainty whereas with horses sometimes not!

Mojo went on to share that everybody would want to shake Toby's hand as he is such a kind and honourable man – that received nods all round and especially from Bob who knew that from the employee aspect. Just as things were going so sweetly, Mojo volunteered,

"He was a great trainer, but, boy, oh, boy, when things went wrong…" I was given the distinct impression that Toby would let people know his displeasure, with a certain amount of volume added, but then all would be forgotten and it would be back to work again. Toby laughed, as did Bob, and this was borne out by that day at Salisbury racecourse I mentioned at the beginning of this story.

For his contribution, he wanted to point out that some of the horses knew and would recognise Toby and that Toby knew of this himself. Toby nodded in agreement. I thought this was a lovely fact to point out as, although as a trainer Toby would have had to deal with large quantities of horses, this just shows that he still had the personal touch – such an important thing to an animal that is trying to do the best it can for you too.

Gerald thanked me for chatting to Mojo and left us to carry on. Toby then went to get the retired guard dog, Mungo, who he had so kindly brought into this ever-expanding home. Mungo had been at the racing yard for years, so Toby, being the animal lover, offered to let Mungo enjoy his last days here at home with him. We were enjoying a cup of coffee when Mungo (thought to be about thirteen) was brought in.

Far from being standard 'guard dog' material, like an Alsatian for example, Mungo was this big, and I mean really big, soppy looking Labrador cross. I could see straightaway how I got the 'waggy tail' picture as he came and lay at my side and licked my hand. He was black with these huge feet; he made me think of a big cuddly bear. Things were a bit quieter now with the children having also gone and so I introduced myself to Mungo and asked him to tell me about himself.

"I may be big but I am not that bold. Everything was a game and I am very affectionate." Toby smiled and said that Mungo was everybody's friend but had this impressive bark which gained him the job of the yard's guard dog. I asked Mungo how he would describe his vocals.

"Very throaty," he replied, "rather like a baritone," he smartly added. Toby laughed and said that summed it up and then Mungo whispered something to me which made me say to Toby,

"Would I be under the right impression that you are not the best singer in the world?" He laughed and nodded accordingly and I thanked Mungo for his cheeky comment. He went on to tell us about the yard.

"Some people came for a quick visit then landed up staying there for days!"

"Oh, yes," replied Toby, "that was a frequent occurrence." I had heard previously from Bob that Toby and Caro were fantastic hosts and people enjoyed their social company as much as the racing side of things. Mungo went on to say that he thought Toby was an honourable man and if someone had wronged him but then apologised, Toby was not a man to harbour a grudge. Toby thought that was a pretty accurate comment, as did others present.

We covered lots more stuff, such as how he felt about another dog who, as a female, actually pushes him around. He wasn't sad about it; he just wanted to say that he was no threat so could they not just rub along side-by-side like the rest of the dogs did. This often happens with animals as it can with people – you know yourself; there is often that person that will try to assert their authority although often it is quite unnecessary.

To finish his chat, what about an alternative career for Toby?

"A peacekeeper," was his excellent reply. This being clarified as he reckoned Toby would firmly, but fairly, suggest to someone that what they were doing was, 'not a good idea and maybe they should think again!' Mungo said he thought his own contribution would show that animals do watch the ups and downs of life and take interest in what people are doing. To me, I think he wanted to emphasise, 'We are not just dumb, not thinking and not seeing animals.'

With that finished we were offered more biscuits and coffee and Toby quietly asked Bob if I could chat to spirit animals as he would really like me to talk to Plover. Bob repeated this to me, which to be honest took me slightly by surprise, but I said that I would do my best and I asked Toby for some details.

Plover was a Corgi that had been given to him and Caro by the Queen and Toby said he had passed over aged nine.

Just at the point of me trying to tune into Plover and ask him to come through, another person appeared, commented that Mojo was looking very attentive on the chair and enthusiastically said,

"Oh, you must meet our kittens!" Within a minute I was presented with two kittens who I think were about five-months-old. My poor brain was scrambled, as I had no idea what I was to be doing next but actually it turned into a bit of a biology lesson. It turned out that the boy had the girl's name and the girl had a boy's. This is not an uncommon occurrence as people sometimes struggle to sex a kitten. So, thanks to my vet nursing days I delivered my simple explanation.

So, here you go readers just in case you ever need to know – If you look at the nether regions of a kitten, a girl will have an oval 'seed shaped' orifice, a boy has a circle which is further away from his anus thus leaving space for two things that will appear in between. So, to help you remember this; a seed is to produce life, so the girl has the seed shape. (Here endeth the lesson.) I have now just thought of all the people stopping reading at this point to 'up end' their cat and check out this fact. Apologies to all cats examined but should this stop future generations being mis-named then, to you, they will be eternally grateful.

I managed to steer myself away from a chat with them, as like the puppy, it is better to chat to older ones who have seen more of life. I somehow managed to concentrate and hoped that it was Plover who had come forward by telling Toby that I thought Plover was a stocky dog rather than a lean one. Toby nodded but then was thrown by my next comment as I repeated what Plover said of himself; he didn't think his coat was always immaculate.

"Oh, I thought he was - he was such a smart fellow."

"I will ask what he means, so please bear with me." I quickly replied.

"I used to run about and get into the thick of things with the others dogs, I wasn't the precious, 'Oh, I can't do that type.' I repeated this to Toby and he smiled in acknowledgment and said now he understood. Toby went on to explain that Plover was really Caro's dog and that when Caro passed over Plover immediately became his shadow. We had a touching conversation about how when Caro was in the hospice Toby decided not to take Plover to see her as he did not want to distress either of them. Plover immediately told me that he knew what was going on and he was fine with Toby's decision.

With that, I saw a picture of a beautiful, and delicate, hand gently combing through his fur. I could only think that he was showing me Caro stroking him and then he told me he had the most amazing eyes. He also declared that he knew when Toby was going to take him for a walk before Toby had even said a word or got up to go. Plover knew and was at the door ready.

Toby instantly recognised these two statements and I felt sure he knew I was connected with Plover for definite.

I was given a vision of a heart but like one of the chambers were leaking/collapsing and a feeling a fatigue. I passed this over to Toby and he said that he thought Plover had eaten poison. I suddenly clicked that this was the dog he had mentioned when we first arrived. I was slightly flummoxed but could only go with the information I seemed to be receiving.

Toby continued saying that he had taken him for a walk and later on that Plover had seemed rather tired, which was unlike him, but nobody thought there was anything seriously wrong. Everyone went to bed as normal and early the next morning Plover died. I thought instantly that this did not sound like a poisoning; anyone whose animal has experienced this will know that a dog doesn't seem 'just tired'. Plover went to lengths to show me pale gums and slightly shallow breathing but expressed that on the walk he had been tearing around with the others like nothing was wrong.

Toby agreed that he had seemed absolutely fine when he was out so I said to Toby that I thought what I was being shown seemed more likely to be the case and this I am sure gave Toby great relief. (I did take the opportunity to check this out with a vet friend and she agreed that a heart issue seemed far more likely.)

Plover gave me more accurate information like he was an even-tempered dog and although not soppy soppy, he loved affection. He informed us that he knew what cows were and told the other dogs to get out of the way! It was so lovely to share this with Toby as I know Plover had a very big place in his heart.

As Plover was originally Caro's dog he was delighted to share with us that he was the 'chosen one' and got to go to many a grand place with her and, of course, was impeccably well behaved. He was a very sociable dog and didn't cause problems with others. He went out of his way to express that he thought he was very individual and good. (I know that Corgis have had some bad press, probably because they are favoured by Royalty and bad news sells better than good. Also, reportedly, Corgis can be rather of a dominant nature). I actually thought I would check this out on Wikipedia as my knowledge of them is very limited and was delighted to read Plover's actual self description of 'even-tempered' and that they were originally cattle herding dogs! No wonder he knew what cows were. It is always lovely for me to find something out after a chat that I know that I had no knowledge of, as again this proves in essence that the animal was passing me the information.

He was very proud of the fact that he was loyal and had shifted his allegiance to Toby when Caro passed over. I told Toby that Plover made me feel like a lot of animals do; that they truly wanted a job to do in life and his was to be loyal to his Mistress and then to his Master. Just then, I was sure I heard,

"I had no children." I asked Toby if this was the case and sure enough, Plover had never had 'a wife'. I am sure he was impeccably bred so this information I thought would have been so unlikely, but yet it was correct.

Most amazingly, and thoughtfully, Plover addressed me personally saying,

"I am honoured to talk to you from spirit and you didn't expect there to be two spirit animals in this book, did you?!" My brain took a second to take this in and my heart was touched. He was so right; the only spirit animal was to be Tony Stockwell's beautiful little Yorkshire terrier, Madonna, so his words were so true and meaningful and I thank him for saying something so beautiful and poignant to me personally. I could see Toby was also touched by this and I thank Toby for asking me and trusting me to try to connect with his beloved dog in the first place.

"Life was a rabble, so exciting," Plover declared putting us back on the upbeat feeling, and went on to tell us that Toby is such an incredible man with a mind like a computer! This raised a wry smile from Toby and acknowledgement from others present. Plover further explained that Toby was able to 'pull' amazing information from his mind and be factually correct. Plover then told me something that I had never even thought of, and from this day forth will remember his view on being in spirit...

"It is not 'rest in peace', it is 'rest in party' – can you imagine the re-unions that go on here?" I ran this through my mind before passing it over to Toby and, you know this makes so much sense - yes, when we live here on earth in our physical bodies we will sometimes meet up with a long lost friend or suchlike and maybe have a celebration but... in spirit, after the initial passing over when we meet up with so many that went before us, these re-unions are going to be an on-going occurrence.

Imagine you are in a place that the ones you loved will all eventually come to that same place - this applies to family, friends, animals and all their offspring and so it continues. The friends you are also with in spirit with will all be experiencing this wonder too, so, yes, 'rest in party' encapsulates the fact that people and animals will keep being re-united anon. We chatted about this view and I say a huge thank you to Plover for such an insight that I can share with others.

Plover had come through to say what he wanted and I thanked him for that. Toby was a little tired but having suffered such a serious stroke and still recuperating, he had done exceedingly well. Toby laughed and said,

"They thought I was a goner!"

"Me too," I replied. "It is incredible, the doctors can only give their opinion by the facts before them but there are so many cases of survivors just like you and I." I told him about me proving my psychic work to the medical profession and the fact that they had even put it in writing.

I have explained that, apart from my hope that this book spreads the word about how animals can communicate, that sometimes devastating illnesses such as cancer/stroke etc. can look very bleak but often can be surmounted - so try not to give up hope.

It is my opinion, and one shared by many, that when your time is up, it is up. Try to live your life in a positive way and do what good you can in what time you have. I follow the path that I have been set to walk and I do, and Toby does according to Mojo, is live with 'acceptance'. If you keep paddling against the flow, you will most likely tire and more than likely fail – choose to go with the flow and deal with what you encounter as and when you do. As my life's motto goes, 'What is for you won't go past you.'

That evening we took Toby out for supper at a local hostelry. I had to laugh - it was only about five miles from his house and Bob knew the area well – and having sat in the back listening to the consistent and accurate instructions of… 'in half a mile you will be turning left, you will be coming up to a sharp bend etc'. I was chortling to myself thinking the 'driving instructor' suggestion of alternative career was probably most apt.

We had such a lovely evening; Toby and Bob reminisced about wonderful racing days and laughed about the things that certainly did not go according to plan. This actually goes with another theory of mine - if you notice, nearly all the funny conversations people have tend to be about the things that went so wrong at one time or another, so, in my mind, when something does go wrong I try and immediately think, 'One day I will laugh about this!' It really does help. Maybe try it for yourself as you generally can't undo the 'mistake' so, in time, at least you may have a funny tale to tell.

I say a big thanks to Toby, his family and, of course, all his pets for sharing their time with me and doing their bit to endorse what I do. I know that horseracing is a tough sport but I hope by listening to this trainer, who the horses and dogs so obviously adore, that it will be another step forward for all the animals out there.

[I had to share this with you... Whilst going through Toby's story to get the information for Jackie to draw her wonderful 'Rest in Party' picture, I found the word 'party' mentioned four times before Plover gave us his heavenly insight, yet the word 'party' is not mentioned in any other story! I truly believe that Plover really wanted to show us that we can celebrate life here on Earth and continue to celebrate life in Heaven too.]

Binderee

Over the years I have realised that many people have preconceptions about racehorses. The words that are often spouted are, 'oh typical thoroughbred.' Then, should they be talking about an ex-racehorse, you hear things like, 'they are 'nutters' - I wouldn't touch one with a barge pole' and so it goes on. Having owned an ex-race horse and spoken to so many - yes, there are a few 'not so easy' (however, that can be said of all breeds) but so many have gone on to make fantastic and versatile horses. They range from doing dressage and eventing to showing, and much more. Over the past few years, there has been a concerted effort to try and help ex-racehorses by re-schooling them to try to give them a second career; after all, most of them have finished racing when they are still pretty young - some, very young, in fact.

There are now recognised showing classes for 'Racehorses to Riding Horses' and Binderee is one such horse. He has this story in his own right as I thought that any horse that had won something as prestigious as the Grand National deserved to be in this book.

Celebrity Pet Talking

Binderee (affectionately known as 'Binders' by everyone) was now in the care of Caroline, who had contacted me. He had been living not far from her as, although retired from racing, Binders was still at Nigel Twiston Davies's yard who had trained him to win the Grand National and many other races. Binders had now been completely re-schooled by Emma Walker, Nigel' girlfriend at that time, and she had competed him very successfully at eventing him at dressage. Unfortunately, Emma and Nigel went their separate ways so Fergal O'Brien, Nigel's head lad, thought of another option for Binders - perhaps he would maybe enjoy doing the 'Racehorse to Riding Horse' show classes.

With discussions had, Binder's owner, Raymond Mould, was delighted at the prospect as he holds Binders very dear to his heart, so Fergal asked Caroline if she would be interested. This made perfect sense as, apart from Caroline's wealth of experience in this field; he would be living just down the road from the racing yard.

Caroline said she would be delighted and as he was still only in his mid teens, and looked very fit and well, that he might well enjoy yet another type of career.

Binderee won the Grand National in 2002 ridden by jockey, Jim Colloty. This is one of the world's toughest horse races and, although it does court controversy (it always has), I have to say that this horse was extremely proud of his achievement. Now anyone reading this might be thinking he only did it as he was one of those 'nutters' but actually Binders managed, by circumstance on a different occasion, to show how intelligent and sensible racehorses can be.

Not only did he win the Grand National but the following year, he won the Welsh National too! On the day of that race, his journey was down the motorway and across the Severn Bridge, to get to Chepstow racecourse. The traffic for some reason was horrendous and the box driver realised, due to sitting in queues of traffic, time was running out fast. For anyone not au fait with racing - on the day of the race, the horses have to be stabled on the racecourse and declared as a runner at least forty-five minutes before the 'off'. Then there is the preparation to be done: putting on their saddle, bridle, number and weight cloths and making them look immaculate. The horses then go into the pre-parade ring for people to watch them walking round before setting off to the starting line.

The driver kept looking at his watch as he was now sitting at the wrong end of the long and very busy bridge. So, after much delay, with such an important race ahead, it was decided that the best plan would be to unload Binders and lead him, in hand, over the bridge and to the racecourse itself. With this option taken, Binders calmly walked the length of the bridge, with the public (I'm sure many of whom were trying to get the races also) watching and marvelling at this stunning racehorse taking this, very unusual, walk in his stride. How often do you think you would hear a car driver say, 'Today, whilst on the Severn Bridge, I was overtaken by a racehorse!' The other question that I would put here to horse owners reading this is, 'Knowing your own horse, do you reckon leading them over a large suspension bridge might make you think twice?' What a dependable horse Binders was.

I can recall seeing pictures of this happening - I don't know if people had videoed him on their mobiles or a TV crew had got there. I cannot quite remember and, to be honest, I am not an avid racing follower although Bob most certainly is. As I am writing this on a Saturday afternoon, I can hear the echoes of the familiar increasing and decreasing tones of a racing commentator. I also have to admit that it was only during a conversation when we took Toby out to supper that I was reminded that it had, in fact, been Binders. (Thank you, Toby, and quite right Plover, 'Toby, is man with a mind like a computer' was a perfect description!)

Caroline heard of me on the Alan Carr radio show on one Saturday night. He had asked people to phone if they had been told anything psychic that had actually come true. The lady that does the artwork for my books, Jackie Fennell, originally came to me as a client. She decided to phone Alan and tell him about my chat with her horse, Harry, as I had given her information that she didn't even know about.

The long and short of it was that Harry had loaded and travelled to a show in her latest lorry but refused to load to come back home. This was very uncharacteristic of him. He told me that the brakes were faulty and that he thought it was dangerous. She sent it to the local garage and asked them to give it the once over. She phoned me and said, "I can't believe this, the garage have found the brakes are faulty; the master cylinder has gone."

Alan and Melanie were in fits of giggles about 'Harry the mechanic' as he is now referred to, and at the fact I had to convince him that the lorry was now safe to travel in again. He now travels in it without a problem! The show was such a hoot and Jackie even landed up doing a cartoon drawing for Alan of his dog.

When Caroline sent me a formal booking for Binders, I immediately recognised this horse's name so I called her and explained about this book and asked would she be interested in turning this into a celeb chat too. She said she would love to but obviously needed to check with his actual owners. (As with everyone in this book, they were assured that everything printed would have their full approval first.) They kindly agreed and so here we are. Caroline and her family's passion are showing horses and this takes such time and dedication. In most other horse events, as long as the horse wins the race, jumps round clear etc. that is good enough. In showing, however, they have to look physically correct, move perfectly, be immaculate and, above all, be very patient to stand in a line-up to be judged.

Bob offered to be my writer for this one as although he rode on the flat, he had a few races over the sticks 'for a bit of fun', as he put it. He said he would love to hear from a horse that had won the biggest Steeple Chasing prize in racing.

Caroline had already sent through Binders's photo which just showed his lovely chestnut head, complete with a full length white blaze and wearing his bridle. He was now sixteen-years-old and had been with her for about four months.

Judging by his first remark to me, apparently he didn't feel his age.

"I know what age I am supposed to be but I don't look my age!" Caroline laughed and agreed he looked in such lovely condition that you could be easily fooled.

"I am gentle and the girls at the yard loved me." I was sure this was a reference to his days at the racing yard. Caroline said that he did have good manners (like most racehorses tend to) and that he was adored by the yard and still is.

Caroline asked me to check with him if he preferred to be retired or to be in work. With no hesitation at all, he said that he was happy to be in work again. He also said that he liked to canter and volunteered he had no pain issues. He then casually said that his right hind leg was slightly thickened, but not sore, and he thought his pelvis was slightly tipped down on the right hand side, but again, no complaints. Caroline agreed with both points and, to be honest, for the work that these racehorses do (they are horse athletes really), they will end up with various imperfections, but as long as there is no discomfort, it is not a problem for them so why shouldn't they still enjoy a working life? This was backed up by him adding,

"I don't find my work difficult and I am easy to lunge." (Lunging is working a horse, un-ridden, on a long line so they exercise in a circle around the person working them. Very often, if a horse is slightly unsound then lunging will highlight it; as going in circles is more physically demanding than going straight.) Having heard, and had it confirmed, that he was in good body shape I went on the riding aspect as Caroline had come to me for a reason - not a general 'what does he want to say' communication.

I gathered from Binders that although he was still a very alert horse, he was a safe and sane ride. Caroline had schooled him and got him carrying himself well and even doing some dressage. Caroline said to ask him about showing and what he thought.

"I want to enjoy myself and thrive on compliments." He told me. I passed this over and Caroline said you could see he was a proud horse but his attitude towards showing had changed. I asked him again to tell me about his feelings regarding being in the show ring. He then made me feel quite put out, giving me the feeling of a slightly nervous heartbeat, and then said,

"I don't want them to pick fault with me!" Now that statement took us both slightly aback as neither of us had thought about the logic behind judging. But, it *is* to pick fault because the more 'faults' you have or mistakes you make, the less chance you have of winning. That is a basic fact; as it is for anything you are judged on. I explained it was nothing personal and 'I am sure that you look and move better than many there anyway.'

"Oh, he does; he won at Stoneleigh last year." (Stoneleigh being one of the major competitions) Caroline told me, "but now he doesn't want to stand there; it's as if he doesn't want to be there." I said I would try to find out more.

I pushed further and the picture he gave me was not so much about him not standing still, but one of him looking left and right instead of keeping his head facing forward. "Yes, that is what he does." She answered. Binders then told me that he was watching the judges as they were moving about and seemingly looking at different things. This technically would have been correct so I explained that they were just doing their job moving about looking at the horses but his job was to stand still to be looked at.

"Why no movement?" Binders asked. "There is a lack of movement," he insisted on pointing out. I was quick to gather that although he gets to move around when it is his time to be ridden around the ring doing his 'show' - he wished there was a bit more to it. He made me think that in his mind, a bit of a speed competition between the other horses would have entailed more fun for him, so maybe he was losing interest. During the first few showing events, it was all a new experience but it had never progressed to the 'faster' bit.

I passed my thoughts over to Caroline and she said that she had wondered the same. Although her life revolved around showing, she would never want to make him compete at showing if he didn't want to. This is why she had come to me. She knew that at sixteen, he would have been too old to take up some other form of competing, but thought that he really might have enjoyed getting out and about again going to the various shows. As she put it, for what he had achieved in his life, he owed nobody anything and he simply deserved to be happy. I agreed with her sentiments and we chuckled thinking of him standing in the show ring with a judge 'picking fault' and Binders (as she affectionately refers to him) saying,

'Yes, I might have a thicker hind leg, and maybe not the best arched neck in the world, but 'Hey - I WON THE GRAND NATIONAL, what did they do?' Maybe it wasn't just the judges he was swinging his head about watching, maybe he was going through the line-up thinking, 'Ah, you just won a couple of hurdle races, and as for you, you only ran on the flat!' Whatever, he was proud of himself and wanted to be noticed and, as he was there, to try to liven up the proceedings.

Having covered what I'm sure Caroline had felt in her own heart, she said she would re-evaluate the situation and decide what was best for him. He was assured that he would never go anywhere; if he wasn't with Caroline, he would just go back to his yard up the road. We decided to do his 'celeb' questions, which I was sure would make him puff his chest out and answer most emphatically.

Bob had given me a good question to ask, which was, 'what advice would you give another horse running in the Grand National?'

"Don't think about it - it is not as bad as you think!"

Binderee had been amazing in that 2002 race - it had been thrilling to watch. He was not in the lead over the last fence and when another horse, cleverly named 'What's Up Boys', moved into the lead in the home straight, it looked like he would go on to win. However, Jim Colloty asked Binderee to lengthen and stride on, and he did. He tried his heart out and didn't just make it over the line; he actually won by a length-and-quarter! That may not sound much but after conquering all thirty of those huge racing fences, and having galloped four and a quarter miles, he pushed on to claim his place in racing history. Incredible. I asked him my question,

"What did you think of the Grand National?"

"It was good - it made me famous!" We laughed, what a superb answer and so true. He will never be forgotten by his owner or trainer, not to mention all the staff on the yard. Also, the general racing public will always remember him, as every year on Grand National day, they replay the race's finales from previous glory years. There are even parades of some of the past winners; which the crowd loves – as, it seems, do the horses themselves.

Caroline thanked me for chatting to Binders. Although it looked like his showing career was now in doubt, she said it was lovely to hear that he was a happy horse and that is all anyone would wish for him. He, in turn, asked me to thank her and said that he knew that she was extremely busy with all her other horses and appreciated the time she had given to him.

I mentioned about needing a photo for this book. Caroline very kindly said if I wanted to come to meet him in person and have my photo taken with him, she would be delighted. So, as you can see, I (and Bob) did travel to meet him and one of the photos adorns this story. I have to say 'one' because I lost count of how many were taken! As Binders was so excited, he would stand for a few seconds and then decide he wanted to wander off (quite hastily!) somewhere. We had great fun – and thank goodness for digital photography as, having checked and re-checked the photos taken, we found some of Binders and me looking forwards in the same picture!

Caroline said she would keep in touch and I said I would ask the last question, which was what he wanted his contribution to the book to say, and his words were,

"We can't be forced into doing something we don't want to do!" I thought that was a great thing to share with us because, at the end of the day, if they really don't want to do something, they won't. (Please note his use of the word 'forced' - some horses are not happy doing the job they are doing, just like many humans, as if you are only doing something because it is expected of you then you will not excel at it.)

Then you meet the likes of Binders, who incidentally, won nearly £500,000 in prize money, and who could ever forget the wonder horse, Red Rum? He won the Grand National three times, yes, three times! A record I would think never to be repeated; it was such an amazing feat that it is emblazoned in racing history.

Another horse, and his jockey, that deserve a mention here are, of course, Aldaniti and Bob Champion. As soon as the music starts to the film, *Champions*, I get 'goose bumps'. The true, and incredibly moving story of a horse that overcame desperately serious leg problems, and his jockey, struggling to beat very aggressive cancer. They both ultimately defied the odds against them and won the Grand National in 1981. It is one film that cannot help but melt your heart. Bob Champion works tirelessly raising funds for his cancer charity, *The Bob Champion Cancer Trust*, and has never forgotten how lucky he was. One of the many websites relating their amazing feat says that although Aldaniti had died in 1997 and Bob Champion had retired from training horses in 1999, they are both legends of the horse-racing world. Their legacy is a sense of hope for all those who follow in their paths. They taught us that even when things look desperate, success can be just over the next fence for those who choose to make the jump.

I know that it was through my illness I was set on this path with my animal psychic work. You never know, maybe one day, there will be a film about an animal that, I as a cancer survivor, will help dramatically change the life of, some animal that goes on to win their own version of a Grand National. (I know that, Zilana, who is featured in the next story, has high aspirations!)

Caroline did come back to me and let me know that as her heart was in showing and Binders's wasn't, he was now back up at the yard which will be his home for the rest of his days. As she said; everyone just wants the best for him, he owes nobody anything. He is as well as ever and was also in the 2011 Grand National parade along with some of the previous winners. Caroline said,

"He was very excited and full of himself!"

No surprise there! I hope he has a long and wonderful retirement at the place where he made people's dreams come true and, having chatted to him, I am sure winning the Grand National meant as much to him too.

I was most touched as although Caroline thought the world of him, she knew a girl who adored him, Sam, who had looked after him in racing. Caroline kindly sent her an email to say he was going to be in this book and Sam wrote to me. She was delighted and just as Binders had said at the very beginning of the conversation that the girls loved him, she most certainly did! She wrote…

'I looked after him and rode him every day for five years when he was in training. I did absolutely everything with him – he is still my hero!'

I think her words say it all.

Alex Hua Tian

From a Grand National winning trainer, and Binderee himself, I continue on the horse theme with my visit to meet Alex and the two horses I would be talking to. As mentioned in Toby's story, Alex is an Olympic event rider. He hit the headlines in 2008 when he qualified to be the first ever Chinese Olympic rider and represented them at the games hosted in Beijing. Media interest was intensified by the fact that he also would be the youngest ever Olympic event rider having already achieved a world ranking of twenty one, and this at only eighteen-years-old!

We know in racing that the horses run a single race and the first past the post is deemed to be the winner, well most of the time anyway. For anyone that is not familiar with the world of eventing, this competition is made up of three riding phases; dressage, show jumping and cross-country. To be technical, the correct title should be 'three day eventing' but as everyone just refers to it as 'eventing' I shall stick to that.

In the 2012 Olympics, Alex, once again, will be doing the honours for China and I know from many of my horse clients the eventing world has been following his progress with keen interest.

Unlike most of the personalities in this book, who had not experienced or even heard of an animal psychic let alone knew of one, Alex, however, did. His knowledge of me came via the owner of a horse, Zilana, who was now in his yard. This dappled grey mare, now aged seven, and standing a good seventeen hands high, had a rather chequered history. Her owner, Rosemary, had asked me to see if I could help this stunning, but rather tricky, mare. Before I share the story of my visit to Alex's yard with you, which, funnily enough, turned out to be just as disorganised as Toby's, I would like to take this opportunity to share Zilana's story with you first. It is obviously a briefer version than in my case-study books but will give you an insight of the serious side of my work and what I try to achieve.

Rosemary had contacted me about nine months previously as Zilana had gained a bad reputation as she was showing extreme behaviour. In spite of what Zilana was doing Rosemary knew in her heart that this was a genuine horse but needed answers, and where best to get them, 'Straight from the horses' mouth,' well, metaphorically speaking.

Rosemary is the owner of a stud and she has been extremely successful with her progeny having bred many champion horses and continues to do so. Zilana, however, Rosemary did not breed but she had been drawn to an advert whilst surfing the internet. (I personally think this is another example of 'if an animal is supposed to come to you, it will!') Zilana was six-years-old, show-jumping bred and had only been broken the previous year. With everything organised, Zilana arrived over from Holland and in spite of being of a lighter physique than she had expected, Rosemary fell in love with her instantly. There was just something so special about her, even with slightly more delicate legs than one would have preferred, Rosemary thought she would make a fabulous show mare. Her intention was to buy her, do some serious showing and hopefully sell her on as a high ranking mare.

The more Rosemary watched her, and got to know her, she realised that this mare was a fantastic mover and rather than just showing her, she was sure she would excel at dressage and maybe even eventing. Rosemary decided to send her to be professionally schooled and then competed to see what she could actually achieve. However, it didn't take long for things to begin to unravel dramatically and this once happy horse was now a very annoyed and unmanageable one. I did not know this prior to the reading but she had been rearing and Rosemary was at her wits end as this just didn't seem to ring true; she was sure that this mare was genuine but why should she show such outrageous behaviour?

Rosemary had read about me on an internet forum and although had not used an animal psychic before, she had read what other people had experienced with my work so thought it worth a try. She had nothing to lose really - she had spent a bomb buying this lovely mare and now nobody wanted to ride her, let alone compete her.

With Zilana's photo printed I tuned in to her before telephoning Rosemary (bearing in mind I knew nothing of her problems) and asked her to tell me something about herself.

"I am forward going and switched on."

"I am definitely not a dangerous horse."

"I am elegance itself."

I passed these statements on to Rosemary and she said,

"I agree. I do not think she is dangerous but other people do!" I said I would come back to that but I would let Zilana chat away and say what she wanted. (I always work this way - imagine sitting a child down and zooming in straight on the negative things, they would more than likely just clam up and prefer to say nothing.)

I got more information which was correct:

She didn't have an issue being in a stable.

She said she knew and understood her paces.

She could jump and liked to keep her feet 'off the poles'.

These things Rosemary recognised but then Zilana 'shouted',

"Why won't they let me go forward?" Suddenly she was making me feel very angst and agitated. I felt a complete cramping up of my body and muscles and then feeling like I wanted to explode.

"That is exactly what she does, explodes; she rears bolt upright and throws a complete tantrum. It has got that bad now that they do think she is dangerous. (Ah, the penny dropped with me; that is why she made such an oddly overt statement at the very beginning).

She made me feel as if this was unjust and so I suggested she tell me what else she was good at. She made me feel that she was sensible in traffic but when asked about hacking out alone, she wasn't willing on that score. She was affectionate but I felt that she was holding back somewhat.

I asked Zilana to try and expand on what was going on that made her feel so angry and upset. Instantly she gave me the feeling of being 'hauled in' by the bit at the front end and being kicked in her belly to push her to go forward. I know there are several ways of getting horses to do dressage and different styles of dressage too, but not all horses are suited to each certain style of riding. I felt that this was the stronger way of riding that many horses often seem to submit to, but not all, and Zilana was one of them. What people are trying to encourage horses to do is; work from their quarters (backend), drop their heads to the correct position for dressage. Many riders seem to use this hold and kick approach but with types like Zilana; they are not submissive and need encouragement to soften with their head carriage. The more you try to pull them into a shape, the more they will fight you. She told us that she was 'elastic' and wanted to stretch out and use herself but felt hemmed in and harried by the rider. The more she was held in and pushed on, the more annoyed she got. She felt she was being pushed to go forward but held back at the same time, so where else could she go? UP! And that is exactly what she had learned to do. Rearing is such a dangerous thing for both horse and rider but I really thought that this mare felt she had no choice. I worded this very carefully to Rosemary as the last thing I wanted to do was to insult anyone's riding abilities or offend someone that was maybe even a friend. Now I had established what seemed to be going wrong, Rosemary said having watched her being ridden, said she felt this did make sense.

"I will bring her home immediately if that is what she wants," ventured Rosemary. On hearing that a wave of relief wafted over me as Zilana was delighted at the prospect, although I felt she was feeling a little disconcerted about where she really lived and who she belonged to. She told us that she had moved about quite a bit in the last six months, so this was understandable.

If you allow me to sidetrack for a minute I would like to follow up on this point. It is something that I deal with so regularly and have found many animals responding well once they know what is actually happening in their life - they feel the need for stability just as we do. Horses get sold day in, day out, and I have even done readings for people who are selling their beloved horse and want me to explain why. I spend my life telling people; these animals do understand what you say and your words will sink into their minds. So, say a horse has had a few homes then tell them your true intentions - even if they are only going to stay with you a while, explain to them and why. At the point of sale, or suchlike, tell them that you are going to do the best for them to try and make sure they go on to a good home. If you have bought that horse with the intention of keeping them for the rest of their days and 'they are going nowhere' please tell them. It can make all the difference to an animal just to know where they stand.

I assured Zilana that Rosemary would arrange collection to bring her back to the stud which, for the present time, was most certainly Zilana's home. I confirmed that also she would (as requested) have a complete holiday to get over this and have some back and muscle treatment too. We left the communication at that and organised that we would have a catch up in a few months to see how she felt and what she wanted to say.

Through the joys of *Facebook* I kept in touch with Rosemary and also did some work for friends of hers too. I knew that Zilana had eventually settled down and she seemed more relaxed in herself. On her next chat I was to try to ascertain what she wanted to do, be ridden or not, and how she felt about life in general.

I was delighted when she immediately said that her stride had lengthened and that she thought she was very scopey indeed. I told Rosemary this and she said she certainly had noticed her stride was far better. I asked Zilana about working again and she clearly emphasised that she needed to be ridden with empathy and not bullied. She went on to say that she wanted to be allowed to use her body and if she went somewhere could Rosemary keep an eye on what was going on? The problem was, the area of England where Rosemary lives is very rural and she could not think of anyone that would be suited to Zilana or would even want to take her on. Zilana now had a reputation (deserved or not) which would make many people that ride horses for a living very wary because if they get injured they are unable to ride or compete any horses at all – it is a tough enough living and sport without added risks.

Rosemary then threw Alex's name into the conversation. She said that she knew if she could persuade him to take Zilana she just knew he would be the man for the job. Having watched him ride and compete, although still young, he rode with such empathy and finesse and horses just floated under him. The more we talked the more exciting this prospect seemed to be.

With Zilana declaring that for Alex she would be 'a golden opportunity' (you never know, she is still pretty young!) we left the chat at that.

I kept in touch with Rosemary and was delighted to hear that Zilana was settling down, and although there had been a few 'blip' moments, Alex and her were getting on well. This was borne out a few months later when in their first dressage outing together, they won the class and went on to become Champion of the day! Rosemary asked Alex if he would like to be in this book and I was delighted when he said he would and to call him to arrange the visit.

The only date that seemed to fit for both Alex and I was the day before he was due to go to compete in France so he would be running around trying to get everything organised. He said, if it was okay with me, then it was okay with him. I had said that I would just fit in around him.

Bob and I arrived slightly early and one of the grooms said that Alex was still out on a horse but shouldn't be long. I asked where Zilana was stabled and they showed us into an American barn. (This, for non-horsey readers, is the descriptive style we use for stabling lined up inside a barn, like in the USA, rather than ones that are actual stable buildings, which is the more British way of keeping horses.)Zilana was very easy to spot down the far end and we were left on our own and hung about waiting for Alex. After a while, to save time, I decided that I would do the catch-up chat with her and then just report my finding to Alex when he got back. (I don't usually work in this way but having had a couple of chats with Zilana previously I knew this would be okay.)

She instantly made me smile because as she was telling me how elastic and supple she was, she gave me proof by seeming to bend double to use her teeth to scratch herself on her hindquarters. She said that she didn't come out of her stable with 'attitude' but with a sort of bounce, I think she meant 'flounce' rather like a model! In between our bouts of laughter Bob scribbled it all down for me to read out. She showed me her being stroked down the right-hand-side of her neck and I heard the words 'good girl' to go with the vision.

She declared that she was easy and 'not a problem' at all. I thought this to be very bold considering I knew her to be one that had to be treated with care and one of those horses that you knew exactly what buttons not to push! At least she thought she was easy, I am sure Alex would tell me his opinion.

"I am extremely gifted!" I had no doubt that this was Zilana giving me the information (bearing in mind we were surrounded by many talented horses) as she always wants to express her plus points, and I thought the model remark would have been pretty spot on, especially, if you remember her original self-description was, 'elegance itself'.

She carried on to tell us:

She was very settled, didn't scream and shout and had a good work ethic.

She thought she had a massive jump but needed to hone this skill. She made me feel as if she was still quite inexperienced but was at least sounding positive about her jumping.

She wanted to point out that she really was a right-handed horse and made me feel that even now Alex was having to use more pressure to get her to work to the left.

Alex was very encouraging and told her, 'You can do it'. Alex rides very much with his body and she was now far softer in her mouth and was not having resistance problems.

She thought her head carriage was far better and to me actually sounded as if she was enjoying her work! (This was from a mare that had been classed as dangerous!)

On a physical point, she did however make me aware of a slight (I would say muscular) discomfort in the upper part of her right hind leg through up into her hindquarter. I certainly didn't think it seemed serious but I had to acknowledge what she was passing over to me.

She said she didn't think she was the bravest horse in the world and if asked to jump combinations she would need very clear instruction until she got confidence in her own ability. Also, if she was over-faced (put at a jump she thought was too big or complicated) then she would panic and lose her confidence again. I felt there really was a fine line here and knowing the empathy that Alex has in his riding skill he would know exactly where this lay.

She did however point out that she was, 'fine with water' which I presumed that meant she would jump or at least go into or through water. (Some horses are absolutely terrible when it comes to water obstacles on a course and I have had many a horse chat on this very subject.)

She declared that there had been a marked change in her balance and that she doesn't 'fall in' on her right shoulder like she used to. (Again, another horse term which basically means, leaning in.)

Apparently Alex doesn't want to fight with horses; it is a co-operation that is achieved and she said he is always two steps ahead of them anyway!

I thought we would leave it there as apparently Alex was now in the arena schooling the horse he had been out on, so we wandered up there to watch him.

As many of my clients have found, I just have a basic knowledge of dressage and I freely admit to having gained limited experience during my riding years. My mare, Misty, like so many, was rather fizzy and very forward going, so found the whole thing too slow, precise and to her, boring! It takes a special type of horse that is prepared to be taught all the paces, complete with intricate moves, and then to be able to do them at different speeds too! As for people like Alex, it has taken years and years of absolute dedication and patience, and once again, patience is something that is naturally in abundance with some of us and far less in others.

With the sun shining through and warming our backs, Bob and I watched and marvelled at the ease and softness that Alex had got this horse moving so freely, but in a beautiful outline with ears pricked to match. You could see this horse listening to his every ask, and, as all dressage riders know, the 'commands' should be barely visible to us spectators. We had been there only a few minutes and my face lit up with a smile as I said to Bob,

"Ah ha, spot on! Alex does do that quick right-side-of-neck reward stroke, which Zilana had told me about." Having seen that this was indeed correct I hoped that all the other information Zilana had shared was accurate too. If so, she had well and truly turned a corner and is the maybe fantastic horse that she always professed to be.

Alex got off his horse, shook our hands and introduced himself, apologising for the delay and the manic activity that was so obvious. I said that it was fine and that to save time I had already done the update chat with Zilana and I would read back to him what I had got. We all headed into the barn and as he was un-tacking the horse he had been on he said,

"You should meet Hazel. She does work like yours; I think she is up at the other end of the barn treating a horse. You should go and meet her; she has had some great results for us." Just then his phone rang (again!) so we moved out of the way and I thought I would go and find Hazel. I have to admit I was slightly worried, whilst getting people for this book I have tried my best to make sure that they do not have their own communicator/psychic, as I would hate to tread on anyone else's toes, after all, they would be their client and I would prefer someone not to do it me. (I try to treat others in life like I like to be treated myself.) I left Bob admiring and fussing some horses and headed off to find her. I popped my head round each stable and eventually found Hazel kneeling down and seemingly applying essential oils to a horse's coronet band (top part of the hoof). I said 'Hi' and that Alex had said that he thought we should meet. I said I was slightly confused as I thought she was a communicator and did she do other treatments as well? Hazel explained that, in the past she had done some communicating but had left it to follow a different path which she felt she was more suited for. This involved E.F.T. (Emotional Freedom Technique), dowsing and this latest type of treatment from the USA that she had studied. It involved using various oils but in a different way from the traditional way they have been used over here for years. We soon got chatting (Alex had dashed off somewhere so I had yet more time) and as Hazel had her notes about Zilana that she got by the dowsing for information technique, I went and got my original notes (fortunately I had brought them with me) so we could compare. We read through them and there were so many matches, we really had both got the same results by different means. It suddenly dawned on me, I could ask Hazel to check Zilana's back-end and see if she, by dowsing, could validate what I had been made to feel. We 'trotted' back down the barn and into Zilana's stable and told Bob what we were doing. I quickly checked that Bob had written down clearly what I had found, and he had so Hazel got out her pendulum.

For anyone that is not into dowsing, it is usually a crystal, (but anything works really) that is on the end of a chain or similar. Although I cannot explain why, when dangles downwards and asked, it will swing one way for yes and a different way for no. For example round and round for yes, and back and forth for no, it works in various ways and differs between persons.

Hazel raised and held the pendulum at various parts of Zilana and it kept showing a swing back and forth result which meant a no. Bob and I watched intently and as she got to the area it starting swinging in a circular fashion indicating, yes, there was indeed a problem. I wanted to see if it would show the area exactly as I had described and do you know? It started where I said and stopped exactly where I had said too! Talk about complementary therapies! Once again, we had got exactly the same result by two completely different means. So if anyone doesn't know about dowsing, have a look on the internet - it is such a fun thing to try and, best of all, costs, zilch to do! (There is actually a company not far from where I live who drill bore-holes to find water for people's land or houses. They have been in business for well over twenty years and when people request them to come and locate water for a bore-hole they produce their trusted old penny which is attached to a chain. This must get some very strange looks from customers and I smile at the thought of this, but they find water, dig the bore-holes and provide people with a constant, and natural, water supply. So, if they can stay in business that long dowsing with an old coin on a chain, this speaks volumes for dowsing.) I hope that by way of validation, as Hazel and I both found the same problem, this shows our work in a very good light also.

Alex appeared back and I took the chance to quickly read Zilana's update and he nodded and agreed his way through the list. He expressed how difficult she had been originally and that eventually she had settled down and relaxed. She gave up putting up a fight when she realised that Alex was not going to battle with her; he just expected her to co-operate with him as he was riding her with the care and empathy that she had wanted all along. She was now showing that great presence and elegance that she always said she had and, we laughed about wondering which model we thought she was referring to. (I leave that answer up to you, dear readers!) As in life, sometimes the overtly beautiful, super talented and maybe genius, often come with quirks but because they are so amazing at what they do, people learn to work round their idiosyncrasies and not rock the boat!

I took the opportunity to say what Hazel and I had both found, and although I didn't think it felt serious it was worth noting. Alex said the osteopath was coming later on that day, so Zilana would be added to the list.

The other horse we had arranged the chat to be with was the stunning big bay, very powerfully built gelding called Furst Love (what a fab name!) Although only nine years old, he had actually risen up the eventing ranks at some speed as apparently was very talented and there was a chance that he could be Alex's Olympic horse for 2012. (As people in the horse world know, which horses get selected or stay sound is a very tough call, so nearer the time Alex will know who he hopes to compete on.)

As I have said, I think the name, Furst Love is so lovely but in the yard, and by Alex, he is called Fred (yes, Fred!) so Fred it shall be. He was stabled next to Zilana so I moved across to start his chat. I thought this would be fun as Alex obviously had a soft spot for him and, having heard a couple of remarks, I thought he may well be a bit of a comedian. I had just started to tune in with him and a lady arrived with a saddle to be tried on... Fred! So, end of chatting again as Fred was quickly taken out of his stable and the saddle placed upon his back. As he stood, with people milling around, the saddler explained that they had eventually found with Fred that rather than putting a truly correct fitting saddle on him, that he preferred it to be slightly looser than would be the norm.

"My back muscles cramp." I am sure I heard from Fred so repeated it.

"Yes, I think they do," said Alex "on the odd occasion, he will suddenly hollow, get himself in a bit of a pickle then sort himself out and carry on as if nothing has happened!" Eventually the saddle fitting was completed with a quick ride by Alex to see that Fred moved happily and freely in it. (This is paramount to saddle fitting. It is no use just having a saddle placed on a horse that seems to fit all where it touches. Just like us, say, with a new pair of shoes, until you walk in them you do not really know how comfortable or uncomfortable they are. A comfortable saddle is, I would say, the most important accessory on a horse. I often get shown images of saddles that slip or seem to be unbalanced etc. and people have been told, 'just put a couple of pads under it, that will sort it out.' My expression I use is back to the shoe thing - if we have shoes that don't fit for whatever reason, the wrong size or shape for our foot, putting on a couple more pairs of socks is not going to fix it and would sometimes actually add to the discomfort. If we expect these magnificent and trusting animals to carry us, jump for us, lift and bend their backs for us, we should take the responsibility and care to make sure that what is between us does not cause any discomfort and or hinder their movement.

"Do you realise I could do this with my eyes shut!" came across one very confident Fred.

"I have great balance, like a gyroscope you know!"

"I don't like to be ignored," and gave me the picture of him being in a lorry with others and if you didn't acknowledge him, he would be most put out!

"Oh yes," replied Alex, "That is him, centre of attention and yes, he does have great balance, he is such a versatile horse". I remarked I didn't think the 'eyes shut' was maybe such a good thing! Alex seemed to be genuinely enjoying the conversation and I have to say, he is all that Rosemary had said; very talented and so likeable with it. I know that he carries huge responsibilities with his appointment as Goodwill Ambassador for the 'Britain You're Invited' Campaign in China, which entailed a lot of media work and promoting of the British Olympics.

Fred made me laugh by showing me a vision of himself, in all his splendour, looking very eye catching and crowd pleasing but then putting his ears back in that childish 'ha ha look at me.' Alex laughed and used a descriptive line that was something like being 'such a plonker!' I truly felt that there was a great bond between them and was most surprised to hear from Alex that Fred, at first, had been a complete twit and proved to be quite a handful. Just then I was given a picture of what looked like Alex coming off the horse's right hand side complete with the words,

"Maybe we shouldn't talk about this." Obviously I asked Alex if he had fallen off him or been 'fired' off his right hand side? Alex turned to the grooms, who by this time seemed to have gathered round, but they shook their heads as they could not recall Alex falling off him. Alex went on to inform me though; that at first, out of temper, Fred would throw himself on the floor, and Alex quickly removed himself, so that would probably explain the picture and most probably why the, 'best not to talk about it'!

"I can seriously change gear and have the most powerful shoulders," stated the 'ever-so-shy' Fred!

"I do get a sore lower back though," he gently commented and gave me this vision of him hollowing for a few strides then carrying on as normal afterwards. Alex said,

"Yes, that's what we were talking about - he gets all discombobulated! Discombobulated! What a fantastic word that I have never used in my life. I too went to boarding school but Alex went to Eton (crème de la crème of boarding schools) so I guess they might have been taught a wider vocabulary there, or I didn't pay enough attention in class - most likely the latter! Anyway, I made sure Bob wrote it down, so here, in all its glory it is – discombobulated! It is such a descriptive word but not one you would want to see it on your dressage score sheet! We had a quick discussion about the back cramp/spasm and Fred seemed to think that he tended to do it to himself by way of over-exertion that wasn't strictly necessary or had been asked for either.

Fred informed us that he knew where his feet were when he landed – he gave me a frightening picture of what seemed to be a jump with a downhill the other side and landing pretty far out as if the ground was running beneath him. I passed this over to Alex and he said,

"Oh yes, that is Fred. If there is a drop-fence he knows exactly where he is and will land far out but safely with it." (If you have ever watched serious eventing, like Burleigh, Badminton and the like, whether on TV or in real life, it takes huge courage - the fences are massive and also can be so narrow and tricky. The thought of being on Fred zooming through the air hoping the landing gear will not fail, makes me glad I decided not attempt this sport which would have probably shredded my nerves into irreparable little pieces!) Listening to Fred describing himself, 'Like a speed boat going through water,' confirmed my sensible decision, although I will give Fred his due, he said that he would slow down/stop if Alex asked and this was correct. Thank goodness for that!

Fred made me feel like he was proud of himself and whilst 'puffing his chest out' showed me what seemed to be two stars. I asked if Alex knew if that represented anything, and it did. Fred was actually competing at Two Star level, again to people that compete at eventing they would know about them, but to me, I recognise them to be somewhere at the serious end of the scale.

It seemed that Fred has really found his niche in life; to be allowed to show off but in the capable hands of Alex. As Fred put so succinctly,

"Alex guides - I do!"

Although we rattled through this chat as fast as possible, knowing that time was of the essence, we covered lots more like; a dressage move that involved two beats with a front foot instead of one. I am sure Fred threw this in to confuse me but it turned out he could do a move called 'Tempi Changes', which needless to say, Alex recognised and gave me the terminology for. Fred said he had given up arguing and, in fact, loved to learn new things however challenging. I thought for the celeb bit I would ask Fred if he wanted to tell us what it is like to be an eventer.

"We have to have a brain to do what we do, but the confidence needs to be stronger than it." I thought this was very clever. As in life, there are often things that your brain would think not possible but it is our confidence that pushes us through the barriers and then our brain knows that, in fact, it is possible.

I asked Fred what he would like to say as his contribution to the book and this is his statement,

"We are all individuals and if we were looked on like that it would make the world of difference."

"Here, here," I say too. I think he had discussed that one with Zilana but it is so true. Different people suit different people because we are all individuals. Different styles of riding suit different horses and different horses suit different jobs.

I thanked Alex for his time, wished him all the best for the 2012 Olympics and continued success with Zilana and Fred. On asking Fred what he thought Alex could do if he was not an event rider, his immediate reply.

"A racing driver, have you seen him drive?"

I passed this to Alex and the look on his face was a picture. He informed us that only the day before my visit he had been interviewed and asked the very same question and his reply to them had been,

"A Formula One driver!"

That raised a smile with everyone and a big thank you to Fred from me.

So, it was off home for Bob and I, covering the many miles of motorways but at a far more sedate pace than a racing car, I might add.

Dean Spink

On my constant quest to find celebrities for this project, during a conversation with Kim, she said,

"I don't know if this is any good to you but I know of somebody who was voted 'Shrewsbury's Cult hero of all time'!"

"Wow, a local person too - that is great, tell me more!"

"He is an ex-premiership footballer whose top job was with Aston Villa, but he played for Shrewsbury FC over 300 times and is still very well known around here and by the footballing fraternity."

"That sounds great to me," I responded, "but how do we get in contact with him?"

"You have already spoken to one of his cats!" she declared laughingly.

"You do remember the cat, Chloe, who you thought dribbled, when in fact, it was her drinking from a tap?" I nodded (how could I forget? I was in a room full of people listening to me doing said communication and felt like I wanted to dribble out of the side of my mouth!), "well, Dean lives with my daughter Sian and Chloe is one of their three cats!"

"Oh excellent, do you think he would be interested?" She said she would have a word with Sian, and this story is the result.

Although Kim lives in Shrewsbury, Sian lives with Dean in Solihull, near Birmingham. He now works for Solihull FC as their sports physiotherapist and also does radio work as a 'sports pundit'. Birmingham is also very central for Sian to travel from as she is a model and budding actress. She has had background parts in *Doctors* and *Casualty* and many other TV shows.

I obviously questioned whether she thought that Dean might think doing this would ruin his 'street-cred' but she said he adored the cats and she would ask and see what he thought of the idea. Dean said he was more than happy for me to come and visit and talk to the other two cats, and also have a catch-up chat with Chloe. He was positively looking forward to it!

I left Kim in charge of the driving and directions as she had obviously travelled the route many times before. The journey took about an hour and, as we were near there, Kim phoned Sian to let her know, and I had to laugh, Sian's first words were,

"Are you lost?!"

"No, I'm not; we will be there in a few minutes, I was just phoning to let you know," Kim replied.

Dean was just back home and getting changed as he had been out working with his industrial window cleaning company. His father has the same type of business and even in Dean's footballing days he often used to work with him - they are not all on David Beckham wages you know!

Celebrity Pet Talking

Sian, unfortunately, was not able to stay for all of the communications as she had a modelling assignment to be at, but was able to listen to the first one which was with Jake. He was four-years-old, black and white and had the longest legs I have seen on a cat for a long time. He was a full brother to Chloe (they were from the same litter) and was off doing his own thing so I worked from his photograph. Jake volunteered straight away that, "I really stretch out and can look like I am 10 feet long!!" I laughed and thought this would sound quite mad, but repeated it anyway. Dean and Sian laughed and said,

"He does. He stretches himself out along the back of the settee and it's true – he looks really long!"

Jake claimed, "I am quite affectionate but I am a boy!" This they totally understood. He was a cat that came forward for attention but then would step back if the others were there as if it was a 'girly' thing to do!

Jake gave me the impression that Dean and Sian's neighbour was not that keen on him going in his garden. The reason I knew of this was because Jake admitted to taking great delight in sitting up on the high boundary fence making his presence apparent but just out of reach. (It is so amazing what these animals do just to be naughtily annoying!). He showed me him scooting up the alley as well and, to be honest, as much as I worry about the cats and traffic, Jake seemed to be pretty 'switched on' to all of it. This may be down to experience as a long time ago Jake got lost for two weeks. It was a horrible time for Dean and Sian as they searched everywhere and could not find him. They put pictures up on lampposts etc. and fortunately someone spotted him and told them that they had seen him hanging around only 800 yards away!! I stopped Sian mid- conversation and said I would ask Jake if he wanted to give us his side of the story. He took me back to that time and to my surprise, he didn't seem distressed about it. It came across to me, that when Sian and Dean tracked him down he greeted them with what seemed a nonchalant 'Hiya!' I repeated this and Dean said that was so right, in fact he had a new friend with him and didn't look worried at all. We can only assume that Jake had strayed, or been chased off his own 'patch'. Maybe after the first few days he decided that it would be safer to make friends with another cat, safety in numbers perhaps. He was brought back to the safety of his home and has never gone off anywhere since.

Sian was running short of time and needed to leave but before she left she got me to ask Jake if he loves his 'Mummy'? A bit of a 'girly' question for Jake but I asked and he replied, in his 'manly' way,

"I get to do what I want, even when told NO! - so the answer is YES!" With that, Sian left and Dean said he would tell her all that was said. I thought I would get on with Jake's Celebrity questions before we started the chat with Phoebe who, incidentally, Jake had said he thought was shy and tended to be most agreeable with her,

"Oh, yes, Jake. Oh, that's okay, Jake," responses. Quick as a flash, Jake enacted posing a question to her,

"Is that food my food?"

"Oh, yes, Jake."

"Ah, that's alright then!" Animals do have a sense of humour, and Jake was showing his. As for his opinion of Dean,

"Grounded and gets what he wants." Kim nodded as she thought that was accurate but Jake wanted also to add something for Sian, who was apparently, "Gentle and delicate and puts a lot of thought into things." Ah, how touching. Kim, as her mum, could vouch for that, as Sian is very petite and of a gentle nature. Having been so sweet, Jake it seemed couldn't resist in having a bit of a laugh at her expense, by adding,

"These fashion magazines; the ones she has so many of - why so many? Aren't they basically all the same?!" Dean laughed and guessed there would be divided opinions on that answer, so I left it at that.

Although I do not follow football, I thought I would ask Jake if he had any impression of what Dean was like as a footballer. Well, the picture made me laugh and I had to be careful. I saw someone with bulging calf muscles making his way through (rather than completely going round) the other players, compounded with the explanation,

"He liked to get in the mix of things!" And that *was* Dean in his footballing days, to a tee. Jake is another animal that would have chatted all day, but we had to give the others a turn, so for his bit for what animal communication can say on his behalf, "Even footballer's have talking cats, it is not unusual!" That caused an eruption of laughter. Well done, Jake, great answer, and so true. You never know, I might get to talk to more of them yet!

So on to Phoebe who was slightly younger at three-years-old. She was tortoiseshell and white and, as I found out, a completely different personality.

Her opening line was,

"I am the odd one out." Which is how I found out she was actually not related to the other two, but she went on to say that she really liked to do her own thing, and was happy with that. She then showed me her walking with rather a 'swagger' which, evidently, she did!

"I like Jake," she declared, "He makes me laugh." Dean said that they did play well and with that comment she added that Jake protects her.

"He does," said Dean, and I could just imagine Jake going, "Oy matey, out my garden and away from my girl – now!"

Dean said he wondered if she would talk about her early days with them. Straight off I heard her say 'spitty' which apparently was a very apt description. I asked her for more and she gave me a rather sad feeling like the impression of segregation. This was confirmed and then she showed me what looked like bars so I asked if she, for some reason, had to be caged?

"Yes," came Dean's reply, "it was very difficult and maybe she will tell you what she did to me." She heard the request and gingerly showed me what looked like being wrapped round someone's arm and not letting go. Dean, I have to say, look sort of amazed, and I have to admit, not all pictures are totally clear, but that one was truly graphic and correct. It turned out that he and Sian had rescued her as she was completely feral and had no idea what people were about. This poor cat had been dumped with another lot of kittens and Dean admitted, she was so horrendous, they did at one point consider taking her back. She had seriously bitten and attacked Dean but, undeterred, he and Sian had spent hours and hours sitting beside her cage until she got used to them. With more patience, they started to handle her and they eventually gained her trust and confidence. The interesting thing about this was, that Dean and Sian had got her because Jake had gone. He, after all, seemed to be lost forever and this one would be a friend for the other cat, Chloe. Now you might think that when a cat came back into his own home, like Jake did, he might have been very antagonistic towards to a new incomer. No, not a bit of it, he actually helped her, and in her own words,

"The cats were kind to me and told me it was okay!" Regarding the biting incident, she took this communication to offer her apology in her own words, which were,

"Sorry about your hand, and you know the difference between you and me? I don't swear!!" I had to laugh; I thought that was so funny in her independent way. She is happy with life and does enjoy a 'fuss' but on her on terms, rather like Jake. Phoebe told us lots of other things that Dean recognised and said of Dean,

"He was my rescuer, and full of perseverance," and she thanked him for it. Dean looked moved, and who wouldn't be? As to what she would like her contribution to show in this, "What I would like people to know most is that when we react badly, we usually do it out of fear and it is nice that we can explain ourselves."

"This *is* a child," Dean announced as soon as I got Chloe's photo out.

"Oh, I know," I said, "I remember her well! This is actually the cat that gets into bed with Dean and Sian, and I mean, in bed! She then pushes at Sian's back, who in turn pushes Dean over towards the edge of the bed.

"She is terrible for that!" Dean exclaimed, "and the worse thing is, Sian would put me in the spare room rather than disturb the cat and ask her to move back over!!" Chloe is a very special cat; she just oozes affection and loves to be adored. She is also very 'on the ball' as she had been listening to the other 'cat chats' and offered to say something about Dean now, if I didn't mind? I said not at all, and to carry on.

"He's a joker, and can say things with such a straight face, a real wind-up merchant!" Dean roared with laughter, this was the truth, he was in fact well known for his 'wind-up' antics. Very proud of the fact that Chloe was calling the shots in this conversation, she then volunteered for Sian,

"Can you tell Mummy I love her, and you can put that in the book!" (If the question was good enough for Jake, it was definitely good enough for her).

Dean said she was such a little 'monkey' as she takes great delight in getting into places where she shouldn't. Be it under the bed, in the wardrobe or shut in a cupboard. All this was of no worry or consequence as she told us,

"I admit I go into places but then I squawk until someone lets me out, I'm not bothered!" A girl full of fun and confidence! Chloe showed me a picture of her behind Jake and mimicking him with his long legs and rolling his hips as he walked. You think of people doing this - animals never cease to amaze me in their similarities of what they do in the name of a laugh. She combined this picture with a statement saying, "Jake thinks he is a clever clogs, well, I'm cleverer than he is!"

A question I wanted to ask was about her drinking from taps, and this was one on Sian's list too. Having previously been given the water dribbling sensation, I found out she will drink from the tap in the bathrooms and the kitchen, but why?

"I do it because it's fun and because it is cold and fresh. See, told you I wasn't stupid!!" Who can argue with that?

Onto the celebrity questions, but she insisted on describing Dean first.

"He is a man's man but with a soft centre, and he can still kick a ball, you know!" I asked her what other job could he do? Although I knew he was the physiotherapist at the club, she suggested that he would be a good coach, and Dean said he helped doing that already. She said that Dean would get his point over but keep it fun at the same time. I think that sometimes that is a hard balance to keep, respect and fun, but I think a good way to get people to listen to you. Chloe then threw me slightly as she was showing me what looked like to be someone being artistic and creative. I couldn't quite match that to the football conversation but as it turned out, it was about Dean's son who is at stage school. It was lovely of Chloe to bring him into the conversation as Brandon loved her and, when he visited, she spent most of her time on his bed.

Chloe decided now was a good time to offer some advice for Sian – the more jewellery she had, the more clutter it would make! But, seriously, she felt on the acting side, to keep sending her letters to the casting agencies, it will pay off and one day she will come from the background into the foreground. Also, that Sian is a fine example showing that you do not have to wear a lot of make-up to look good! So with Sian's career advisement over, the last question was what Chloe wanted her contribution to this book to be. I kid you not, this was her answer,

"To let people know who I am!" Words failed us!

I thanked Dean for his time and for being such a star, as often footballers get bad press, but he was more than happy to show his soft side here.

All we had to do now was drive back home without getting lost...

"Ah, but the motorway suddenly divided," uttered Kim... I say no more - but just writing 'North or South' is really not enough for us!

I mentioned in Jacky, 'The Angel Lady's story, that Kim writes Angel poetry. Having read through her lovely and touching selection I have chosen this one to put here. Kim had been such a great help to me, as have so many other people, which is why you have this book to read today. I, like many others, believe that we are looked after from afar, so here you are:

What is an Angel?

Fluffy white wings
A halo of gold
An aura of light
A sight to behold.

An Angel can be
All of these things
But also a friend
Without halos and wings.

Someone who's sent
When your need is great
An acquaintance, a neighbour
Or even a mate.

It might be a stranger
In the street,
On a train or a bus.
Just someone you meet

Just be assured
They hear if you call
They will send you help
And catch you if you fall.

So always know
They are by your side
To help with your woes
Or just for the ride.

You can choose to ignore them
Or acknowledge that they
Won't go away
You may need them someday.

Kim D Hill

Ami Dolenz

Although there have been quite a few stories in this book that I have done on Skype to America, all the people so far had been British but living in the USA.

I had another lucky break when someone I knew told me that she was in contact with Micky, Ami's father, and offered to mention this book. It turned out that Micky and his wife didn't have any pets but they suggested that Ami and her husband, Jerry, might be interested as they were crazy about their dogs. They were happy to take part and here is Ami's story with their dog, Filly.

Although most of us Brits would recognise Micky Dolenz's name due to his fame through being in the band *The Monkees*, Ami is very recognisable in America in her own right having had, and still having, a great career.

As I do a lot of work for people in the US and my books have a good following over there I am delighted to be able to include her, and her husband, in here. Her husband, Jerry

Trimble, is a well known actor and stunt-man and, as for Amy, she like Jerry, has been in a list of films as long as your arm.

Ami started her career very young and won awards for her acting as Melissa McKee in the 80s series, *General Hospital*. She also played a brilliant role in, *'She's Out of Control'*, playing opposite Tony Danza, and with her numerous TV appearances and guest slots, she is a household name.

As they had two dogs I asked them to choose one for each story and Ami chose Filly who was a hairy crossbred dog. She was slightly larger than a terrier but with a really cute face with her hair drooping forward representing bushy eyebrows. She was a natural choice for Ami as Filly had in fact been Mickey's dog until the age of three. She was now eleven-years-old and her photograph showed a most inquisitive yet gentle face.

Again, this was done via webcam. It was their early morning and our late afternoon and Bob was in attendance with his pen at the ready.

Both Ami and Jerry were excited to hear what their dogs had to say as, like most of the celebrities in this book, they had not experienced a psychic dog chat either.

Filly's opening introduction to me was,

"I am sweet and gentle but I do like my food!" She had also informed me that she was quite independent, not a clingy sort of dog. She indicated a couple of physical things which I thought, I would mention a bit later.

Ami smiled and said that Filly was sweet and gentle and confirmed that she did indeed have a keen interest in food. She said that although she was indeed the independent type Filly had come to live with her as her dad's circumstances had changed. Mickey had taken Filly on as a rescue dog in the first place but thought it would be fairer for her to live with Ami.

This would give her stability and of course, he still would be able to visit her. Having listened to that, Filly volunteered,

"Sea. Awesome!" I asked if she ever went to the beach.

"Oh, yes, she absolutely loves it; we often take her - how lovely to hear about it from her." Filly went on to say that she was the apple of Ami's eye and that she would sit up on a chair like, 'I'm a person too.' She said that, in spite of her age, her eyesight was still good. As Ami confirmed this Filly added,

"I'm a mongrel but beautiful!" Ah, how sweet. I totally agreed. We had a dog called Bruce that looked fairly similar, although a bigger version. He too had long wispy hair and had beautiful eyes that seemed to radiate through in spite of all the accompanying fuzz.

Ami and Jerry didn't have their own children at this point and they were delighted to hear that, although visiting children could be noisy, Filly didn't mind and really welcomed their visits.

She was a very motherly dog, and although she had never had puppies of her own, she had actually had a hand in helping others to raise theirs. It is amazing how often I have heard of this and I know in nature there are various species that will do this and it is the norm.

Filly made us laugh about getting gravy in the hair around her mouth and then showing us her doing her begging impression. With that the conversation came up about Filly being an actress herself. Apparently, she had been in a couple of films as Ami said she was very good at it. She had been in a film called *The Last Sentinel* so I said I would ask her about it.

"I could walk like a model but also do a sad impression too." Filly proudly told me. I passed this over and Ami said that she had been very good and they were very proud of her. (I thought to myself, I will have to get the DVD of the film and watch it for myself.

I did get it a couple of weeks later and although, to be honest, it was not my type of film. (I don't do sci-fi or violence and this was a sci-fi type war film.) Having talked to its starring dog I was still going to watch it anyway.

What made both Bob and me laugh was; on the first three appearances Filly made, each time, somebody seemed to be giving her food! Whether it was a soldier or someone hiding away, they fed her. I truly think she does like her food and there is a film to prove it!)

I asked her what she thought about herself being a movie star as she was revelling in her mini fame.

"I was a star for one," and I kid you not this is exactly what she said next, "and where are my dollars?" I burst out laughing and repeated it. Ami and Jerry thought this was hilarious and said to ask as she hadn't actually been given money for the film what would she maybe like instead?

"I could wear a velvet bandana or collar. Either would do as long as it said No.1 girl!" Ami said she would see what she could do. Filly, however suggested that should that not be possible, how about a really posh dog bed?! She was such a little character, and as she had said earlier, was just 'like a person', and a very cheeky happy one at that.

I asked Filly, if Ami was to do a different job from her acting one, what she did she think Ami would be good at? She said that Ami would be very good working with kids. Jerry and Ami's faces were a picture as they declared,

"We were only talking about that yesterday!" As for Ami's best quality,

"She is naturally beautiful and that doesn't apply to a lot of people!" I thought that was lovely, and yes, Ami is incredibly attractive. Maybe this goes to show, that even dogs are aware of the radical efforts people are putting themselves through to try to look good. I have to say, this call was taking place pretty much at their breakfast time and she looked absolutely lovely.

We covered Filly's physical side as she had pointed out to me what I took to be a slight arthritic problem with her right paw. I felt it wasn't a serious problem, just an age related one. (I always pass what I am given, so if, at any point in the future an animal does start to show a problem with that specific area, the owner will be aware of what I had informed them of earlier.)

Ami, however was aware of it, and glad to have it confirmed as what they had thought, nothing to worry about. As it is said, 'age doesn't come on its own.' It was certainly not affecting her life, just like us if we land up with a bit of a dodgy ankle; we learn to take care where possible and when the time comes, that we need to take some form of pain relief, then so be it.

If I can take this opportunity to point out there are so many alternative pain relief things on the market rather than traditional medicines. I point this out, not because I am against orthodox treatments (I have had tons of the stuff!) but something that became increasingly apparent when I started this work. I ask animals to tell me what treatment they think would help them.

Rarely do they propose conventional medicine but they have, through their own suggestion, shown me amazing results from acupuncture, homeopathy and things such as devil's claw for pain relief. The advantage of these is that they don't tend to have the side effects that many of the orthodox drugs do.

People will often ask me, 'how would an animal know?' This is a hard question to answer, but I can say, that in the wild, animals will self-medicate and that is fact.

I would suggest that animals are maybe more highly evolved than people think - we, as people (well, the majority of people), have to learn or be told what to take to heal themselves.

It was time to move on to Jerry and his dog, so back for Filly's contribution of what she wanted to say,

"People may think it is hard on the animals in movies; it is not - it is fun." We thanked her for talking to us and sharing in what she thought was a very special little life with her owners. Before we 'wrapped up' (see the movie bit has rubbed off on me – ha ha.) Jerry said, just before I finished that they would still dearly love to make a movie with Filly themselves.

Could I please ask her, as they would love to hear what she thought she would be good in? Immediately she gave me the idea of a film about a dog that was lost and with all the ups and downs that would go with it.

"Oh my goodness!" they declared, "we have even thought of the name, "*Lost in* ………" The title epitomises exactly what she had thought about but, obviously, I cannot give away the full title should they get the chance to make it. What I will say is, I bet your bottom dollar there would be at least more than one occasion when we would see a very forlorn looking Filly, searching for…food!

Jerry Trimble

This was now Jerry's turn with their other little dog, a fawn coloured Brussels Griffon called Titan. I thought this was a great name - sounding rather like a title for the type of film Jerry, in his stuntman days, might have worked on. I knew that Jerry, like his wife, Ami, had been in numerous American films and TV series but had also been a very well known and respected stuntman. To give you an idea of how athletic this man was (imperative for stunt work, needless to say) - he is an expert in Taekwondo and Kick-boxing. He won many championship titles and in his early film career managed to combine his acting and martial arts skills gaining him the lead in the action film, *The Master*, alongside the fabulous Jet Li. The stunt work on films is something that I had not really thought much about, although I have heard that a lot of actors take pride in doing their own stunts. In reality though, firstly, most are not allowed to due to insurance reasons, and secondly, there is a lot of skill and training involved. You would be mistaken to think they can't get injured because, in reality, they can. There have even been reports of fatalities, so for all the car-chase sequences we see and the people jumping from the places like the Golden Gate Bridge, they deserve utter respect. Although lots of Jerry's film work involved him being a tough man, he was a real softy when it came to his animals.

It soon turned out that Titan, now aged two, was similar to Filly in the respect that he had not come to them as a puppy; he came to them when he was five months old. In other ways, he was very different.

Jerry was telling me that Titan had come all the way from Arkansas and as he told me that I immediately felt an uneasy sensation about travelling. I passed over my feelings to Jerry and he agreed. Jerry said that they knew all about his travelling angst and they had actually got him a special seat, which seemed to have helped him.

I said, according to Titan himself, that although he liked to run around and play he was rather precious (which I took to mean in the sensitive way). Jerry smiled and said I was so right; Titan was rather precious, whereas Filly just seemed to take things in her stride.

As soon as he said 'take things' Titan showed me being taken to what seemed a park.

"Oh, yes," Ami interrupted, "My mum and I are always taking him there - he loves it, they both do."

"I am mischievous, a bit of a scamp," he volunteered. Ami and Jerry laughed but with that, I felt that although Titan would run around merrily, he needed always to know where people were for a fear of getting lost.

"Oh, yes, that is him." Jerry replied. "He always seems to be checking out where we are, and that is in the house too."

Although he had shown me the happy/fun side, including the cute picture of Jerry giving Titan's little hairy beard a gentle tug, I felt he was a slightly complicated dog. I didn't know anything about his background and had no idea if he had maybe come from friends of theirs. What was becoming very apparent was that he was nervous of loud noises and things being unexpectedly dropped to the floor, especially if anywhere near to him. I put this across the best way I could.

"Oh, I know what one thing definitely is - my gym bag. Sometimes if I am rushing and just drop it down to the floor, he runs off in total panic." I explained to Titan that no one would ever drop anything on him and that there was nothing to worry about on that score. Jerry said he would try to be more thoughtful about it in the future. I suggested Titan take the lead from Filly (she would love that line being an 'actress' herself) as she doesn't worry, this shows that he need not either.

Jerry asked me to ask him how he felt about children coming to visit. As soon as he had posed the question I was feeling rather reticent and was pretty sure that he would be uncomfortable in the presence of children. This was correct and Jerry said it was such a shame as Filly has great fun with them but Titan just wants to get away from them. I suddenly got a picture of what seemed to me like a dog that was confined, yet children were able to surround him, but he was unable to get away.

"Yes, he was kept in a cage at his first home so that makes a lot of sense." Jerry replied and with that Titan then showed me a rather unhappy awareness of feet. "Oh, yes, he is very wary of feet too." I didn't feel he had been cruelly treated in the past but, if you could imagine a little puppy shut in a cage, then children playing and banging/kicking the cage to get his attention. This had set up a fear of them and their feet. I offered to see if we could help him. I suggested a scenario where children would gently put a biscuit on the floor for him and not throw it. Jerry, or Ami, would then say to Titan, 'It's okay, they won't hurt you.' This we hoped, in time, would re-enforce that the visiting children were not something to be afraid of. He said if he was worried he would just sit back and watch them from a distance. He was relieved to know that it would be explained to the children to leave him alone too. I hoped this might help and I will find out in due course.

Having suggested he watch them, and maybe learn from Filly, Ami then asked if Titan would maybe like to be dressed up? (I think this was to put him more on an even keel with the 'Miss Filly Film Star'.) I put it to him,

"Titan, what would you think of being dressed up, would you like that?"

"I'd look very stupid as Batman, wouldn't I?" He answered cheekily and then gave me a silly picture of a black gangster style outfit, complete with a large silver $ on an extravagant belt! They laughed and said they did occasionally dress him up but in nothing as audacious as that. (When, about a year later, I received Ami's picture for this book I had to smile to myself – there she was with Titan in her arms and him dressed in a little doggie t-shirt!)

I asked him what his favourite sign of love was which turned out to be Ami's long nails running up his back like 'spiders' as he put it. He showed me lying on a pillow and Ami said,

"Oh, yes, he sleeps above my head!" This gave rise to an odd question as to why he does not ever sleep above Jerry's head. The answer I got was a cross between too much hair product (!) and that Jerry gets hotter than Ami. I swiftly moved off from that one but not before Titan volunteered that he loved Jerry anyway! Although little Titan had got his worries, he knew he was truly loved. I found out that he followed Ami everywhere he could and loved being a 'Mummy's boy' (sorry, Jerry!), as he put it. He loved Filly and I hope that our chat would maybe help regarding children and the other little things.

We moved onto the celeb questions and, as Jerry had mentioned he was going on a trip, I asked Titan what he thought Jerry was now doing for a job.

"Jumping from buildings to buildings," was his reply.

"He has actually picked up on your past career and not what you are off to do." I replied. Jerry smiled and said,

"But he is right, I am off to do some stunt work."

"Oh, I thought you had retired from that," I replied

"Oh, yeah, I had but you know what it is like…" so Titan was actually completely on the mark!

Titan wanted to let us know how well he knew Jerry by telling us that he has this amusing quality of answering a question with a question (I, myself, wonder if that is a man thing? But as you are a boy, Titan, we will let you have that one anyway). He went on to tell us that he thought Jerry treats people as equals, which makes for a more peaceful/less conflicting life. For the book he wanted to point out something, which was very relative to a problem brought up earlier during the chat.

"To let people know that even what people think looks small - it is often bigger to us." I think that is such a valid point. These little dogs can be so small; sometimes even a well-laden designer bag can be bigger and weigh more than them!

I say a big thank you to Jerry and Ami for participating in this project. I know, over the US, people will love reading about their little dogs and what a wonderful way to spread the word about animal communication.

Matthew Rhys

"I never thought I would be wanting to talk to a 'blue-arsed fly' but I do!" That was my reply to one of several quick emails that had passed between us. Probably not the most usual thing you would hear from an animal psychic - so written to a Hollywood actor, this might come as a bit of a surprise too.

This was, in fact, in direct reply to Matthew's email saying, 'Am like a blue-arsed fly! How's tomorrow? Similar time to this?' Although Matthew lives in Los Angeles, and his horses were there, he was over filming in London and trying to fit this into his extremely tight schedule. (Funnily enough, the locality of his horses to him was the opposite of Melissa Porter's - her dog was in the UK and she was in the US.) Time for me was running out too as this book was near to completion, so it was all systems go. I also needed to have Bob with me to take notes so had to re-schedule some of his work appointments too.

My introduction to Matthew was a joint one as he is great friends with Nicola (the lady that put me in touch with Paul McKenna) and keeps his horses with Clare Staples. Clare had recently emailed me to book to a chat the four horses: Buddy,

Celebrity Pet Talking

Elvis, Bono and Jimmy. (Some definite musical influence going on there, although I did have to ask Matthew which 'Jimmy' it was, which was, of course, Jimmy Hendrix). Clare owns the first two, Matthew owns Jimmy and they co-own Bono. I knew of Matthew through Nicola and it suddenly struck me that he might want to join in with this project too. Nicola assured me he would and Clare thought it was a great idea. What I didn't know at this point was; that although my book is designed to really prove that animals can communicate, this was actually to lend itself to a cause; the appalling slaughter and desecration of the wild Mustang population.

I knew that Clare was doing much to raise awareness of their terrible plight, as are many famous people like Clint Eastwood, Sheryl Crowe, etc. We all think of the 'good old USA' with its wild and rugged mountains and plains where the buffalo and wild horses roam, all beautifully encapsulated by the wonders of the Hollywood film industry. This, unless serious action is taken, will soon be gone forever. The sickening fact is that 100 years ago in the US there were estimated to be approximately two million mustangs in the wild, but they have been persecuted so much they reckon there are less than 30,000 left. How shocking is that? Now, you might be forgiven for thinking that maybe the cowboys have been rounding them all up, domesticating them and people are having them as riding horses instead but this is as far away from the truth as you can get. Just like it is the in the rainforest, where swathes of trees are disappearing along with the animal's habitat too, well, in the US, land is systematically being sold off to the people with the most dollars, and these beautiful horses are simply in their way.

So, how do they get round this problem? With all their richly lined pockets, do they help relocate them or humanely persuade them to land further away? No – they chase them with helicopters, round them up and most get slaughtered! How inhumane and disgusting is that? Words fail me! When this reading was booked, I said to Clare that I would ask these two beautiful mustangs for their opinion.

I do know that this is a 'bone of contention' for some cowboys and landowners as they don't want wild horses amongst their stock, this I can understand. But, if here in the UK, where there is way less land than the US, we can manage and monitor our wild forest ponies, then surely they can set up some protection programme and have areas that these wild horses are allowed to live, and live in peace.

As I said, I knew of Matthew ages ago as he was a good friend of Nicola and her partner, Buster. I knew he was Welsh and had made his name in America in films, the theatre and for his directing skills. Apart from playing Kevin Walker in the hugely popular American series *Brothers and Sisters*, he was critically acclaimed for his theatre role in, *The Graduate* alongside Kathleen Turner. I also found out he played the lead in a London based drama called *Metropolis*, which, if you recall, was the very word that Sir Roy's cat gave me that I couldn't pronounce. What tickled me also was in *Whatever happened to Harold Smith?*, a quirky comedy which he played alongside Stephen Fry, and his character's father found out he was psychic and became a celebrity because of it! Of all the film stories in all the world…

Having got the details and pictures of the two horses (that Clare had wondered if they were brothers), I decided to start with Bono first. According to Clare, he was the more outgoing of the two. He was a five-year-old, jet-black mustang with quite a white blaze down his stunning head. I ran through the outline of how this works as, Matthew had not experienced animal communication before either and, I am sure, didn't quite know what to expect. I think he might have been under the impression that I was going to just tell him things about his horse, and he looked delighted when I confirmed that I was tuned in with Bono there and then. Here were the intro things he told me about himself: He was solid, reliable, didn't fight and was sociable.

Matthew's face was a picture and his smile matched his words,

"You got him; that *is* him!"

I went on to say that Bono didn't think he had the best gait (action) in the world and gave me the feeling that he relied on people for support and to give him confidence.

"Yes, very true," Matthew said and with that I felt a surge of emotion. I said I didn't know if I was picking it up from Bono or him, or both. Matthew was getting the gist of this very quickly and was keen to hear more. I said that I felt that Bono had a huge heart as he had told me that he felt treasured and likes to feel needed. Bono was very proud of the way he had come on in the seven months Matthew had had him as he informed me,

"I am not the same horse."

Matthew agreed and Bono said that he thought that he would improve more and that you would look back and never believe he was the same horse.

Although Bono was sociable to people (in spite of him having been rounded up an ill treated) he declared that he didn't kick or bite the other horses. This was true but was also accompanied with a picture of him eating his hay but making it quite clear to the others, 'This is mine!' Matthew laughed and said he has seen him do that.

The next line made me laugh so much I had trouble getting it over,

"I can see between my legs!" was Bono's very strange comment. I had no idea why he would say such a thing and had Matthew ever seen him standing with his head down looking back through his legs? The answer was no, but Matthew offered that maybe because they ride up high and he is looking downwards? Not according to Bono; he was sticking to his guns giving me the same picture so all I could say was to look out for it!

"Tassels *are* good." Bono emphatically passed to me. Again I had no idea what he meant and I actually presumed it was either on the western saddle or an item of clothing. No – it was 'fly' tassels, which is the American name for a horse fly fringe as Matthew explained what the comment referred to.

"I have to admit, I make fun of the whole fly tassel thing. Other horses there wear them but I laugh and tell mine that I won't put them on them as they make horses look rather silly." I added that maybe he wouldn't mind 'looking silly' as he thinks they are a good thing. Matthew laughed and said he would maybe have a re-think. Matthew had been bursting to ask questions. I felt at least Bono had been able to share what he wanted and had given a true account of information that I was able to get from him with no guidance from Matthew at all so I said to go ahead.

"Can you ask him about when he is in his stall (stable). When I approach him he…" I asked him to hang on a second until Bono showed me how he would react to Matthew's appearance. Bono made me feel he was suspicious as if he was trying to weigh Matthew up. He would also want to back away but not in a very anxious way, just as if he was wary. This was exactly how it was and Matthew asked me to ask him why. Bono made me feel he was fine if it was a female that approached him (true) but as he put it,

"It is because you look similar." I told Matthew that I thought this was a direct reference to the people who had forcibly rounded them up. Matthew said that made complete sense and volunteered that he always wore his cowboy hat so maybe he should take it off before going into the stall. I said I thought that might help and I would ask him for some words for Matthew to say to remind him that it was only Matthew and not to worry. He gave the words (bonding key),

"Hey, buddy it's me." As I write this I realise there could be great confusion as one of Clare's horse's is called Buddy – oh, what fun! Bono was quick to say he *did* trust Matthew and it was just instinct. I hoped my words would help.

"Can you ask him about me picking his feet out too, please?"

The vision I was given was of Bono, not refusing to lift his feet, but a definite pause as if he was again wary to let it happen. This was correct so I said I would ask more. It turned out, again, it was a male – female thing. He said that his mind would always question why Matthew was trying to do it and was it because Matthew was trying to dominate him. (Lifting horses' feet is quite against instinct as their natural escape from fear is flight.) I also said to Matthew that I didn't think he spoke to Bono at the time to say what he was doing. Matthew agreed and said that he probably just supposed that a horse would know what he was going to do anyway. That was a valid point and as I said to Matthew,

"I am thinking that I have managed to show you that they really can understand you."

"Oh, yes," he enthused, "this is amazing!"

I said to treat Bono like you would another person or child; just tell him what you are going to do, and remember if you do say something that is not right, he will know too! He laughed when I told him about Tony Stockwell saying 'five minutes' to his terrier Archie, as Archie always knew if it was actually longer than five minutes!

Matthew really had got into his stride and was asking me questions to pass on as if I was just talking to another person on the end of a phone line.

"Can you ask him, why, when we take him away from his stall and if he has not finished his hay, he seems very reluctant, can you ask him why?" I had to laugh, I said I think I could give him the answer without even asking Bono, but I did and it was as I had thought; he just wanted to munch his way through it there and then. He *was* happy to be ridden but if he had hay he would have preferred to eat all his hay before he went anywhere. Matthew laughed and said that was fine, it was just because both of them could look a bit grumpy when asked to leave it behind. With that Bono made us both laugh by giving us the analogy of a mother taking away their child's cornflakes before they had finished. Bono did say, however, that he knew he would never be starved so I think Matthew felt better about that.

"What does he think of Clare and me as riders?"

Bono made me feel as if Clare was very natural and carefree and Matthew, he keeps worrying if his horse would be okay. Matthew agreed that maybe he did worry too much and I said to remember that Bono had told us that he relied on people for his confidence. Just at that point, Bono gave me a fabulous vision, accompanied by the sound of Matthew saying, 'Go on, boy.' This was them having a damn fine canter with a real sense of freedom and joy with the wind in their hair and not a care in the world. Matthew, I could see, was so touched to hear about that and told me that those were his exact words. On a serious point, Matthew asked me to see if Bono got bored with the rides they go on as, to be honest, they can be quite repetitive. Bono responded without hesitation.

"It's kinda like jogging really, it's okay." I laughed at his analogy and said that he seemed to be fine with it. Matthew was smiling broadly and said,

"There are lots of joggers on the trails!"

"Gosh, they must be fit," I commented.

"Oh, yeah, they are hardcore." He said laughingly as we were marvelling at the fact that Bono knew exactly what jogging was!

He went on to say that he felt secure then admitted to pretending to ignore Matthew if he goes into the field to catch him! He clearly showed me him keeping his back to Matthew, with a clear, 'yeah, yeah - I know you are there,' and then feigned surprise. Matthew couldn't believe it, he *did* do that although he had always thought it was because Bono could be a bit wary of him, but to find out this was done on purpose was just so funny. Bono did at this point say that Matthew was kind and gentle to him and looked after him well. I can just imagine what it is going to be like now - as Matthew strides into the paddock, Bono does his, 'I can't see you bit' and Matthew then tells him, 'I know you are acting - I do that for a living!'

I said to Matthew that I would go on to the serious issue about the Mustangs and see if Bono wanted to say anything about it, adding that, obviously, I would not push him on it. Bono heard the conversation and immediately gave me the terrible picture of people using electric cattle prods on them. My heart sank and I have to admit I hesitated before telling Matthew. I said that it was a disturbing picture and did he know if they were guilty of using cattle prods on them?

"Oh yeah, they do." He gloomily confirmed. Bob and I were horrified; we had no idea how horrendous the situation was. I asked Bono what he, as a previously wild mustang having had first hand treatment from these people, would like the world to know about what is happening - in the hope that this can be stopped. These words shot deep into my soul and I hope they do yours.

"We are families; this amounts to the same as ethnic cleansing." I tried to move swiftly on to get to the cheerier stuff but Bono insisted on imparting this bit of knowledge too.

"They are destroying generations of history." This was not about the 'wild west' culture, what he meant was the lineage of breeding that has survived since the horse was first introduced to America, which incidentally, was by the Portuguese. (I have to admit to doing a 'google' as Bob and I had a debate between them and the Spanish.) This was hundreds of years ago, so, yes, history was being destroyed and not just American.

"Don't look so sad, Matthew," Bono volunteered much to Matthew's amazement, but it had the desired effect and made him smile. (Animals are so fabulous at doing this, when things are sad, they will try to make someone feel better.) Bono said to be positive and to remember that 'people force' has managed to change other things in history for the better, so why not this? Hear, hear!

He suggested that as people really had no idea of the abuse going on and maybe even think that these celebrities fighting the cause are 'puppy huggers!', that someone infiltrate these heinous people, video what they are subjecting these horses to and put it up on a big screen somewhere for the public to watch. He said that way the truth would come out and people could not avoid the issue. (I had to laugh at this horse's expression of 'puppy huggers' and am not sure if it is an 'Americanism' or simply a 'Bonoism'!)

I pointed out, however, that I was not sure he was totally aware of American law and whether that would be legal or not – but a great suggestion anyway.

"Does he miss his family?" Matthew forlornly asked.

"They are long gone," was his instant reply, adding, "you are my family now." Which I know was about not just Matthew but Clare and the other three horses. Matthew thought that was so lovely and was cherishing those words just as Bono decided to say something that would be only really suitable from a family member.

"If you don't mind me saying, Matthew, I think the un-shaven look, is not a good one!" Well, I couldn't believe it. I had to do a quick 'double-take' and yes, Matthew was sporting the latest fashionable look and was now in raptures of laughter. How wonderful, his horse was giving him personal advice and I got to tell a Hollywood actor that apparently his beard didn't suit him! What fun!

I said we had better do the celeb questions so I asked him for an alternative type of work for Matthew.

"He could be a comedian, you know; he has a great sense of timing and often laughs at his own things"! (I don't know if technically comedians should?) I passed this over to Matthew but said it was so like his line of work anyway that I would ask again.

"He could set up treasure hunts; he is good at searching for things." As I told Matthew, he roared with laughter saying that Clare and him have an ongoing banter as he keeps mislaying hoof-picks, mane combs and the like.

For his contribution to this book as what he would like people to know,

"To be dominated is not nice, but if you are asked, you will often want to do as asked." Wise words from a horse and that should apply to the human race also.

At some point in Bono's conversation I had mentioned that Jimmy seemed quite a different character. Although younger, at only four, he seemed more confident about things. This indeed was correct. Jimmy was of the same colour and physique as Bono but his white blaze was finer and looked just like someone had painted a seven on him.

Jimmy told me he was a pleasure to have and quite soft really. He said he was good to saddle up and was the, 'ask and I do' type. Matthew said I had nailed him again (what an unfortunate, now very popular, saying that is, when you actually think about it) but I was delighted to be on the mark and let Jimmy chat away, which he did.

"I am still a baby," he declared with a funny lift of his upper lip to show me he still had baby teeth on his outer two teeth. (These, corner teeth, start to change anytime from four-and-half onwards.) Matthew laughed thinking of Jimmy doing that and asked if I could check with him about his teeth. I said that I didn't feel they were dreadfully sharp but a bit 'up and down'. Matthew confirmed that the horses had had their teeth done about seven months ago and said he would book the dentist again. I gave a quick dentistry explanation about how when teeth are changing from the premolars (baby teeth) often they don't all change exactly when they should. A dentist will correct this as the horses' mouth matures which helps avoid a problematic wave mouth in the future. Jimmy, having listened to our teeth conversation then volunteered,

"I have quite a big head, you know." This was an odd remark and it turned out to be nothing to do with teeth. Matthew admitted to cracking several jokes about the fact that Jimmy's, and Bono's heads were way bigger than the other horses. I had to laugh at Matthews face and said that things would never be the same for him again! He agreed and I said I loved it when people do realise how much the horses understand, it adds a whole new dimension to the relationship. In our house, we often say silly things to Sally, our dog and Stan our cat, and then laugh and say, "Imagine if they repeated that to a communicator"! As you have gathered by now, animals do not tell people's secrets, they have respect just as we humans are supposed to do. In my *Animal Insight* book it was one of the first things I wrote by saying, 'Don't worry, they won't say, 'Oh I saw mummy kissing the postman.' They just don't do it.

I said to Matthew that Jimmy came across to me as a good ride and that nothing much seemed to faze him. The reason I got this was his way of showing me a bush with wind rustling through it and nonchalantly saying, 'Oh yeah, it's a bush.' Matthew said that was so spot on; Jimmy was like that whereas Bono is more spooky, like, 'Whoa, where did that bush come from?' I said that is why Bono said he needed someone to rely on to look after him, but Jimmy, he thinks he can look after the rider. Matthew laughed when I suggested that maybe Jimmy could have a word with Bono to tell him not to worry so much. Can you imagine it?

"Bono, it's *just* a bush."

"But, it is a *moving* bush!"

"Yeah, it's called *wind*, Bono."

"I know but it makes the bush move."

"Of course it makes it move. Oh, I give up. Come on, let's canter really fast then all the bushes will look like they are moving then maybe you won't notice!"

They really do chat too, and about one another, which we did come to.

It occurred to me at this point, as I said to Matthew; originally I was going to do just one horse and suggested he and Clare chose the most outgoing of the pair because that tends lead to a more upbeat type of story, which is what I wanted, if possible, for this book. However, as we now see, it does seem to be the other way round. (That for me is good for a sceptic's point of view, because, had I been swayed by prior information and then tried to alter my answers to suit, I would have been totally off the mark on them both.)

Jimmy said he wasn't maimed or scarred, he just felt he was such a lucky boy to have landed up where he has. With that, Matthew asked the question that I knew Clare wanted answering, 'were they brothers?' As soon as Matthew had posed the question I heard an immediate, and distinct, NO. Matthew made me chortle as all he could do was laugh at what Clare would say to this answer as she seemed convinced they were. Jimmy went on to point out that if you checked his dentition and Bonos' also, he was under the impression that their ages were too close for the possibility of them being brothers. I said to Matthew that I could really put my head on the block here as I know that they can DNA horses, so that would provide the answer, and see if Jimmy and I were right, or wrong.

I explained to Matthew, I had only found out about the DNA thing literally a couple of weeks ago thanks to a lovely dog, Rosie. I had been chatting to her and her owners had had the test done. In fact, her picture was on my desk, as I was hoping the publishers for this book would let me use her picture as she was so gorgeous and had such an amazing long tongue. She was so eye-catching and that is what book covers are all about. I held it up for Matthew to see and he thought she looked fantastic.

"I am a celebrity too, you know; I have had my photo taken with the celebrities." Jimmy had butted in with and seemed so proud of this fact.

"Oh, yes, he had," Matthew beamed; that is part of Clare's project to help the mustangs. She is asking them to have their photograph taken with the boys for the campaign. For these two lads, who had been herded and brutally pushed about, divided from their families, what a lovely outcome that they got to pose with these lovely ladies and help their fellow mustangs. Matthew asked if the horses had grown up together and I had to say I felt that they had not. I was led to believe that Jimmy had bonded with Bono in the way that often happens; during a terrible situation you just seem to find that someone that can comfort you, or you them. (I think Jimmy was like Bono's Angel on earth.)

When I asked the sensitive question about the Mustang plight, Jimmy simply said,

"It is a disgrace – I can't say more than that." I left it there.

"So, Jimmy, what other job do you think Matthew could do apart from acting?"

"A chauffeur," he confidently replied and gave me the impression of Matthew beckoning people to get in the car and go. Matthew thought this was funny and said that he was forever picking people up and taking them up to the stables. (Well done, Jimmy, you got that one spot on. Bono however took the safer option and had to be asked twice, but that is him, bless him.) Jimmy wanted me to let Matthew (and Clare) know that he was very happy and did not find life stressful in the slightest.

Jimmy went on to say,

"I know I talk too much (!) but I am very knowing and pick things up very quickly!" I asked him for his contribution to this book and what an answer he gave,

"Just because we are big, it doesn't mean we hurt any less." I think that is such a huge statement. If you think of it in human terms, people are horrified when someone says about a poor child being beaten, but in the end, pain and abuse hurts every living being, big or small.

We had to finish off as Matthew was on a filming schedule but not before Matthew could resist asking the horses to say about the other horses in the group. He was now totally converted to the fact that animals can communicate and people, like me, can hear them. He thought this would be such fun. As soon as he said that I heard 'six' whereas Clare had always said 'four'. I asked Matthew why he though Jimmy would say that.

"There are actually six!" he exclaimed and went on to explain that another two girls ride with them a lot so their two horses often stay too.

"What does he think of Buddy?" (Clare's horse.) With no hesitation whatsoever came Jimmy's reply,

"He's a ponce!" I burst out laughing and said it as it was. Well, Matthew's reaction was so funny and he said,

"Oh, that is brilliant – he is; he is a palomino and gets all on his toes. Oh, wait till I tell Clare!" And as for Elvis, Clare's other horse, (great names eh? That would make for an interesting but rather diverse pop group should they all have been alive today!) Jimmy declared that Elvis was not as fast as he thought! Matthew said he knew exactly what that was about as they do try to race each other. He had to admit though, that Elvis being a quarter horse, does have the edge with his burst of speed.

I thanked both the boys for chatting to me, and Matthew too. I have to say my face was sore from laughing, as I think Matthew's was too. Although this story contains a very serious message, I hope that these two mustangs have shown you how truly funny, utterly wonderful and forgiving animals can be.

Stephanie Beacham

As with some of the other stories, an introduction came through another celebrity who was kind enough to contact someone on my behalf. In this instance, it was William Roache as Stephanie had played his 'love interest' in *Coronation Street* a couple of years ago. I obviously knew that William would know many celebrities but I had asked about Stephanie specifically. You might think that is because she is the glamorous actress who, on Wikipedia, has a list of her acting achievements as long as your arm, but it was actually something she had said on *Celebrity Big Brother* (*CBB*) in 2010. During a conversation she mentioned that when her two little doggies, as she calls them, are at home in the United States and she is abroad elsewhere, she will Skype home every day just to be able to see and talk to them! My ears pricked up on hearing that and I thought, 'Now, that is an animal lover if you have ever heard one!' Also, although being famous, especially for the role as Sable in *The Colbys* and then later in *Dynasty* opposite Joan Collins, which incidentally got labelled as 'the battle of the bitches', she came across as a very decent and thoughtful lady. In *CBB* there were many funny incidents as she teamed up with Ivana Trump, the other more senior lady of the household, both showing their class and decency by not getting involved in any needless backbiting that, sadly, people on these types of shows often seem to sink to. (Later on we did talk about her time in the *Big Brother* house and what it was like being cooped up in such an environment.) For anyone that has never seen *Big Brother* – a group of complete strangers are put into a house with cameras covering everywhere so their every move is watched. They have absolutely no contact with the outside world, they are subjected to various tasks to earn treats and purposely, life is made rather difficult. We, as the public, get to watch what is going on, who is cracking under the pressure, or not, as the case maybe and the housemates then get voted out one by one. The celebrity version is a slightly kinder one (only slightly!) and it is interesting to watch these people showing their real personalities once away from the glitz and glamour that we would usually see them surrounded by. This often throws many of our public preconceptions to the wind.

William emailed Stephanie on my behalf and she was delighted to take me up on my offer. Apart from wanting to hear what her two little dogs had to say, apparently one of them was being aggressive to other dogs and was 'a bit of a handful' according to her email, Stephanie sent me the most stunning picture of her and the two little ones (which is the one I have used here to accompany her story) with their names and saying that they were both three-and-a-half years old. We booked a date and, you know I say there is no such thing as coincidence, well, someone from the *Celebrity Big Brother Bit on the Side* (their after-show) contacted me in that very same week. They asked me if I would like to go on the show and chat to one of the contestant's dogs. I have written 'contestants' as, not to be rude, but 2011 was of a very different calibre from the previous year. They wanted an animal psychic to ask the dog prediction questions, like, who would win? What did that contestant's future hold and so forth.

That to me, is NOT what our work is about (yes, occasionally we do get offerings about their future, like the month of Jacky Newcomb's house move from her cat) but I do not ask those types of questions and would not want to do anything that would trivialise animal communication. I have to admit, I laughed to myself thinking that I was soon to be doing a proper communication for one of the celebrities who was on the show last year.

I had organised Kim to come and write for me but the day before she had broken her foot and was in a lot of discomfort. She had not done it by means of any heroic or sporting action, no, she had dropped her iron on it! This goes to show that ironing can be a dangerous sport and as I don't do dangerous sport I now have my avoid-the-ironing excuse and I will stick to it! Bob, bless him, stepped in to help me out.

It was morning for Stephanie and early evening for us. With the sun streaming through her windows (lucky her, summer 2011 here in the UK was yet another non-event!), she had one of the dogs on her lap ready for the chat. I explained their company was not a necessity but Stephanie was quite happy to have Nutrina, a Jack Russell cross Shih Tzu, poised on her lap anyway. Nutrina was fluffy with a light tan head, complete with white hair randomly mixed through it, dark inquisitive eyes with a black button nose to match. I knew Stephanie had had her some time before she got the other one, Sienna, who she had told me was a rescue dog. Stephanie also had never experienced a psychic animal conversation either so after explaining things to her I gave her what Nutrina had told me.

"I am very alert; I can hear a pin drop!" Stephanie immediately nodded and I added that I thought she was a rather vocal dog too.

"Oh, yes, like when a pin drops, she doesn't miss a sound and then barks at it," laughed Stephanie. She continued, "but seriously though, that is one of the things I am hoping you can help me with. I know from Bill (William) that you helped one of his dogs to settle down." Back to Nutrina's intro information,

"I am very important." She declared. I then asked her why. "Because if people are there you cannot ignore me, I am so delightful!" Was her reply complete with a picture of her running round and round as if this would make Stephanie laugh. I added that although I felt Stephanie was protective of her that Nutrina also felt that she had a job to do in this relationship too. This all made sense and as Stephanie said,

"Yes, she is delightful but as for the 'can't ignore me' that is so true but not so delightful, and quite frankly can be annoying like last night for example." She carried on, "she most certainly does think she has a job; like raccoon duty for one! They were on the roof and she barked and barked, kept running up as if to tell me about them. She did not give up until I got up and went over to where she insisted on vocally directing me to. She then sat down, stopped barking and stared up as if to say, 'There are raccoons on the roof, you know!' She will then do 'her job' which is to stay there transfixed for hours like a terrier waiting for something to come out of a hole – this complete with bursts of noisy excitement and she would stay there all night if she could! It is so annoying - I know they are there and as much as I try to ignore her, she is not happy until she has made me get up and go and investigate what I know is there already! Seriously though, I am worried that should she get the opportunity she would try and attack one of these racoons and get seriously hurt." Bob and I were listening intently as, firstly, we had not even thought about raccoons being in America let alone going on the roofs of houses and secondly, having seen them on cute cartoons didn't think that they would be much of a threat to a feisty little terrier like this.

"They are much bigger than you would think; they can be as large as a fox and have claws like bears. They cause serious damage to roofs and the little bandits have no fear, and I mean, no fear. If you see them and try to shoo them away, they just look at you with their beady eyes, like, 'And?' Could you please tell her how dangerous they can be and that they could seriously hurt her." I did my best but whatever I, or Stephanie said, it was like Nutrina had her own thoughts on the matter and seemed to want to have the last word, whatever.

"Oh, yes, she always tries to get the last word. If tell her off, and believe me I do, she will still get the last word by means of her doggie grumble." Although this conversation was a serious one, we could not help but laugh, Stephanie spoke of Nutrina like she was a naughty child and to be honest, she was! She was so loved, and knew it. I know there are people that love and adore their dogs but who would fly theirs to England with them as they could not bear to be parted for such a length of time? Stephanie had; but on their return this time Nutrina had become bossier and noisier than ever.

I told Stephanie that I was sure Nutrina was vying to be top of the pecking order including over Stephanie too! It seemed she really didn't know her place and in her mind she thought it was the right thing to do – gaining superiority and all that. Stephanie agreed so I suggested that I explain to Nutrina that it is actually 'us humans' that are in charge. That meant Stephanie is there to look after her, decide what is right and wrong and, by all means, Nutrina, be a dog and bark to alert your owner when someone comes to the door, but, when asked to be quiet, do! Earlier she had mentioned to me something about how nice it was lazing in the sun so I tried to use this information in a positive way. I suggested she imagine how it would feel if whilst peacefully sunning herself she was suddenly disturbed by some unnecessary and voluminous noise? I had hoped for the 'Oh, that would be so annoying' answer, but instead it was rather like a 'So?' with a shrug of her little hairy shoulders. This was one strong character!

Nutrina then gave me, what is often a common misperception from animals, that she thought Stephanie says sorry, or seemed to imply by her actions that 'it doesn't matter really' after having reprimanded her. Having listened to the steps Stephanie had taken in the past to try to teach this little dog (and a couple of things did work and still were effective with her) this would have surprised me. Sure enough, Stephanie assured me that she definitely did not. So, here goes the misconception - after say, five minutes of a behaviour correction, in our minds all is forgotten so we go and give our pet a cuddle or maybe throw a ball for them or suchlike. Nutrina, like so many, linked this as either 'sorry' or, 'oh, you didn't mean it' and then they dismiss what they were told off about and the behaviour continues. I did the same as I have done before; explained to her that this is not the case and asked for something to be said so she would hopefully remember what the reprimand was about now that a little time had passed. Nutrina offered,

"Lesson Learned." I passed this on to Stephanie and suggested she refrain from being too quick to initiate fun or affection just to try to help the message filter through that she had been told off due to unwanted behaviour. Just at that point, Nutrina who had left Stephanie's lap a while ago was now obviously blocking the way for Sienna (who apparently she loved) to come through to where Stephanie was sitting. She was not being aggressive but she didn't need to be, her body language made it obvious and Sienna didn't want to challenge her. Stephanie immediately told Nutrina that she was being unfair to Sienna. I said to Nutrina that I thought it was a very unkind thing to do and imagine if someone had made you feel that you couldn't come to Stephanie, how hurtful that would be. Stephanie then went and picked up Sienna and, funnily enough, Nutrina went and sat down with no attitude or pushiness.

We covered other misguided bits of 'I'm in charge' behaviour and one example was shown to me in picture form of Stephanie answering the door, complete with a very young Nutrina tucked under her arm. This was before Sienna had arrived and it would have been quite normal for someone to just pick up a little pup/dog whilst they answered the door. Unfortunately, to one like Nutrina, this was a sign to her that she was on a level footing with Stephanie. This was her house too as she was there to greet the visitors, they were obviously there to see her just as much a Stephanie and this, in her mind, made her an equal. Stephanie had mentioned things were worse since they had come back from England, which made sense as I felt Nutrina was trying to reinforce her territory and boundaries once again.

I had mentioned earlier that Stephanie had flown the two dogs to England with her. She told us that she had been there playing *Maria Callas*. I heard 'three' in my head, so said,

"Were you there for three months?"

"Yes, we were." She replied. "It was lovely. Can you ask them about the travelling?"

"Yes, by all means. I take it you are talking about the plane journey as you'd said you thought the twelve hour flight was such a long one for them."

"Yes, I do. Thanks."

Nutrina was quick to inform us,

"Our every need was catered for! We were most comfortable thanks!" I repeated this and said this seemed slightly unusual as most animals are flown like cargo, although safe, it can be quite a lonely experience. Stephanie was quick to explain that these two lucky dogs had actually travelled in the cabin area, so that explained that. It just seemed like a long car journey the way Nutrina had put it by adding,

"We were not shocked by the whole thing!"

"What did they think of being theatre dogs?" We chuckled at this point remembering the story I had sent over to Stephanie (to show her an example of the book content) was Jenny Seagrove's. In her story, we talked about the problem Louie, her dog, had encountered being left in the dressing room at one particular theatre. Stephanie's dogs however, told me they had no such problems; they just slept a lot and thoroughly enjoyed being spoilt by everyone that came and went. What I also established was Nutrina, having been off her own territory, had been much milder in her manner. This was a good indication that her behaviour was as I had deduced from all that she had shown and said to me.

Still on the subject of *Maria Callas* and the theatre, Nutrina gave me a picture of a glass of water!? I had no idea of the significance but she gave it again so I, using my logic, asked Stephanie if the show used to make her thirsty and maybe this is why I was being shown a glass of water? She looked perplexed (she can still look stunning even when perplexed – oh, how unfair life is!) and said maybe she had been but could not quite recall anything obvious. As I have said before, I don't look up information on people before a call as I want any info to be 'off the cuff' and from their animal and not from the internet. We did, however, after the call go online as Bob said that he had never heard that Stephanie could sing (neither had I) so we did some research.

The list on Wikipedia makes for such interesting reading and apart from Stephanie being known as a stunning actress with class and a velvet voice to match, I had no idea that she had been in *Tenko*, which I remember from my childhood. (Sorry Stephanie, I am only twenty-one, honest!) It was a gripping series about a prisoner of war camp - it gave the true depth of the awful conditions of the POWs (prisoners of war) and their survival and resourcefulness. Then, skip on a few years and Stephanie is a prisoner yet again in *Bad Girls* but this time it was more of a comedy role. Behind those bars she played Phyl Oswyn who was teamed up with actress Amanda Barrie to make the, 'Costa Cons'. They provided us with endless laughs of their various scams fooling the dim-witted and not so dim-witted. It was such fabulous viewing and they gave much light relief in what was also a very gripping prison drama set in a more modern era. Naturally, neither series would give room for fantastic costumes and fashion, but Stephanie's role in *The Colbys*, and later on in *Dynasty*, I think may have used up her full allocation for life!

Having found *Maria Callas* information and write-ups, it was a play about this Opera Diva's career, life and her heartbreak over her romance with Aristotle Onassis. This is something I would have loved to go and see, a very poignant story by all accounts. Further down the page a very kind person had written a review which read…'I've seen the play and it is amazing. Stephanie is perfect as Maria Callas; it is like the play was written for her. I especially liked the line "I'm just drinking a glass of water and I have presence!" Oh so true!'

Ah, mystery solved - she wasn't drinking it, it was a line she said as Maria Callas! (Oh thank you lovely reviewer!)

As I had gathered, from other things, Nutrina was a fabulous and funny little dog and I felt that she would be just as happy (like most animals) if she knew exactly where she fitted in - like a child knowing its place and who to respect and be able to rely on, thus able concentrate on the more fun things in life. I knew that Nutrina liked to try to have the last word, which had been confirmed earlier, so I suggested to Stephanie that she could solve this by simply turning away from her. I even managed to get words to go with this, so suggested that, should Nutrina get 'on her high horse' that Stephanie simply turn her back on her so there would be no option of a debate, and say, in Nutrina's offered words, "You are so annoying, I don't like annoying dogs." (This is on the principle of *not* rewarding bad behaviour, ignoring it where possible to avoid wrongful attention seeking, so, when they are being good, you reward them with your attention and interaction.)

This might have sounded like tough love but what I also did was to establish what Nutrina's favourite sign of affection Stephanie gives her so this could be incorporated with her behavioural training. The most common from animals is the kissing of their head, certain words or food treats etc. but for Nutrina what I got, demonstrated by moving pictures, was the hide-the-ball game. Stephanie immediately recognised this and said she was brilliant at finding it, even in the most obscure places - she was so very clever. I joined these two things together. If Nutrina had been good, say for example, stopped barking when asked, then she would be rewarded with her game and this would show just how really very clever she was. This point should be very important to her as she would be given the best reward as stated by herself!

I really hope that this would work. I, as usual, had to say I couldn't promise it would, but it has before and I have tried my best - so only time will tell. I always think, what will be will be, and if this doesn't work for Nutrina, as I know from experience it can work, that maybe someone reading this might find putting things like this into action can help with their wilful little dog.

What a lovely reading this was, Stephanie clearly loved her dogs and had us in fits of laugher when I mentioned about the *CBB* Skype comment, she said,

"Oh yes, it's true but they are 'not good Skypers!' They lose interest especially if it goes out of focus. I know they can hear me but how much they see of me I am not sure but it is so lovely to see them - I miss them so much."

I immediately had this silly cartoon scenario (of my own imagination I might add) of these two little dogs, pulling up their chairs, dragging the keyboard towards them and pressing the appropriate computer buttons. Having found and selected Stephanie's name and had a quick debate about who was going to speak first (Nutrina winning that one for sure), a paw clicks on the 'answer with video' button. They are then most delighted to see her face only for it to do that 'out of sync' thing where sound no longer fits the words. Then, worst of all, the 'freeze' happens making the screen resemble a version of some poor, over-pixelated photograph, or perhaps a version of modern art?! After a minute of, 'Bark bark, can you hear us?' a quick confab is had and the decision is made, 'Let's play ball instead.' So, with a swift hit of the paw to press 'end call' Stephanie is now disconnected, computer buttons re-pressed and keyboard re-shifted, they pop off their chairs to go and find that ball.

Stephanie explained that when she is working away, her assistant looks after them and they do seem happy with the arrangement. On a serious note though, she had worried that the England trip might have been too much for them. I said, judging by the earlier remarks, that maybe it wasn't?

I just had to compliment her on her *CBB* appearance (which incidentally she had thought was the last one and was not aware that another channel were trying to continue with it after all) as it was a joy to watch. I am not one of these people that enjoy watching others being bullied and sided against and that actual one had a feel good factor and a lot of camaraderie. Stephanie told us, in her words,

"It was an extraordinary experience. I loved it. It is the biggest confrontation with yourself - I enjoyed it all." She said she learned so much about people, and herself, in such a short space of time and under intense pressure. On the reality shows, I believe that people can only pretend to be what they are not for only a certain length of time and then their true personality will show through. I, as did the rest of the country, thought Stephanie came over as a really decent and thoughtful person.

So many people that live the celebrity lifestyle lose themselves in a false sense of grandeur and these types of people you could not rely on to be a true friend.

Talking of friends, we spoke about William and what a lovely man he is. Stephanie was acting with him in *Coronation Street* at the time William's wife, Sara, suddenly and, most unexpectedly, had passed away. Stephanie said she felt that there was no coincidence that she had been playing that part at that time so was there to be able to support him during such a sad time in his life. She said that William had been there for her previously when she needed support and that is what I call friendship, which is only deserved by people that are true and thoughtful to others.

I knew that Nutrina would rather avoid another certain conversation but Stephanie now brought it to the fore.

"Can you ask her not to be so aggressive to other dogs?" (I had already said in an email that this is a tough one but I would try). I went onto my 'tough love' approach saying that I knew how much she loved Stephanie and should a big dog attack her, it could be so serious or even fatal so please think of what the consequences could be. I got back that familiar feeling of, 'yeah, as if.' I had to share my thoughts and findings with Stephanie and she said,

"Oh yes, typical. She picked an argument with a large Alsatian the other day and it bit her on the neck!' I stopped Stephanie there so I could get a true feeling from Nutrina as about this retaliation and being bitten. I hated to admit this, but she seemed to simply shrug it off as if it was nothing that a quick bathe of salt water had sorted out! No trauma, no major damage, just a little skirmish that did nothing to frighten her.

"Absolutely right," said Stephanie, "it just broke the skin but she didn't need any veterinary treatment, and she most certainly did not seem upset by it at all. Ask her about Kelsey." I duly did and for a dog that apparently didn't like other dogs this looked like Nutrina merrily running round with a feeling of glee. I said, with that slight 'Oh lord, I hope I have the right tone',

"This is strange, but it looks to me like she is happily running about with, who I presume to be, Kelsey."

"Oh yes, she does, she loves him and his friend. He is a big Labrador and she has known them both since she was a puppy - they are great mates." I suggested that I should ask what was different about them to other dogs in the park.

"They won't want to come and take over my house; they have their own homes," was her somewhat strange reply. After discussing this reply we could sort of see where her logic was coming from; as Stephanie had known these dogs from pups, as she was friends with their owners, that Nutrina didn't feel threatened as they definitely had their own home and she had hers. I tried to explain about the others dogs again but felt I was getting nowhere really and apologised as I couldn't seem to make headway on this. As I write this, it reminds me of William's Jack Russell, Oliver, when presented with the same line of questioning said, 'Just don't even try!' (Hey, maybe these dogs are 'good Skypers' after all, and this line of defence has already been discussed?! I must remind Stephanie to ask William to check his contacts list!)

Nutrina had already taken up about an hour of chat and so onto Stephanie's celeb questions. 'If she hadn't been an actress?'

"A great debater," and the reason, "because she could give either side of the argument and put forward facts without getting upset." Stephanie, with her velvety voice, agreed that she supposed she could. As I write this, I think Nutrina cheated slightly there, that does sound like acting to me! In fact, this is what I think politics is made of - acting! If you are on a certain side, even if you don't agree with what you have to say, you say it anyway! Mmm, maybe an easy second career and I reckon they could claim for expenses there too!

I asked Nutrina to say what she thought of Stephanie's appearance in *CBB*,

"She didn't play up to the cameras; she was simply herself." Good answer, and quite right.

As for her contribution to this book, what would she like people to know?

"Animals can travel the world; they are far more versatile than you think."

I thanked her for talking to me and said to Stephanie that all doubts about them travelling might have been answered too.

As I said earlier I had received the age of the dogs but the 'how long have you had them' was missing. As we are going to be moving on to do the other dog (as you can see in the photo, she is tiny and looks so cute) I asked Stephanie how long she had had her. She said,

"I often wondered if getting her put Nutrina's 'nose out of joint' but let me see, er, how long after it was…"

"Seven months?" I ventured. Stephanie looked surprised and said,

"It could well have been," and a surreal moment occurred. Here was I chatting to this very famous lady and now, she, Bob and I were counting on our fingers how many months it was from March, when she got Nutrina, to September when she got Sienna. SEVEN!

"So it was seven months," I laughed.

"How on earth did you know that?" Stephanie asked incredulously.

"Nutrina told me. If you remember earlier, she also told me correctly you were in England for three months too!"

"Oh yes, she did, how would she know such things as length of times?"

"To be honest I don't really know but I often get told numbers. I am terrible at hearing names but animals are always volunteering relevant numbers, such as what they cost, how long something took to heal, their height/weight, and all sorts of things. There is so much more to animals than meets the eye and that is why I am doing this book to try and share this and show people." So, now we knew how long Stephanie had had Sienna I said to Nutrina that I really needed to speak to Sienna now.

"Why did you call her Sienna?" for some reason I felt compelled to ask.

"She was found as a near-dead stray in a deserted house in a place called Sienna Plantation in Texas, so hence Sienna." She continued, "I was working over there and the cleaner turned up one day with this emaciated little dog, handed her to me, begging me to take her and do what I could for her. So that day, Sienna left with me, wrapped up carefully and placed in a

Louis Vuitton dog carrier. She was flown here by plane and was put on a drip at my own vets." The leap from the squalid home and then travelling by plane in a designer carrier made us smile especially with Stephanie's accompanying words, "It was a real Cinderella story with her own carriage."

She went on to say that this little dog, who was judged to be about a nine months old, was literally skeletal and had lost all her hair from her waist down and was clinging onto life by a whisker. Stephanie held Sienna up showing us her beautiful soft wispy coat that she never dreamed would ever have grown. Stephanie said, in fact, she thought, even if this poor little being did survive that she would probably resemble some prehistoric creature for the rest of her life with a just smattering of hair at her front end and nowhere else. Poor little soul.

What an amazing tale of kindness on Stephanie's behalf and survival by such a tiny creature whose life hung in the balance for three days. But survive she did and blossomed into the cutest little dog you would ever see.

During Nutrina's conversation I had mentioned that I felt that Sienna was very different from Nutrina and had described herself as 'the cutie, girlie sort' that wanted to please. At this point, I also repeated this lovely picture of Sienna up on her hind legs with her front legs bobbing like, 'Hello, it's me.'

"Yes, she does; she is just like a Meerkat!"

I knew Sienna had been a rescue dog but, given her young age, the other bit of information slightly threw me.

"Do you know if she had had puppies?" I ventured.

"Not that I know of," replied Stephanie. I added,

"I have to admit, she seems very young to have had puppies but I can only go on the information she is showing me."

"Actually, I have known dogs younger than that to have had puppies, so it could have been possible." I explained that she had shown me tiny puppies in the corner of a very insalubrious room but had repeated to me twice,

"It's okay," but with that feeling of being resigned to a sad, but unchangeable, fact.

"Oh, how sad. Maybe she had left the puppies behind?" I said it made me feel like she was starving and was torn between finding food for herself to survive which meant leaving them and hoping they would still be there when she came back. Again I stressed that she felt calm and resigned to whatever had happened. We would never truly know, but at least she was safe now. I suddenly thought to say,

"Just a thought, but are her nipples more pronounced than Nutrina's?" As by this time Sienna had once again got pride of place on Stephanie's lap so with a quick look she declared,

"Oh, goodness, yes, they are! It had never crossed my mind as she had been so ill I had never thought about it. Oh, poor her, what a sad life she must have had. I know she was abused; she has problems with her hips. I think she was kicked in the pelvic area - can you ask her about it?" I said I would as, although I tend to avoid delving into sad past issues unless they are affecting their present life, this was relevant and she had already 'taken' me there anyway.

Sienna quickly drew my eye to her right hind leg as if that was the one with more of a serious problem and then gave me a drastic picture to accompany it. What she was showing me was not her being kicked but some ignorant, unfeeling, thoughtless person grabbing her by the hind leg, at speed, and lifting her up into the air that way. Although this sandy coloured little girl thought to be a Chihuahua crossbred would have weighed very little, this was still most of her body weight being whiplashed against her own hip in this most inhuman action. I also thought that this injury had occurred sometime before her being rescued as I could see muscle wastage.

I passed over this information as sensitively as possible and Stephanie agreed that it made complete sense and yes, there was muscle wastage and to this day, when she runs, she tends to do it on her other three legs still. I was quick to say that I sensed no tenderness; it was like the damage had been done and, at this point in time, was causing no physical pain.

This was the most darling little dog, and although Nutrina can be bossy, they loved each other and I said I felt that in no way had Nutrina been put out by her arrival. Stephanie went on to tell us that once Sienna was well enough she was obviously very concerned about how they would get along.

All seemed fine until one day they had a 'spat', and a full-blown one at that. There was actually no physical harm done but, as Stephanie was going to England to work, she was very worried there might be a re-match. Blow me - Stephanie told us that, although they were being cared for by her assistant and she had been assured that they seemed happy enough, she was still worried about what effect this fight had had on them both, she actually flew back from England after a week to see them personally herself. Having found that they were both were indeed very happy and there was definitely no sign of animosity, she then flew back again! Now that is dedication with no expense spared!

These two little dogs now truly adore each other and there have been no raised fists - well, paws – since!

Talking of raising things, Bob and I were amazed to see that little Sienna will sit balanced on Stephanie's one hand. She just stays there like a little statue, so trusting. As we were admiring and cooing about that, Sienna volunteered,

"I love to be babied." I passed this remark over and the next minute we were then cooing over this little soul upside down in Stephanie's arms just like a baby. (I have to say, people go to fabulous parties and red carpets dos but the hour and half we spent doing this, in my mind, far surpassed the joy of any glittering event. It was such a joy, and honour, to share in such love and personal moments with Stephanie and her animals.)

Another fact that was correct was that although Sienna had obviously had a horrendous start in life, she was not a clingy dog. She said she was quite happy with her own company. Stephanie said that often she will go off and sleep or relax on a chair on her own. We covered so many more things - one being that although Sienna had managed to conquer most of her fears I still felt there was an underlying uncertainty that would still occasionally go through her mind. I told Stephanie what she was conveying to me and that I hoped one day that she would truly let go and know that nothing could ever happen to her.

"I know exactly what you are referring to," she replied. "It is very much like she is frightened to do something wrong so suddenly she gets all nervous and worried." Stephanie went on to say that whatever Sienna did, she could never do anything wrong - she is a little angel and she should never worry. I was so pleased to know that Sienna would have heard that and I assured her that it was the truth. Please believe that this is your life now and will be for the rest of your days. You are so dearly loved, so relax and enjoy. We know you could never do anything to upset Stephanie and I quietly pointed out, 'Hello, look at what your mate gets up to!' So, by comparison… impossible!

Sienna made me feel that she would present Stephanie with things, I didn't know if she meant toys or suchlike.

"No, it is not toys, but she is amazing. She never returns home from a walk without having given me some sort of present, whether it be a leaf or a feather or just some delicate thing she can find."

"For you, for you!" I could hear Sienna saying to let Stephanie know the words to accompany the gift. Ah, how sweet. On the subject of 'walkies' Stephanie asked Sienna, who was still in her arms,

"Do you want to go for a walk?" And with that, I kid you not, she waved her front paws.

"Are you hungry?" asked Stephanie - no reaction. "She is obviously not hungry because if she is, she will lick me for a yes!" So, as if to re-affirm this, again she was asked if she wanted to go for a walk and again she waved her paws but still lying in this gentle slumber position. Simply adorable. I could feel the warmth and intensity of love and gratitude this dog had for Stephanie. Such a lovely feeling.

I took the opportunity to ask her what she thought of Nutrina.

"She is bonkers!" was her immediate reply. I said that I knew she could be rather overbearing at times, but was this okay with her?

"Yeah, she is bossy but I've met far worse than her." A very succinct answer and when you think how her canine life had started. Sienna then took her opportunity to say that she trusted Stephanie implicitly and knew that whatever she did would be for the right reasons. I said to Stephanie that I hoped Nutrina got the gist of that and takes the easier option of letting us humans decide what is best in the knowledge that knowing that Stephanie only has her best interests at heart.

"Me too," she replied, "and while we are talking about Nutrina, please ask her about squirrels."

"Oh, yes! Smell, smell, smell!" Nutrina delightfully shared with us, complete with anticipation but then added, with an air of innocence, "but I don't catch them though." I laughed and said she may be fibbing about the catching bit, but actually it was the truth and as for her sense of smell, apparently she will search and seek out every gopher hole she can. (We don't have them over here in the UK but thanks to kids television with 'Gordon the Gopher' we have a pretty good idea what they look like.)

As wonderful as this was and, as diverse as two dogs could be (which I like as it validates my work as you could not really swap anything to suit the other), it was time to thank Stephanie for sharing such a special relationship with me and to thank Sienna too, but not before her final questions.

For her, most importantly, I found out that her favourite sign of affection was having her head stroked whilst being called 'darling girl'. For the book she told us,

"Dogs hearts are huge. Even though we get hurt, we still go on and try." From this little girl, a statement no truer said. The story of her former life has sadly been a reality occurring every day. If we all try to do our bit by helping in whatever way we can, we will also be the winners.

These amazing animals really are here on earth to show us love, loyalty and what true forgiveness is. Maybe one day we will tip the balance so there will be far more joy and understanding than exists in this world today.

Postscript

This book has been a labour of love and I hope it has achieved what I set out to do. These stories were designed to share in the fun and everyday life of celebrities and their pets and some even have updates:

If you remember when I visited Jacky Newcomb, which was in June 2010, her cat, Jasper, volunteered that they would be moving to Cornwall in October. This didn't seem to ring true at the time as Jacky was sure they were, in fact, moving in that next two weeks. A few weeks later, Jacky put a note on *Facebook* saying that the house sale had fallen through and how very disappointed she was. As time carried on, there were yet more delays, and I could see the date rolling on towards October. I sent her an email in late August saying, 'I wonder if Jasper is right after all?'

"Oh no," she replied, "It can't be October, that could be a worse time to move; I have got so much on that month with two books coming out at the same time."

Although Jacky is renowned for her Angel books this one was co-written with her sister, Madeline Richardson. *Call Me When You Get to Heaven* is a true and fascinating account of how their father, after he passed over, visited various members of the family and made his presence known. It is a fabulous and uplifting book, and how funny that my father chose Jacky's house to make us aware of his presence too.

I was now following her house moving date with keen interest. By the time the first week of September had arrived I could not resist sending Jacky another note on the subject. She made me laugh with her reply,

"Are you ready for this? Drum roll…We move into our new house on…1st of October!!" And they did! So Cornwall has gained another angel and I have to say through doing this I have also gained an amazing, and lovely friend.

Barrie John's cat, Milo, suggested Barrie's other type of work could be doing interior design and guess what? He landed up with a monthly magazine column about offering advice about interior design! I dropped him a line when I spotted it. His reply,

"I had totally forgotten about that – wow!"

Jenny Seagrove's dog has stopped weeing under the piano – long may that last and how although Louie forget himself and still tugs on his leash but at least his 'stays' are exemplary.

Clare Staples dog Mr Big, was found to have some physical issues. After having him treated and put onto a supplement, he got the bounce back in his stride.

William Roache's dog, Oliver, did quieten down slightly but then decided to do some sporadic barking instead! As William put it, 'He makes me jump out of my skin!' I offered to have a chat with Oliver to see if I could shed any light on what was going on and hopefully help him, and William. Whilst talking to Oliver he made me aware of the effect of Tinnitus in his ears which was making him hypersensitive to sound in a way that he would try and bark over them. William said this made perfect sense and also he could see Oliver was more edgy than he ever had been.

I remembered I had experienced this scenario before with a dog called Bracken in a story called 'Ringing True' in my *Animal Talking Tales* book. I looked up my files and called Neshla, her owner, and she told me what the vet had prescribed for Bracken, which had done the trick. It was a herbal form of calmer which is designed for animals of a nervous disposition, and as Tinnitus can be a most annoying condition, this helps relieve the stress of it. I noted it down and said I would pass the information to William.

Neshla made me laugh by saying that Bracken was now 'famous' in Cyprus as her mum, who lives there, had recommended my book there and now lots of people have read it. This brought up the conversation of this celebrity book and what it was about and why. I said it was completed and just needed the pro-editing done and that was it.

"If you haven't got an editor I would be delighted to do it for you." Neshla offered (I had completely forgotten that, in fact, was her job, but usually on medical books) saying that it would be her way of helping this book and my cause too. How very kind and wonderful. So a huge thank you to Neshla for her professional editing skills and to William's Harry for prompting the phone call in the first place – another wonderful piece of synchronicity!

Jenny Smedley was delightful and having written about my chat with her dog, KC, in her latest best-seller, *Pets are Forever*, people have contacted me. She has also been so kind and referred people to me who have got in touch with her because of the books she writes. One was a very angry Jack Russell who, after a chat, is now far happier as it was not her nature; it was due to a complete misunderstanding of circumstance. This, in turn, directed her neighbour to me whose cat had turned rather angry too. His case of 'flying' at her totally unprovoked on a warm summer's day was solved by his simple, yet crucial, information,

"She does know there are ants in the garden doesn't she?!" Ah, then all became clear and harmony was restored.

I know you will have gathered how grateful I am to all the people who have helped pass letters on for me and their help in so many other ways. As for the people above, they have been kindness itself. Throughout this project they have been there for me and supported my efforts. I truly believe that, without their help, this book would have been nigh on impossible.

If you have enjoyed this book and see the good it can do and just happen to know a celebrity, be one or know someone who knows one, then you too can help make the next book happen and spread the word even more. I have had amazing help from Matthew Rhys (one of Wales's best exports to Hollywood), who, although so busy working and filming, has found the time to introduce me to other famous people as he can see the true potential of what my dream and work can achieve. Please feel free to contact me through my website and we can go from there - between us all, we can, and will make even more of a difference for the animals out there.

I would like to thank Jan, my friend in Scotland who has given her time to check over my spelling and grammar for this, and my other two books, before they went to the editors. (Every time a story comes back I open it with anticipation to see how much red is splurged across the page denoting my mistakes. Also for her odd funny comments like, when for some reason I typed 'conflab' instead of 'confab', she suggested that maybe my diet efforts really were playing on my mind!) When I sent Anna Forrester's story to her, I put a note saying that she might be surprised as it is about rats. She replied, informing me that, as she was originally a Manx person (born on the Isle of Man), that they do not use the word 'rats', they say 'long tails'. Here is some Manx folklore she wanted to share with me…

'The refusal by Manx people to say the word 'rat' came about in the 1600s when the Duke of Athol returned to Douglas (Isle of Man's capital) after receiving a knighthood from Queen Elizabeth. Disaster struck as he stepped from the ship to the landing jetty, when he inadvertently trod on a rat, which then bit his foot. He stumbled, tripped, and fell face-first onto a stack of barrels, breaking his nose. Under the ancient Manx law, no man with a facial disfigurement is allowed to be a ruling member of the nobility so the newly knighted Sir was forced to step down and hand the Dukedom to his eldest son instead.

From that day forward, it has been considered unlucky for any person to say the word 'rat' on the Isle of Man. Instead of the word 'rat' Manx people say "long tail", and upon hearing the dreaded word uttered by someone else Manx people may do one of three things to ward off the bad luck: knock on wood, whistle or tug a forelock – and sometimes all three!' So folks, you now know what not to say if you ever set foot on their island.

Talking of things to say; Sian, the partner of Dean the footballer, has started to have more success in her acting work and is coming to the foreground as her cat suggested. Whittled down from thousands, she is the face of a certain wood preserving product that says, 'It really does what is says on the tin!' I think that sort of describes my way of doing my animal psychic work. This was eloquently put in an endorsement for me by William Roache, saying,

"There are no pauses, or staring into the Ether, she just relays in a very matter of fact way, usually with humour, what the dogs are thinking." Remembering what his dog offered about Williams painting efforts, so, if he were to buy this preserving product, do you think he might land up with only a half painted fence? Bless you, William; you have been so very kind to me.

There are numerous people to thank which I have tried to do personally. I should mention that I am very grateful for efforts many clients made on my behalf.

Also huge thanks to Kim for all her note taking, organising skills, being such great company and for having a Sat Nav that obviously did know more than us!

This is 2011, and all across the world there is an apparent financial crisis and publishing houses are not exempt from the effects. Having found out that most of the celebrities had not heard of this type of psychic work, publishers too were being cautious as it is now a very difficult and unsteady market. I decided to go it alone and publish this myself as I feel that is the best way to get these stories out and let this book 'speak' for itself. I have lost count of how many people I contacted and how many times I had to explain what to so many people seemed utterly impossible, and even ridiculous, and some even thought so!

I do hope my efforts pay off and will spread the word on behalf of animal communication. I also hope in time, that monies from this book will enable me to make donations to some animal rescue centres. I have chosen small ones to benefit from this as, although all animal charities need help, the larger ones have higher profiles and the smaller ones often get overlooked.

I have managed to get the ball rolling on this already as some celebrities I approached (or were approached on my behalf) wanted me to chat to their pet, but not have it publicly in a book. In these instances, they gave me a donation for my chosen charities. This has been wonderful as I was still able to share with these celebrities what an animal psychic can do, and how lovely the experience can be. They in turn have told their friends, so the word has still spread and the charity coffers benefited from it as well.

Thanks everyone. If you had not experienced the world of animal communication before, I am delighted to have been able to add another facet in the wonderful relationship you have with your own pets. To quote what someone recently wrote to me:

'Thank you so much for showing me that my animal does really and truly understand what I am saying. We have a wonderful relationship and you have now added another dimension to it. To know that when I tell her I love her; she truly understands me. The joy that has brought to my heart is immeasurable.'

Jackie Weaver

www.animalpsychic.co.uk

For the cover I would like to thank the gorgeous dog, Rosie, (with the longest tongue in the world!) who I had the joy to chat to as a 'doggie client'. When I received her picture, I asked her kind owner, Kirsty, for permission to use it. Rosie was actually a rescue dog, found as a stray, so how fitting that her eye-catching look would be the face to spread the word for the animal kingdom. She is extremely proud and, as is her owner. The cat is our own little Stanley, who looks like a little Angel but is really our own 'little monkey', and on the back are myself and Binderee, again with kind permission of his owner.

Photographer credits:

Jenny Seagrove - Gill Shaw Photography

Jacky Newcomb - Nick Richardson Photography

William Roache MBE - David Tipton (Silver Image Photography)

Alex Hua Tian - Laura Ness Photography

Once again, more fabulous bespoke drawings by my friend, and very talented artist, Jackie Fennell. Thank you.

www.jacksart.co.uk